D1046837

DISCARD

PRIVACY-ENHANCED
BUSINESS

PRIVACY-ENHANCED BUSINESS

Adapting to the Online Environment

Curtis D. Frye

Q

Quorum Books
Westport, Connecticut • London

Library of Congress Cataloging-in-Publication Data

Frye, Curtis D., 1968–
    Privacy-enhanced business : adapting to the online environment / Curtis D. Frye.
      p.   cm.
    Includes bibliographical references and index.
    ISBN 1–56720–321–3 (alk. paper)
    1. Electronic commerce—Security measures.   2. Internet (Computer network)—Security
measures. I. Title.
    HF5548.32.F79   2001
    658.8′4—dc21   00–032810

British Library Cataloguing in Publication Data is available.

Library of Congress Catalog Card Number: 00–032810
ISBN: 1–56720–321–3

First published in 2001

Quorum Books, 88 Post Road West, Westport, CT 06881
An imprint of Greenwood Publishing Group, Inc.
www.quorumbooks.com

Printed in the United States of America

The paper used in this book complies with the
Permanent Paper Standard issued by the National
Information Standards Organization (Z39.48–1984).

10 9 8 7 6 5 4 3 2 1

Copyright Acknowledgments

For my twin, who helped make this possible

Contents

Figures and Tables

FIGURES

TABLES

Preface

This book was first conceived in 1997 by John Blaber, then of O'Reilly & Associates, as a companion piece to a Web log analysis tracking software package. With Dick Peck, I had just finished my first book-length project for O'Reilly, a market research report entitled *The State of Web Commerce*, and, as much as John wanted to write the book, he just did not have the time and entrusted the project to me. Unfortunately, the package was never released, so the book was never put on the schedule and I was free to find another publisher. I found Quorum Books over the Internet, fittingly enough, and had the great pleasure of selling my proposal to Eric Valentine who, to my utter delight, writes his letters on a typewriter. His patience and guidance have made this book a reality and for that I will be eternally grateful. I'd also like to thank Gerry McGovern, founder of Ireland's Nua Ltd., for publishing Nua Internet Surveys. That newsletter, managed by Sorcha Ni hEilidhe and Kathy Foley, provides the best coverage of research about the Internet and should be on everyone's reading list.

Every writer has a history of well-wishers and mentors who made it possible for him to do what he does. In my case it started at Syracuse University with a graduate assistant and debate coach named Peter Loge. Pete taught me to research and to see connections between seemingly unrelated issues, a highly valuable skill. While at Syracuse I also had the pleasure to study under Dr. Murray S. Miron, a noted psycholinguist. Dr. Miron's rigorous instruction and mentoring gave me insights into the human mind and the world of Washington, D.C.

While at the MITRE Corporation in McLean, Virginia, I had the pleasure to work for two forward thinkers: Bill Ruh of the Workstation Systems Engineering Center and Tom Barksdale. Bill took me, a political science major, under his wing and helped me learn information systems and databases, while Tom brought me into the world of economic and competitive analysis and let me delve into a variety of subjects, enhancing the research skills I'd developed in college. But if you're looking for someone to blame for my being a writer, call Brad Cox, then of George Mason University. I did my graduate work there and, after grading a software documentation project I'd lead, Brad said, "You know, you should do this for a living."

I'd also like to thank my agent, Neil Salkind of StudioB Productions, and the agency's founders, David and Sherry Rogelberg, for taking me on, keeping me busy, and helping me make it as a writer.

Special thanks as well go to my twin brother Doug, whose support got me through the lean years, to my parents for never letting me forget what I mean to them, and to my cat Mirrors for keeping me humble.

Introduction

As the Internet and its progeny the World Wide Web continue to grow and affect the business world, some writers have predicted the end of the Industrial Age and encouraged leaders to throw off the shackles of the physical and embrace the virtual. The Information Economy is the wave of the future, they argue, and those companies which best manage their data will gain a decisive advantage over their competitors.

Their argument is valid, but it brushes aside two fundamental truths. The first truth is that information cannot be eaten, nor driven to a child's soccer game. As physical beings, humans will always require food, clothing, and shelter. Once those needs are met, attention turns to making existence more bearable by building relationships, securing transportation, and storing goods of all kinds against future need. The second truth, and perhaps more to the point, is that business success has always depended on marshalling information effectively. When Henry Ford designed an assembly line that reduced the time to build a car from two months to two weeks, he organized the automobile manufacturing process so applied knowledge flowed smoothly down the line. To pretend industrial innovation is anything other than information management ignores how innovation comes about in the first place.

That said, we do not live in Henry Ford's world. The days of endless columns of black Model T's are gone; consumers are accustomed to choice and exercise it freely. They demand new features and products built more precisely to their specifications. They comparison shop and trade information about vendors with other consumers, both in person and over the Internet. They use information to their advantage in the marketplace and derive significant cost and usage benefits from that information.

Consumers are also becoming increasingly aware of how businesses acquire and analyze their personal information. They pay cash and resist register clerk's attempts to solicit their phone numbers or addresses. They screen telephone solicitations efficiently with CallerID and toss direct mail into the recycling bin 99 percent of the time. They understand that a receipt is all that is needed to claim warranty protection. They even, on occasion, submit false information to fight back against what they feel is an invasion of privacy.

Shaver states the problem this way:

The focus of management's attention is what will determine the quality of the relationship between seller and buyer. In hindsight, it is now clear that the focus of attention as the nationwide databases were being loaded with ever more personal information during the 1970s and 1980s was in the wrong place. In those years, our intensity of focus on growing computer power and the application of statistical expertise blurred our ability to see how customers really felt about what we were doing. Instead of building strong relationships built on personal human feelings and personal trust, we were building *weak relationships* based on *impersonal electronics* and *impersonal mathematical calculations*. . . .

Nothing symbolizes this misplaced focus as strikingly as the way most database marketing experts explain what they do and how they do it. A lack of peripheral vision typified by a persentation given to graduate students from leading business schools in the United States by one of database marketing's acknowledged experts. When describing how his company implemented database marketing for their clients, he cited the following key steps in the process between seller and buyer: . . . [initiate, manage, optimize]. . . .

Think about those words for a moment! They all reflect what the seller is doing "to" the buyer, rather than something the seller is doing "with" the buyer. . . . Control and manipulation are *not* the source of relationships based on good feelings and trust.[1]

The uneasy dance between producer and consumer is complicated by constant changes in the technological and legal landscapes. Consumers demand products built to more exacting tastes but are reluctant to surrender the information manufacturers need to design and build those products. Governments, including those in foreign countries, pass laws that affect how domestic businesses use their customer's personal information. Then, in the middle of it all, new companies spring up and offer their services as intermediaries to buffer the buyers from the sellers and ensure personally identifiable information is never given out except under the most exacting conditions.

Vendors can excel in the online economy by paying heed to a number of facts that make electronic commerce vastly different from traditional marketing:

- *Consumers care about privacy and are aware of what can be (and is) done with their information.* While most Internet users have been online for less than two years, the amount of information available on the Web, and circulated via electronic mailing lists, means that the average Internet user is much better informed about how much information is collected and how it can be used to identify them.

- *Consumers have the tools to protect their privacy online.* Unlike with traditional direct-marketing channels like direct mail and telephone solicitations, where users are limited to signing up with mail and telephone preference services, users can take active steps to protect their privacy online. For instance, they can configure their browser so it does not accept *cookies*, small files placed on users' computers to track user preferences and movement throughout sites. At a more basic level, site visitors can protect their privacy by entering false information into registration forms, hence the saying, "they want personal information, but they didn't say whose."

- *Organizations who are or who might potentially do business in European Union (EU) countries must protect consumer privacy.* Every EU country either has or will pass strict personal-data protection laws. Companies that want to operate in EU countries and be able to transfer personally identifiable data back to the United States will need to have a strong, verifiable data protection regime in place.

- *Preparing for domestic data protection legislation will prevent surprises later.* While the near-term prospect for any kind of data protection law in the United States is somewhat remote, there is a real possibility that Congress will pass legislation limiting how companies can gather, analyze, and distribute personal information. The sooner companies have a policy in place, at the very least in anticipation of new laws, the smoother the transition to the new regime will be.

- *Businesses will benefit by protecting customers' personal information and earning their trust.* In electronic commerce, companies that get ahead tend to stay ahead. By earning consumer trust and taking advantage of the information consumers do provide, knowing that information will not be circulated without their permission, companies will be in a wonderful position to benefit themselves and their clients.

Privacy-Enhanced Business analyzes the forces at work in the online world and offers advice on how businesses can earn consumer trust, maintain positive relationships with their customers, and operate under the attitudinal and legal constraints imposed on doing business in an increasingly interconnected world.

Chapter 1 introduces the Internet as a social and technological phenomenon by briefly recounting the early days of ARPANET, how the network's developers interacted as a community, and how their interactions have shaped the online world. It also looks at the demographics of the current Internet population. While the online population is far less homogeneous than it was even five years ago, certain trends remain. One of those trends is the online community's attitude toward privacy.

Chapters 2 through 4 fill in the policy background from a legal standpoint, explicating the legal theory of privacy that has developed in the United States through legislation as well as Supreme Court and inferior court decisions. Chapter 3 looks at the European Union's Data Protection Directive, which proscribes transferring personally identifiable information about EU citizens to countries without sufficient safeguards. Chapter 4 compares the American and EU approaches, identifying the differences and analyzing potential paths for reconciliation. Switching gears, Chapter 5 examines the economics of the Internet, from pricing strategies to the phenomenon of *increasing returns*, where companies that gain a market advantage tend to further their lead and those companies who trail fall farther and farther behind. One way to prevent that sort of loss is through Internet-based advertising, the subject of Chapter 6.

The next two chapters examine the technical aspects of Internet commerce, advertising, and information gathering. Chapter 7 demonstrates what information can and cannot be gained by maintaining activity logs for every visitor to a Web site. The chapter also looks at the software and services organizations can buy to make sense of the logs. This chapter also examines cookies, the much-debated files that can be used to track user movements through a Web site, and other user-tracking technologies. Chapter 8 reverses the focus by looking at Web users and what they can do to visit Web sites without leaving crumbs. Chapter 8 also introduces the *infomediary*, a type of organization that could allow consumers to maintain their anonymity while still allowing businesses access to detailed demographic and behavioral information.

In Chapter 9, *Privacy-Enhanced Business* returns to the policy realm by describing the range of legislative scenarios for the next ten years, and offers concrete steps businesses can take to improve consumer confidence, maintain the flow of information about their customers, and demonstrate their compliance with consumer expectations as well as the law. The two appendixes hold the full text of two documents that are vital to senior managers mapping corporate strategies: the European Union Data Directive and an EU Working Paper on the use of contracts to ensure the security of personally identifiable information transferred from the EU to third countries that lack adequate protection.

NOTE

1. Shaver, Dick, *The Next Step in Database Marketing: Consumer Guided Marketing* (New York: John W. Wiley & Sons, 1996), 81.

The Internet as Business Environment

There is no shortage of literature describing the Internet's history as a social and technological phenomenon. Likewise, books on doing business over the Internet abound, though it is interesting that most of the electronic-commerce literature focuses on how technology affects business transactions but ignores the social dimensions of the Internet and how the medium's early years affects its users' knowledge, values, and expectations today.

This chapter presents a quick history of the Internet, from the early years as a Department of Defense project to the commercial transition engendered by the World Wide Web and rapidly falling computer prices. It also examines how that history has affected the knowledge and attitudes of Internet users, as evinced by the open-source software movement and Internet users' appreciation for how computers can be used to gather, process, and distribute information. Finally, Chapter 1 examines the economics of the Internet in both its pure form and as an extension of traditional industry.

A QUICK HISTORY OF THE INTERNET

The Internet began as a U.S. Department of Defense (DoD) project to ensure national data communications in the event of a nuclear war with the Soviet Union. As with many other inventions, more than one individual foresaw various aspects of what eventually became the finished product. As related by Katie Hafner and Matthew Lyon, Paul Baran first conceived what was to become the Internet in 1959.[1] Baran, a Hughes Aircraft engineer who had left the defense contractor to take a position in the RAND Corporation's computer-science department, knew full well how fragile the United States' nuclear command and control systems were. That fragility, with the associated risk of an accidental or deliberate nuclear exchange, led him to consider methods of preserving data transfer even if large sections of the U.S. communications infrastructure was destroyed.

One of Baran's key insights into the problem was the nature of the American telecommunications grid, consisting almost exclusively of lines controlled by AT&T, and how its configuration was particularly vulnerable to a counterasset nuclear strike. At the time, telecommunications traffic was carried on either centralized or decentralized networks. Figure 1.1 illustrates the two network types. In a centralized network, all communication between points on a network (nodes), be they telephones or computers, is routed through a single point. If that central node fails, all communication in the network fails. A decentralized network offers a bit more redundancy: Each central node might be connected to two or more other central nodes and, in the event a node was down, the sender could choose another route to send a message. The network was still vulnerable, however, if communication between network segments depended on the availability of a single node. In Figure 1.1, the decentralized network depends on node B to pass all data from nodes in the left half of the network to nodes on the right.

As part of his investigations into finding a new network structure, Baran engaged in lengthy discussions with Warren McCulloch, a psychiatrist working in the Massachusetts Institute of Technology's Research Laboratory of Electronics, about how the brain formed new neural pathways in the event brain cells associated with a particular function were destroyed. This distributed network design, patterned after neural nets, would help preserve data transfer within the United States even if significant portions of the national communications grid failed. Figure 1.2 illustrates how a simple distributed network might be configured.

In its pure form, a distributed network would have connections from every node to every other node in the network. The obvious drawback of such a design is that once the network grows to more than four or five nodes, the expense of creating and maintaining that many links becomes prohibitive. Baran ran a number of simulations to determine how many connections each node required to approach the reliability provided by a pure distributed network, finding that each node required connections to no more than three and four other nodes to approach the theoretical limit. His results demonstrated that, at least in theory, a reliable distributed network could be built at an acceptable cost.

By 1965 Baran had won RAND's support for the project and the company sent a recommendation to the Air Force that the network be considered.[2] Re-

Figure 1.1
Centralized and Decentralized Networks

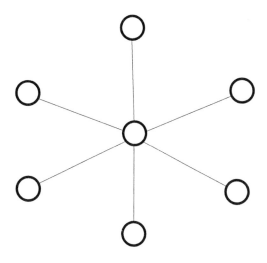

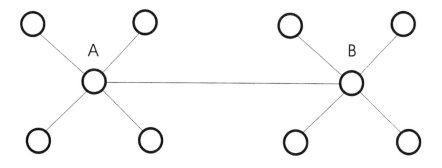

sistance from AT&T, the company the Air Force originally approached to build and maintain the network, and the prospect of turning the project over to the old-school Defense Communication Agency (DCA) caused the project to be put on hold until an organization better suited to running the endeavor could be found.

Figure 1.2
Distributed Network

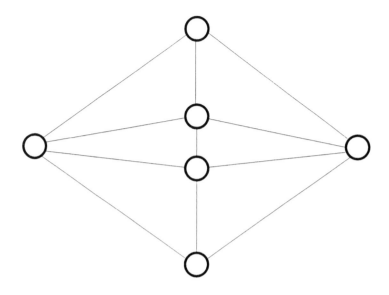

Parallel Developments

In late 1965 a British researcher named Paul Davies published his ideas on efficiently transmitting data on a distributed network. Davies, a physicist at the British National Physical Laboratory, proposed to break messages into packets, or data blocks of uniform size, and send each packet across the network individually. Each packet would contain the identity of the message it belonged to and its own place within that message, so the recipient computer could reassemble the packets in the proper order and request the originating computer resend any packets that failed to arrive within a certain interval after the first packet. A few years earlier at RAND, Paul Baran had envisioned a similar transmission scheme. Each packet would move through the network independently and, at every node, recompute the best path to the destination machine. Baran based his idea on the shipping industry, especially long-haul truck drivers using the new interstate highway system. If a driver discovered the most direct route between two cities was clogged or completely blocked, that driver could pick a different route and actually save transit time by avoiding the congestion.

The theory for a distributed national telecommunications network was in place. All that was needed was an organization that could turn theory into reality. That organization was the U.S. Department of Defense's Advanced Research Projects Agency (ARPA).

ARPANET

President Dwight Eisenhower formed the Advanced Research Projects Agency in early 1958 as a response to the Soviet launch of the Sputnik satellite the previous year and as a way to overcome the interservice rivalries within the American military that threatened to undermine DoD research. Later that year the National Aeronautics and Space Administration (NASA) was formed and took over most of ARPA's programs. Faced with untimely extinction, ARPA redefined itself as the DoD's clearinghouse for long-term research programs that, because they promised no results that could be integrated into military systems immediately, the services were not interested in pursuing themselves. The agency's commitment to basic research and its separation from the traditional military hierarchy made it the ideal home for the new distributed-data network project. In 1968 ARPA awarded Bolt Beranek Newman (BBN), then a small consulting firm, a contract to develop the Interface Message Processors (IMPs) that would be the actual nodes on the network.

It was at this point that the ARPANET moved from a theoretical exercise to a physical network. It was also at this foundational moment that the ARPANET became a social construct. While BBN built the first IMP in Cambridge, Massachusetts, that computer was destined for the University of California, Los Angeles (UCLA); ARPA's ties to the academic research community had led the agency to fund UCLA as the first ARPANET node. The academic community of the late 1960s was about as different from the military as possible, both from a social and an organizational perspective. In the military it is customary for a program office within an agency or service to "own" a particular technology. Work on that technology is controlled by that office, often quite closely, as the billets assigned to that office often depend on the work assigned to it the previous year. The academic community is much more used to sharing work among different departments. While the struggle for funding in the academic community can also reach epic proportions, the instinct to share the research load among project teams and to publish results is still in place. It was in this environment that the ARPANET took shape.

Bootstrapping

Through the 1970s computer scientists from UCLA, the MITRE Corporation, the University of California, Santa Barbara, NASA's Ames Research Laboratory, and other organizations established ARPANET nodes and used the network to share their work. Building a network from the ground up meant that the programmers needed to write all of the software from scratch as well. For instance, after creating the File Transfer Protocol (FTP), one of the first applications ARPANET programmers wrote was an electronic-mail (e-mail) program. Hafner and Lyon note that Stephen Lukasik, who directed ARPA from 1971 to 1975, was an electronic-mail pack rat who hated to throw anything away. The problem was that the primitive e-mail handling program used on the ARPANET at the time stored every message as part of a single file. To read a new message, Lukasik had to page through a large and constantly growing file. After Lukasik complained to Larry Roberts (then head of ARPA's Information Processing Techniques Office) about the difficulty he had handling e-mail, Roberts wrote a program named RD (short for "read") and presented it to Lukasik the next day.[3] RD presented the contents of a user's inbox as a series of messages that could be saved as separate text files, printed, or deleted. Other users heard about the program, obtained its source code, and added new features. After a short time there were myriad different versions of RD, plus entirely new programs that built on RD's features.

The ready availability of RD's source code, as well as the programmers' willingness to distribute their creations, continues to play an important part in the culture of the Internet. In *The Virtual Community*, Howard Rheingold notes that Internet Relay Chat (a program that allows users to type messages in one of many common areas, called "channels," in real time), Usenet (a network of computers which distributes the contents of newsgroups like sci.econ), and Multi-User Dungeons (shared online gaming environments where users could play characters in a fantasy or science fiction milieu, usually referred to as a MUD) as examples of collective goods that have been distributed through the Internet.[4] While these applications have certainly had an impact on the Internet, the first application to take off was electronic mail.

Robert Young relates a similar tale from 1996:

Grant Guenther, at the time a member of Empress Software's database development team, wanted to enable his co-workers to work on projects from home. They needed a secure method of moving large files from their office to home and back. They were using Linux on PCs and using Zip drives. The only problem was that at the time (1996), good Zip drive support was not available in Linux.

So Grant had a choice: throw out the Linux solution and purchase a much more expensive proprietary solution, or stop what he was doing and spend a couple of days writing a decent Zip driver. He wrote one, and worked with other Zip drive users across the Internet to test and refine the driver.[5]

Much of the ARPANET's utility came from its users ability to share their research agendas and results. The initial goal of the ARPANET was to allow users on the network to share the computing resources of other machines connected to the network, including processing power and file storage. Even so, e-mail use grew rapidly and in short order accounted for most ARPANET traffic. The literature of the ARPANET and the Internet relates numerous stories of how researchers used e-mail in the 1970s to transcend institutional and geographic frontiers. One incident, which occurred in September 1973, illustrated how the traditional geographic barriers could be overcome using the network. In this case, Len Kleinrock, a UCLA researcher, had left an electronic shaver at a conference in Brighton, England. By that time there was an ARPANET node at Brighton, so Kleinrock was able to connect to the computer there, find an acquaintance online, and ask that user to locate the razor and send it back with another UCLA researcher. This type of international transaction seems routine today, but at the time it bordered on the miraculous.[6]

Continued Growth

The number of computers connected to the ARPANET grew at a slow but steady pace through the mid-1970s, adding about one node a month. That steady level of growth continued until about 1984, when the number of nodes on the ARPANET began doubling about every year. Table 1.1 illustrates how the growth of the ARPANET (later the Internet) has accelerated since 1981.

In addition to an exponentially increasing number of computers on the network, the ARPANET, and its successor the Internet, underwent some significant changes in the 1980s and 1990s. As more universities, research institutions, and government offices were added to the ARPANET, knowledge of and demand for e-mail and other services spread. In the early 1980s several companies, most notably America Online, CompuServe, and Prodigy, started offering online services that, while not ARPANET or Internet connections, offered users a community and shared resource base individuals and businesses could access from home or work. In the mid- to late 1980s, entrepreneurs began to establish true Internet Service Providers (ISPs). Rather than offer access to a closed network, as was the case with CompuServe and other online services, ISPs offered a direct link to the Internet. At first the online services did not interact with the Internet, even by e-mail, but over time every online service provider extended its offerings to include Internet access.

It was also in the mid- to late 1980s that businesses began to follow and even host customer support and discussion forums hosted by online service providers and in Usenet newsgroups. Consumers who owned products from companies with discussion areas could enter into real-time discussions (called chats) with other consumers to compare notes, discuss the products' features and benefits (as well as problems and limitations, as appropriate), and provide feedback to manufacturers. As will be discussed later in this chapter, consumers' ability to publish and exchange information about companies and their products has had a profound impact on commerce.

The increasing commercial presence on the ARPANET caused many government officials and observers to question whether it was appropriate for the U.S. federal government to continue subsidizing an increasingly private network. Even though the number of commercial computers connected to the Internet did not exceed the number of noncommercial computers until 1994, the U.S. federal government decided to halt its support for the ARPANET in the late 1980s. The final host was removed from the ARPANET in 1989, though many of the network's computers were immediately connected to the Internet.

Table 1.1
Number of Hosts on the ARPANET/Internet

Date	Hosts	Date	Hosts
08/81	213	10/92	1,136,000
05/82	235	01/93	1,313,000
08/83	562	04/93	1,486,000
10/84	1,024	07/93	1,776,000
10/85	1,961	10/93	2,056,000
02/86	2,308	01/94	2,217,000
11/86	5,089	07/94	3,212,000
12/87	28,174	10/94	3,864,000
07/88	33,000	01/95	5,846,000
10/88	56,000	07/95	8,200,000
01/89	80,000	01/96	14,352,000
07/89	130,000	07/96	16,729,000
10/89	159,000	01/97	21,819,000
10/90	313,000	07/97	26,053,000
01/91	376,000	01/98	29,670,000
07/91	535,000	07/98	36.739,000
10/91	617,000	01/99	43,230,000
01/92	727,000	07/99	56,218,000
04/92	890,000	01/00	72,398,092
07/92	992,000		

Source: Network Wizards. Available <http://www.nw.org>.

Transition to Commercial Use

By the 1980s communicating via computer networks had spread far beyond the core group of the ARPANET's computer scientists. Online services like AOL and local bulletin board systems (BBSs) allowed users to exchange e-mail and engage in real-time chat with users with similar interests. What began as a military network to preserve American communication capabilities in the event of a nuclear strike had become a medium where (then) thousands of individuals could interact on a daily basis. While the definition of what was acceptable use of the Net expanded first to include nonmilitary research and then personal communication, the Net community was far from embracing commercial activities as acceptable practices.

One characteristic of contemporary computer networks is that once a connection fee is paid there is no marginal cost to the user for each additional byte of data sent over the network. In other words, it costs a user just as much to send an e-mail message to a colleague in Singapore as it does to send the same message to someone in the next office. By the same token, it costs just as much for a user to send one message to a colleague as it does to send ten messages—unless an account holder consistently requires a lot of bandwidth, Internet Service Providers rarely meter their customers' usage. Network capacity is considered a common good, to be shared by the network's users. Such was not always the case, however. A number of ISPs and online service providers charged their users based on the amount of data they sent and received. Unwanted messages represented a real cost to the recipient, as did unnecessary information within those messages.

Because of these charges, and the limits on ARPANET and Internet bandwidth, it was considered very bad manners to consume excess bandwidth. E-mail signatures were, by common consent, to be kept to under five lines; whenever possible, large files were to be sent during off-peak hours; and, even after the scope of acceptable activities expanded to include nonmilitary and other research, commercial uses of the ARPANET and Internet were not allowed. The prohibition was based on the nature of the network. Since message recipients were often charged to receive e-mail, sending advertising messages over the Net shifted the cost of the advertising from the advertiser to the prospective customer, regardless of whether they made a purchase. In short, despite the presence of FTP, Gopher, and Wide Area Information Service (WAIS), the technology was not in place for users to request only those files they wanted to receive. The technology that made it possible for users to request only those files they wanted to receive came about in 1989 when Tim Berners-Lee, a researcher at the CERN's High Energy Physics Laboratory, developed the protocols for the World Wide Web.

The World Wide Web, often abbreviated WWW or simply "the Web," is a network of computers that runs on top of the Internet. Not every computer on the Internet is on the Web, but every computer on the Web is on the Internet. Much like with FTP, a user types in a network address and is granted access to the files at that address. The Web's access software, referred to as a browser, offered a much more attractive user interface than did FTP, Gopher, or WAIS. Even so, the text-only, command-line interface and presentation lent itself to the technically savvy computer scientists and not to the general public. It wasn't until 1993 or 1994, as Frances Cairncross relates in *The Death of Distance*, that the Internet became a popular medium.[7] This popularity was brought on by Mosaic, the first graphical Web browser software. Created by Marc Andreesen, who later went on to help found Netscape Communications, Mosaic allowed Web site owners to present their documents through a graphical user interface. Much as the Macintosh operating system, and Windows after that, had introduced graphical user interfaces to personal computer owners, so did Mosaic make the computer-scientist-oriented World Wide Web accessible to the common user. Web browsers also created caches of images and text so that if a user revisited a page that had not changed since the user's previous visit the browser could simply load the image and text from the cache instead of requesting the host site send the page again.

Another benefit of the World Wide Web was that no information was transmitted over the Internet unless a user requested that information. When a user wants to visit a Web page, they type the page's address (the technical term for which is a Uniform Resource Locater, or URL) into the browser and press Enter. The browser software then looks up the address of the computer hosting the page. Once that address is obtained, the browser connects to the foreign machine and requests the desired file. This consideration was the driving force behind the explosion in commercial use of the Internet. Not only could companies make their information available on the Web, they were able to make that information available without foisting unwanted pages onto users who may have had to pay for the privilege of receiving information they would delete immediately. It is also worth noting that by 1995 almost every ISP had gone away from charging for bandwidth consumed by their individual users and only charged users (usually companies) whose Web sites generated more than two gigabytes (GB) of traffic a month. As competition increases and technology advances, the amount of bandwidth available for a given price increases as well.

THE INTERNET TODAY

There is no doubt the Internet has captured the collective attention of the industrialized world. Literally millions of new users are acquiring Internet accounts every year, with some ISPs and online service providers even offering connectivity "for free" with the purchase of a personal computer system. As of September 1999, Ireland's Nua Limited estimated the number of Internet users was 201 million, distributed geographically as shown here:

World Total	201 million
Africa	1.72 million
Asia/Pacific	33.61 million
Europe	47.15 million
Middle East	0.88 million
Canada & United States	112.4 million
Latin America	5.29 million[8]

This number has grown rapidly over the past few years. The first statistically defensible survey, conducted in 1995 by Trish Information Services and O'Reilly & Associates, indicated there were 5.9 million Americans over the age of eighteen who had direct access to the Internet through an Internet Service Provider, work, a library, or an academic institution. America Online, Prodigy, CompuServe, and other online service provider subscribers were excluded because, at the time of the survey, only Prodigy had an effective World Wide Web browser available for its subscribers.[9] Since then a number of research organizations have conducted studies to determine how many people use the Internet; researchers are also interested in tracking Internet-user demographics to determine the age, income, education, and professional characteristics of Internet users and see how this correlates to corporations' target audiences. One firm, IntelliQuest (http://www.intelliquest.com), conducts a quarterly poll to classify current and potential Internet users. On March 5, 1999, that company released a report that indicated that 79.4 million adults in the United States had Internet access, with another 18.8 million adults expected to go online over the succeeding year. Since the Nua estimate includes children, the two figures seem consistent. As Figure 1.3 indicates, Nua expects the number of Internet users to increase to 350 million by the year 2005.

Internet Demographics

Other demographic information gleaned from an AC Nielsen study show why the Internet is an exciting market for advertisers. Results quoted in *The Internet Advertising Report*, a December 1996 document from Morgan Stanley, indicated the average Internet user at that time was

Figure 1.3
How Many Online Worldwide

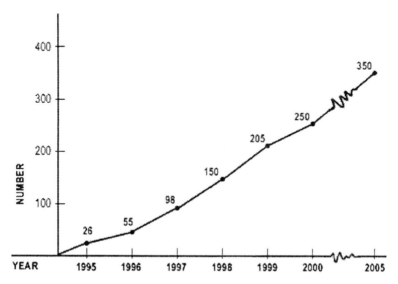

Source: Nua Internet Surveys. Available <http://www.nua.ie/surveys/analysis/graphs_charts/comparisons/how_many_online.html>.

- Between thirty and thirty-four years old (with only 10% of the population under eighteen).
- 64-percent likely to have a college degree.
- In a household with an income of at least $60,000 (25% have incomes of $80,000 or more).
- 50-percent likely to have a professional or managerial job.
- 60-percent likely to spend more than two hours per week online.
- 50-percent likely to have access at work.[10]

An SRI study released in February 1997 corroborated most of these results, indicating that more than 65 percent of Internet users had household incomes of $50,000 or more, versus 35 percent of the U.S. population as a whole, and that over 75 percent of Internet users had attended college, versus 46 percent of the total U.S. population.[11]

As the Internet has become more popular, the demographics of the Internet-user community has begun to resemble the national average more closely. In August 1999 Morgan Stanley Dean Witter issued an update of *The Internet Advertising Report* entitled *The Internet Data Services Report*.[12] The updated report combined U.S. Census data with the results of the GVU Tenth Internet Survey (examined in more detail later) to illustrate how the average Internet user looks a lot more like the average U.S. citizen than they did four years ago. Table 1.2 presents the results of that comparison.

While new Internet users are closer to the national average for income, age, and education than their counterparts with more than four years of Internet experience, they still have, on average, significantly higher incomes and more education than the average American. Economically speaking, Internet users are a valuable slice of the general public. Table 1.2 provides specific figures for comparison.

What Internet Users Care About

Internet users are more educated than the average American, but they also benefit from a strong tradition of mentoring. In the early days of the ARPANET most of the network's users were extremely capable programmers, but many times they could use tools created by others to complete their tasks without building their own software. Users taught each other how to use their programs and, as new users were introduced to the network, their predecessors shared their knowledge and encouraged the newcomers to write and share their own software to strengthen the community. This spirit of mentoring continued through the ARPANET years and into the era of America Online, CompuServe, and the Internet. Discussion areas on AOL, the Internet, and other services, such as the San Francisco Bay Area's Whole Earth 'Lectronic Link (WELL), were established with the purpose of allowing more experienced users to share

Table 1.2
A Profile of Users by Experience

	U.S. Avg.	Internet Avg.	Years on the Net	
			< 1 Year	> 4 Years
Median Household Income (US$)	34,076	65,250	51,920	71,060
Average Age	35.8	37.8	40.7	35.7
Male/Female Ratio	48/52	66/33	52/48	74/26
Education				
High School (%)	81.7	96.4	92.7	96.4
University (%)	23.6	33.6	25.3	33.6
Race				
Caucasian	71.8	88.1	86.5	87.8
African-American	12.9	2.3	3.5	1.6
Asian/Pacific Islander	4.1	2.1	2.0	2.5
Hispanic	11.2	1.8	2.2	1.8
Other	n/a	5.7	5.8	6.3
Urban/Rural				
Metropolitan (%)	79.9	86.2	83.9	88.2
Rural (%)	20.1	13.8	16.1	11.8

Source: U.S. Census, *GVU Tenth Internet Survey*. Available <http://www.gvu.gatech.edu>.

their knowledge with new users. The end result of the mentoring process is a knowledgeable online population with a firm grasp of what kind of information gathering and processing is possible with computers.

PRIVACY CONCERNS:
MAIL, TELEPHONES, AND THE INTERNET

Direct marketing via the Internet is a logical extension of the lucrative direct-mail and telephone marketing industries. *Economic Impact: U.S. Direct Marketing Today*, a study commissioned by the Direct Marketing Association (DMA) and undertaken by the WEFA Group, illustrates just how much money is invested in traditional direct-marketing campaigns and, perhaps more importantly, how successful the efforts are. Several statistics stand out:

- In 1996 direct-marketing campaigns costing approximately $144.5 billion (up 6.3% from 1995) generated an estimated $634.6 billion in consumer sales and $498.1 billion in business-to-business sales.

- Direct-marketing advertising accounted for 58.3 percent of the estimated $247.8 billion spent on advertising in the United States in 1996.
- Telephone marketing outlays were expected to grow to $57.8 billion in 1996, representing 40 percent of all direct-marketing costs.
- Direct-mail advertising, commonly thought to be the most prevalent form of direct marketing, accounted for $34.6 billion in 1996, 23.9 percent of the total spent on direct advertising.
- Of 1996 direct-marketing expenditures, 54 percent, or $78 billion, went for business-to-business campaigns.
- Over 56 percent ($81.4 billion) of 1996 direct-marketing dollars were earmarked for generating sales leads.[13]

That's all well and good, but how are the addresses and demographic information collected? In her 1994 book, *Who Owns Information?*, Anne Wells Branscomb gives a detailed account of how consumer contact information is collected and disseminated among direct-marketing companies.[14] While magazine subscription records and information garnered from retail mailing lists are excellent sources of demographically segregated consumer information, many direct-mail marketing lists are formed with the direct assistance of the U.S. Postal Service (USPS).

Direct Mail

Every change-of-address postcard filed in the United States is entered into computers at the USPS's approximately 200 regional centers and sent to Memphis, Tennessee, to be added to the National Change of Address (NCOA) database, which contains almost all of the deliverable postal addresses in the United States.[15] Once the addresses have been added, the changes are shipped off to more than twenty mailing-list management firms who pay the government for the updates.

Interestingly, the Postal Service does not give its customers the ability to opt out of the mailing lists provided to direct marketers. According to Sandra Harding, spokesperson for the Postal Service, the USPS "is not in the business of censoring mail." Harding went on to say that it is much easier for the customer to throw unwanted mail away than it would be for the USPS to maintain lists of the types of mail each customer wants to receive. She also questioned how postal employees were to determine which mail should or should not be delivered.

Buttressing Harding's arguments is a USPS survey that reported that 60.3 percent of U.S. postal customers were not bothered by unwanted solicitations and that one-sixth of Americans had purchased six or more items by mail order.[16] However, for those postal customers who do want to have their names removed from direct marketers' mailing lists, the Direct Marketing Association maintains a list of individuals who do not want to receive any direct-mail solicitations. DMA members must buy these lists and ensure the listed parties do not receive any mailings. Harding claimed that entering one's name with the Mail Preference Service reduces junk mail by about 80 percent, though Branscomb indicated at least two barriers to effectively removing one's name from mailing lists. First, many direct-marketing organizations are not members of the DMA and do not honor the association's removal lists. The second barrier is that individuals may not pick and choose which lists to be removed from: it is an all-or-nothing proposition.[17] Since some mailings are bound to be of interest, it is perhaps not unexpected that only 3.3 million Americans have asked to be removed from DMA members' mailing lists.

Harding notes that rather than filing a change-of-address form, postal customers may individually notify each sender they wish to have their new address. While this tactic may keep commercial solicitations away for a while, it is only a matter of time until the marketers catch up with the mover. Harding uses *Time* magazine as an example. *Time* pays one of the USPS's list-management agents to check the publication's subscription list and note any changes. *Time* takes the revised list, updates its own files, and sells the "new movers" list to other firms.[18] What the processing centers do not do is sell lists of all individuals filing change-of-address forms; to receive a new address, the client must have had the customer's previous address. The USPS ensures the data centers do not violate this provision by "seeding" the updates with addresses monitored by postal employees. In addition, the practice of selling individual addresses for $3 apiece, which Branscomb describes in *Who Owns Information?*, ended in 1994.[19]

Even though the Postal Service is "not in the business of censoring mail," it should be noted that the USPS does have a vested interest in ensuring direct marketers are able to reach postal customers with bulk mailings. In 1995 third-class mail made up 39.3 percent of mail in the system and generated $11.8 billion in revenue, with the added consideration that third-class mail is often much easier to handle than standard first-class mail. As Table 1.3 shows, the 1995 figure represents a steady increase in the amount of third-class mail sent, revenue generated, and the percentage of all U.S. mail that has been sent third class since 1992.

One advantage of handling bulk mailings is that the letters do not have to go out on the day they arrive at a local post office. Rather, they are delivered when the carriers have the time to mix the mail in with the hand-sorted first-class mail. Third-class mail's lower priority means that the cost of each third-class letter is appreciably lower than if it were sent first class. In addition, bulk mailers may lower their costs and further speed USPS processing by adding computer-readable bar codes, using ZIP+4 postal codes, and presorting mailings so carriers are able to add the bulk mail to their load for the day quickly.

Table 1.3
Volume, Revenue, and Share of Third-Class Mail in the U.S.
Postal System

Year	Volume of Third Class Mail (in millions of pieces)	Revenue (in millions of dollars)	% of Total Volume
1995	71,112.1	11,791.5	39.3
1994	69,415.5	10,513.8	39.2
1993	65,773.2	9,816.7	38.4
1992	62,547.2	9,490.2	37.6

Source: USPS Annual Reports.

Telephone Solicitations

Contrary to popular opinion, the telephone, not direct mail, is the most-used direct-marketing medium. Consumer-targeted direct telephone marketing expenditures increased from $15.2 billion in 1991 to $19.3 billion in 1996 (an annual growth rate of 4.9%), with revenues increasing from $124.5 billion to $168.8 billion (6.3% annual growth) over the same period.[20] With an average positive response rate of 6 percent, telephone marketing is a significantly more efficient means of generating positive responses than direct mail's 0.25–4-percent efficiency.[21]

The downside to telephone marketing is that phone calls are significantly more intrusive than direct mail. While unwanted mail may be thrown away, it is much harder to distinguish unwanted telephone calls from desired ones. Because unsolicited telephone calls require the recipient to drop what they were doing to answer the phone, it isn't surprising that a Walker Research poll indicated that 70 percent of respondents considered the calls an "invasion of privacy" and that 61 percent of those surveyed hung up within seconds of determining a call was a solicitation.[22] Consumers may use Caller ID, a service that displays the caller's phone number and (sometimes) identity, but if the recipient is not near the unit when the call arrives there may not be time to read the display and decide to answer the call before voice mail or an answering machine takes over.

Some practices, such as using computerized dialers with prerecorded messages and calling cellular phone numbers where recipients pay for air time on incoming calls, were outlawed in the Telephone Consumer Protection Act of 1991. Other provisions of that act prohibited anyone from calling hospital or nursing home rooms except for emergency purposes, "curtail[ing] the most egregious abuses of the telemarketing industry" without prohibiting telephone direct marketing altogether.[23]

Even though many intrusive practices have been eliminated from telemarketing, a surprisingly high 28.2 percent of telephone customers nationwide request unlisted phone numbers. The rate jumps to well over 50 percent for customers in Los Angeles and Las Vegas.[24]

THE ONLINE ENVIRONMENT

Georgia Tech's Graphic, Visualization, & Usability (GVU) Center's WWW User Surveys, cited earlier in Morgan Stanley Dean Witter's *Internet Data Services Report*, offer publicly available information about Internet demographics and are frequently consulted as barometers of World Wide Web user attitudes toward electronic commerce and other policy issues. The tenth annual survey ran in the latter part of 1998 and provided useful insights into how consumers viewed online commerce and privacy.[25]

One telling statistic is that 58 percent of respondents to a questionnaire on electronic commerce and privacy indicated they were "very" concerned about security when they made online purchases or banked via the Internet. Online banking and electronic commerce are sensitive applications, but user concerns spread to their personal information as well. Fully 75 percent of users indicated they would not provide personal information while registering at a site if the site did not disclose how the information would be used. A similar percentage (73.1%) said they refused to register at a site because they did not perceive the value offered in exchange for their personal information as being worth the risk of having that information misused. Finally, 67.3 percent of respondents noted that they have refused to register at a site because they did not trust the entity collecting the data.[26]

Respondents to the GVU survey were also strongly in favor of new laws to protect privacy on the Internet. Of the 1,482 respondents to this yes/no question, 40.6 percent indicated they strongly agreed that new laws were required, with another 30.8 percent agreeing somewhat.[27] Opinions over what rights companies should have with consumer information follow a similar pattern. Table 1.4 summarizes the results from a number of questions regarding personal information and user opinions on how their data should be handled.

One somewhat troubling result from a marketing perspective is that nearly half (44.6%) of respondents did not agree with the statement that information about users improves the marketing of a site.[28] It is an article of faith in the business world that the more an organization knows about its customers, the easier it is to service those customers' needs. That fully 28.5 percent disagreed at least in part with that statement (and that a further 16% were neutral or had no opinion) indicates a fundamental division between consumer attitudes and those of the marketers trying to reach them.

The 1996 edition of the GVU survey went further, asking how often visitors had deliberately provided false information when registering at a Web site. A significant number of respondents (33.5%) said they had provided false information at least once. While most respondents from that group (66.5%) indicated they do so less than 25 percent of the time, the wasted effort and expense of failed attempts to reach site visitors could significantly

Table 1.4
Internet User Opinions on Privacy and Electronic Commerce

	Agree Strongly	Agree Somewhat	Neither Agree nor Disagree	Disagree Somewhat	Disagree Strongly	No Opinion
Information improves site marketing	10.7	44.7	13.7	14.3	14.2	2.3
Reselling magazine subscription info OK	1.8	6.5	6.5	19.2	65.1	0.9
Users should control their info	72.9	17.6	4.9	2.3	1.0	1.3
Using info in other media is acceptable	2.6	9.9	6.2	19.4	61.3	0.6
Like receiving targeted direct mail	2.0	11.9	11.5	21.8	51.3	1.5
Like receiving mass emailings	0.5	2.3	5.4	14.4	75.9	1.4
Should be able to use aliases on the Net	31.9	26.9	22.1	6.8	5.2	7.0
Value the anonymity of the Net	66.1	21.7	8.4	1.1	0.8	1.5
Should be able to communicate privately	81.6	11.6	4.7	0.3	0.7	1.1

Source: U.S. Census, *GVU Tenth Internet Survey*. Available <http://www.gvu.gatech.edu>.

impact a firm's bottom line, not to mention making it much less attractive for other firms to buy or trade for the list.[29]

Internet Users and Personal Information

One reason the Internet is so popular is that it makes it possible to communicate rapidly and inexpensively with large groups. Whether by newsgroups, mailing lists, or online chat rooms, important information makes its way around the Internet at lightning speed. Many users have received multiple copies of the same electronic-mail message warning against the latest virus or "threat" to the online community. While many of these messages are hoaxes, there have been a few substantial campaigns against perceived abuses of personal information. The following section details those cases.

Lotus Marketplace

In April 1990 Lotus Development Corporation sent out press releases announcing their plans to team with Equifax, a consumer credit information bureau, to build *Lotus Marketplace: Households*, a CD-based collection of demographic information and estimated income of 120 million Americans. The project progressed smoothly until January 1991, when a firestorm of protest erupted on the Internet, resulting in more than 30,000 letters being sent to Lotus and Equifax protesting the product. On January 23, 1991, *Lotus Marketplace: Households* and a companion product with equivalent information for American businesses were removed from the market.[30]

So what went wrong? Why should consumers react so negatively to a product that simply gave small businesses access to information larger (and richer) companies had been buying for years? Mary Culnan, a professor at Georgetown University's School of Business Administration, noted that many consumers were clearly "surprised and shocked" that a company had accumulated so much information and was willing to sell subsets of it to small businesses for $695.[31] What was common knowledge in the business community, that any one of literally hundreds of direct-mail firms or consumer information bureaus like TRW, TransUnion, National Demographics and Lifestyles, and Acxiom Integrated Marketing Systems could have provided the same data, was a completely new and frightening prospect to many consumers.

It should be noted that the negative reaction took place even though Lotus and Equifax had taken several steps to safeguard consumer privacy. Branscomb notes that the firms

- Removed telephone numbers, actual income, and purchase-history data from the product.
- Screened purchasers to ensure only legitimate businesses acquired the product.
- Advised purchasers on the legalities and ethical aspects of using the information.
- Provided Lotus- and Equifax-funded means for consumers to remove their names from the database.[32]

The *Lotus Marketplace: Households* case illustrates how consumer concerns can proliferate at lightning speed over the Internet. While mass communication and discussion of issues on a global scale is in most cases beneficial to both consumers and businesses, the potential for rumormongering and spreading misinformation about products and services also exists. One such incident involved Lexis/Nexis' P-Trak Person Locator service.

Lexis/Nexis

Designed as a tool for attorneys, law-enforcement agencies, and private investigators to locate heirs, fugitives, and debtors, the P-Trak database came under fire in the popular media only days after its debut on June 1, 1996. For $85 per search, in addition to Lexis/Nexis's monthly subscription fee of $125, subscribers could access a database licensed from TransUnion, one of the big-three consumer credit information bureaus (along with TRW and Equifax). The database contains up to three previous addresses, phone numbers, maiden names, aliases, and Social Security numbers (SSNs) for over 300 million individuals.

Some privacy advocates took exception to making SSNs available in a public database, citing the potential for criminals to enter a target's name and address and use the person's SSN to apply for credit cards or for other fraudulent activities. These objections led Lexis/Nexis to make SSNs invisible if the database were searched by name, though subscribers could still search by SSN. The company took this action even though several other sources, such as the International Research Bureau, CBD InfoTek, and West Publishing Information America sell personal information, including SSNs, for as little as $13 per person.[33]

If the debate over the P-Trak database had ended there, little if any damage would have been done to Lexis/Nexis's reputation; instead, a wild variety of rumors cropped up on the Internet. Some of those stories stated falsely that mother's maiden names (which are often used to access bank accounts and credit cards) were available through the service, while other messages claimed that individuals' complete credit records could be obtained. The misinformation resulted in Lexis/Nexis's 800 number being jammed for two days with calls from angry consumers demanding their records be removed from the database. Eventually the company set up separate 800 number, mail-in, e-mail, and WWW-based mechanisms for individuals to request that their information be removed from the P-Trak service.

Social Security Administration

In a situation remarkably similar to the uproar over the availability of SSNs through the P-Trak service, the Social Security Administration came under fire in April 1997 after rumors that SSNs and salary histories were generally available on the SSA's Web site. In fact, the Web site did offer citizens the opportunity to obtain a Personal Earnings and Benefit Estimate Statement (PEBES), a projection of the user's Social Security benefits after retirement, online. To get the information users were required to establish an encrypted link with the SSA Web site and provide their SSN, name, date and place of birth, and mother's maiden name to verify their identity. The exact same information is required to receive a PEBES by mail, an SSA service offered for the past ten years with virtually no security-related complaints.[34]

As with the P-Trak database, rumors proliferated after published reports of the database's existence. According to a C|Net story, several legislators wrote the SSA requesting the agency stop using the Internet to disseminate Social Security–related information despite the complete lack of known security problems with the service. The C|Net article goes on to quote Karen Coyle, a privacy expert with Computer Professionals for Social Responsibility, who said the online hysteria, in this case, was not well-placed.[35]

Conclusions

As the public furors over the Social Security Administration WWW site, Lexis's P-Trak database, and Lotus Marketplace products demonstrate, concerns among and reactions from Internet users do not always take information providers' privacy-protecting measures into account; in the worst case, popular opinion may be shaped by hearsay and partial information. There are mechanisms available to Internet advertisers and WWW hosts to help avoid similar perception problems, but concerns over user privacy have also been heightened by a recent increase in "junk" e-mail.

POISONING THE WELL: THE CYBERPROMOTIONS CASE

Though the Internet bears increasingly little resemblance to the tightly knit academic community of the 1970s and 1980s, many users have an aversion to unsolicited commercial e-mail. Unlike direct marketing using the U.S. Postal Service's bulk-mail services, literally millions of e-mail messages may be sent for next to no direct cost to the sender. The indirect costs of such mailings, however, are significant. They include the following:

- Machine resources. Since e-mail messages usually pass through several machines on the way to their destinations, each of those computers' other tasks is affected by the time to process the messages of a user on another system.
- Network bandwidth. Just as large numbers of e-mail messages consume machine cycles, the data also clog the transmission channels between machines, slowing the overall functioning of the Internet even further.
- User fees. Although many online services and Internet Service Providers have adopted flat-rate pricing or allow generous amounts of access per month, downloading and reading unsolicited e-mail takes time paid for by the message recipient, not the sender. So, unlike bulk mail sent via the post office, Internet users subsidize junk e-mail senders' operations through their subscription fees. For users outside the United States the cost of downloading and processing junk e-mail is even higher, as most telephone services charge a per-minute rate for local calls in addition to a base monthly fee.

Many ISP's terms of service agreements stipulate that subscribers may not use their accounts to send unsolicited commercial e-mail (known as "spam" in the vernacular of the Internet), though there are a handful of companies that allow their subscribers to do so. One of those companies, Cyber Promotions, has had run-ins with, among other Internet access providers, America Online, CompuServe, and Prodigy.

Cyber Promotions versus AOL

Cyber Promotions, based in Philadelphia, Pennsylvania, has sent literally hundreds of millions of unsolicited commercial e-mail messages to subscribers of AOL, CompuServe, Prodigy, and numerous ISPs. Over one eight-day stretch in November 1996, AOL's mail servers processed 1.9 million messages from Cyber Promotions every day.[36]

The conflict between Cyber Promotions and AOL flared up on January 26, 1996, when AOL sent a letter to Cyber Promotions indicating the online service provider's dissatisfaction with Cyber Promotions' solicitations. To reinforce the inconvenience caused by the unsolicited e-mail, AOL gathered a large number of undeliverable messages from Cyber Promotions and e-mailed them back to Cyber Promotions as a series of large files. As a result of AOL's e-mail "bombing," two of Cyber Promotions' access providers canceled the firm's accounts and a third refused to sell the company an account at all.[37]

A round of lawsuits followed, including a request by Cyber Promotions on May 8, 1996, that the U.S. District Court for the Eastern District of Pennsylvania find that the bulk e-mailer "has the right to send to AOL members via the Internet unsolicited advertisements" and to "permanently enjoin AOL . . . from . . . directly or indirectly preventing AOL members from receiving [Cyber Promotions'] e-mail messages."[38] The latter request was based on AOL's implementing PreferredEmail, a tool that required AOL subscribers to click a box stating "I want junk e-mail!" before messages from Cyber Promotions and other known bulk e-mail advertisers would be allowed into that user's mailbox.

Despite several different theories presented by Cyber Promotions' lawyers, the court found in decisions issued on November 4, 1996, and November 22, 1996, that

- AOL was not a state actor, so the PreferredEmail tool did not violate either Cyber Promotions' or AOL subscribers' First Amendment rights.
- Customer complaints and the technical problems of processing Cyber Promotions' e-mail gave AOL legitimate business reasons to block the advertiser's e-mail.
- Cyber Promotions has numerous alternative Internet-based avenues of reaching AOL members, such as the World Wide Web, as well as non-Internet avenues including the U.S. mail, telemarketing, broadcast and cable television, newspapers, magazines, and leaflets. That none of those methods is as cheap as e-mail was, in the court's opinion, irrelevant.
- AOL had a legitimate interest in selling the right to advertise on its system and in refusing ads from individuals and companies that do not pay appropriate fees.[39]

As part of its decision to grant a temporary restraining order, the District Court adopted an interesting analogy offered in one of AOL's briefs, writing,

AOL's private system is akin to a private resort swimming pool that has a "channel" leading to the "ocean" that is the Internet. AOL has permitted persons swimming in its "pool" to transmit messages to and receive messages from the Internet ocean. AOL has, however, taken steps to prevent sharks such as Cyber [Promotions] from entering AOL's pool from the Internet ocean.[40]

AOL and Cyber Promotions eventually settled the matter out of court in a manner both sides described as a "victory": Cyber Promotions was free to send unsolicited commercial e-mail to AOL customers from a limited set of addresses, which the customers were then free to block with the PreferredEmail tool.[41] Unfortunately for Cyber Promotions, AOL isn't the only online service provider fighting against unwanted commercial e-mail.

Cyber Promotions versus CompuServe

Like AOL, CompuServe subscribers had been receiving thousands of e-mail messages from Cyber Promotions every day. Unlike the AOL case, however, Cyber Promotions had, on October 17, 1996, modified the header information in thousands of e-mail messages to read as if the messages had come from CompuServe. In addition, the advertisements' return address was altered to "102673.01425@compuserve.com," meaning that thousands of undeliverable messages were "returned" to CompuServe's system, not Cyber Promotions'. The resulting deluge of e-mail crippled CompuServe's servers, causing messages that would normally arrive in minutes to take up to three days to reach their destinations; inspired 9,970 complaints from CompuServe members in November 1996 alone; and led "many" CompuServe customers to cancel their accounts.[42]

On October 24, 1996, the U.S. District Court for the Southern District of Ohio issued a temporary restraining order that prohibited Cyber Promotions from sending e-mail to CompuServe accounts and from altering its messages to appear as if they originated from CompuServe. On February 3, 1997, the court issued a preliminary injunction affirming its earlier decision, holding that Cyber Promotions

- Sent numerous unsolicited e-mail messages to CompuServe's proprietary computer equipment.
- Continued to send a high volume of unsolicited e-mail after repeated demands to stop.
- Deliberately evaded CompuServe's attempts to block the unsolicited e-mail.

Based on those conclusions, including CompuServe's reduced ability to use its private property (servers) as a direct result of Cyber Promotions' actions, the court found that the online service provider "ha[d] a viable claim for trespass to personal property and [was] entitled to injunctive relief to protect its property."[43]

That the court based its decision to grant the temporary restraining order on the proposition that Cyber Promotions' unsolicited e-mail violated CompuServe's property rights is extremely significant. If other online services and ISPs were to sue successfully on the same grounds as part of a class action suit or individually, the practice of "spamming" could be curtailed sharply. However, the difficulty in enforcing the ban, as exemplified by CompuServe's inability to block Cyber Promotions' messages, would lessen the effectiveness of such a finding.

On May 9, 1997, CompuServe and Cyber Promotions entered into an agreement that barred Cyber Promotions from sending unsolicited e-mail to CompuServe customers and specified fines of up to $35,000 if such mailings did occur.[44]

Implications for Online Marketers

While the District Court for the Eastern District of Pennsylvania's decision simply affirms AOL's right to block unsolicited commercial e-mail from a number of sources, the District Court for the Southern District of Ohio's findings in the CompuServe case raise a number of questions regarding e-mail-based online advertising. These questions include the following:

- What constitutes "solicitation"? Is signing a guestbook at a particular Web site sufficient? Signing up for e-mail about related products or services?
- What is the minimum number of messages that constitutes trespass? The CompuServe court found that Cyber Promotions' e-mail barrage had significantly reduced the value of CompuServe's property by impairing their computers' ability to perform their usual functions. Would a single message be sufficient for a trespass finding under that doctrine? One hundred? One hundred thousand?
- What constitutes "notice" that a trespass has taken place? The decision indicates that a party must be put on notice that a trespass has occurred and that CompuServe's policy statement on its network "may be insufficiently communicated to potential third-party users."[45]
- What application, if any, would these precedents have to cases challenging direct mail or telephone solicitations?

CONCLUSIONS

In 1994 Anne Wells Branscomb accurately predicted in her book, *Who Owns Information?*, "The more computer networks that come on line, the more likely is the public to become aware of how their personal data is being gathered and used for business interests. With this awareness will come a greater demand for more personal autonomy over such information."[46] As the junk e-mail lawsuits and consumer concerns over the Lexis P-Trak database, *Lotus MarketPlace: Households*, and the Social Security Administration's online PEBES service indicate, consumers have become more concerned over how their personal information is used by marketers. Despite these difficulties, an April 1997 Forrester Research report indicates that direct-marketing companies expect their Internet-based sales volume to increase from its 1996 share of 7 percent to 36 percent by the year 2001.[47] The economic advantages of the Internet make it too attractive not to be used as a means of getting information to customers quickly and inexpensively, though marketers must make efforts to gain and maintain consumer trust through several means. They include the following:

- Educating consumers on what information is being collected, how it will be used by the company, and whether it will be sold or traded to other organizations.
- Understanding that consumers, especially Internet users, are very concerned about personal privacy.

• Using the Internet to publicize privacy protection efforts and, in the event of a rumor flare-up, to disseminate accurate information.

NOTES

1. Katie Hafner and Matthew Lyon, *Where Wizards Stay Up Late: The Origins of the Internet* (New York: Simon & Schuster, 1996), 54.

2. Ibid., 63.

3. Ibid., 194.

4. Howard Rheingold, *The Virtual Community* (Reading, Mass.: Addison-Wesley, 1993), 13.

5. Robert Young, "Giving It Away," in *Open Sources: Voices from the Open Source Revolution*, ed. Chris DiBona, Sam Ockman, and Mark Stone (Sebastopol, Calif.: O'Reilly & Associates, 1999), 122.

6. Hafner and Lyon, *Where Wizards Stay Up Late*, 188.

7. Frances Cairncross, *The Death of Distance* (Boston: Harvard Business School Press, 1997), 97.

8. Nua Ltd., "How Many Online?" 1999. Available <http://www.nua.ie/surveys/analysis/graphs_charts/comparisons/how_many_online.html>.

9. O'Reilly & Associates and Trish Information Systems, *Defining the Internet Opportunity, Phase II: Internet Users* (Sebastopol, Calif.: O'Reilly & Associates, 1995), 2.

10. Doug Arthur, Chris DePuy, and Michael Russell. *The Internet Advertising Report* (New York: Morgan Stanley & Co., 1996), 4–4.

11. SRI Consulting, "New Study by SRI Consulting Maps Consumer Use of New Media," 4 February 1997. Available <http://www.sri.com/press-releases/2-4-97.html>.

12. Jeffrey Camp and Stephen Flynn, *The Interned Data Services Report* (New York: Morgan Stanley Dean Witter, 11 August 1999). Available <http://www.morgan stanley.com/techresearch/index.html>.

13. Direct Marketing Association and the WEFA Group, *Economic Impact: U.S. Direct Marketing Today* (New York: Direct Marketing Association, 1996), 5.

14. Anne Wells Branscomb, *Who Owns Information? From Privacy to Public Access* (New York: Basic Books, 1994).

15. Ibid., 9–10.

16. Ibid., 15.

17. Ibid., 10.

18. Sandra Harding, telephone interview with author, 14 May 1997.

19. Branscomb, *Who Owns Information?* 10, and Harding, interview.

20. DMA and the WEFA Group, *Economic Impact*, 22.

21. Dick Peck, vice president for business development at O'Reilly & Associates, interview with author, 14 November 1996.

22. Branscomb, *Who Owns Information?* 31.

23. Ibid., 33.

24. Ibid., 43.

25. Georgia Tech Research Corporation, *GVU Tenth Annual Survey*, October 1998. Available <http://www.gvu.gatech.edu/user_surveys/survey-1998-10/graphs/privacy>.

26. Georgia Tech Research Corporation, *GVU Tenth Annual Survey*, October 1998. Available <http://www.gvu.gatech.edu/user_surveys/survey-1998-10/graphs/privacy/q48.htm>.

27. Georgia Tech Research Corporation, *GVU Tenth Annual Survey*, October 1998. Available <http://www.gvu.gatech.edu/user_surveys/survey-1998-10/graphs/privacy/q59.htm>.

28. Georgia Tech Research Corporation, *GVU Tenth Annual Survey*, October 1998. Available <http://www.gvu.gatech.edu/user_surveys/survey-1998-10/graphs/privacy/q61.htm>.

29. Georgia Tech Research Corporation, *GVU Tenth Annual Survey*, October 1998. Available <http://www.cc.gatech.edu/gvu/user_surveys/survey-10-1996>.

30. Mary Culnan, *The Lessons of the Lotus MarketPlace: Implications for Consumer Privacy in the 1990's*. Available <http://www.cpsr.org/dox/conferences/cfp91/culnan.html>.

31. Ibid.

32. Branscomb, *Who Owns Information?* 18.

33. Rose Aguilar, *Service Still Provides Sensitive Information,* 19 September 1996. Available <http://www.news.com/News/Item/0,4,3608,00.html>.

34. Janet Kornblum, *Social Security Site Closed*, 9 April 1997. Available <http://www.news.com/News/Item/0,4,9555,00.html>.

35. Ibid.

36. J. Weiner, *Memorandum Opinion and Order in AOL v. Cyber Promotions, Inc.*, C.A. nos. 96-2486, 96-5213, 948 F. Supp. 456 (Eastern District of Pennsylvania, 26 November 1996). Available <http://www.jmls.edu/cyber/cases/aol-cp2.html>.

37. J. Weiner, *Memorandum Opinion and Order in AOL v. Cyber Promotions, Inc.*, C.A. nos. 96-2486, 96-5213, 948 F. Supp. 436 (Eastern District of Pennsylvania, 4 November 1996). Available <http://www.jmls.edu/cyber/cases/aol-cp1.html>.

38. Ibid.

39. Weiner, 948 F. Supp. 456 and 948 F. Supp. 436.

40. J. Weiner, *Memorandum Opinion and Order in AOL v. Cyber Promotions, Inc.*, C.A. nos. 96-2486, 96-5213, 948 F. Supp. 456 (Eastern District of Pennsylvania, 20 December 1996). Available <http://www.jmls.edu/cyber/cases/aol-cp3.html>.

41. CNet News.com Staff, "Spam king, AOL agree to disagree," 4 February 1997. Available <http://www.news.com/News/Item/0,4,7648,00.html>.

42. J. Graham, *Temporary Restraining Order in CompuServe Incorporated v. Cyber Promotions, Inc. and Sanford Wallace*, C.A. no. C2-96-1070, 962 F. Supp. 1015 (Southern District of Ohio, 24 October 1996). Available <http://www.jmls.edu/cyber/cases/cs-cp1.html>.

43. J. Graham, *Memorandum Opinion and Order in CompuServe Incorporated v. Cyber Promotions, Inc. and Sanford Wallace*, C.A. no. C2-96-1070, 979 F. Supp. 482 (Southern District of Ohio, 3 February 1997). Available <http://www.jmls.edu/cyber/cases/cs-cp2.html>.

44. J. Graham, *Final Consent Order by Stipulation in CompuServe Incorporated v. Cyber Promotions, Inc. and Sanford Wallace*, C.A. no. C2-96-1070 (Southern District of Ohio, 9 May 1997). Available <http://www.jmls.edu/cyber/cases/cs-cp3.html>.

45. Ibid.

46. Branscomb, *Who Owns Information?* 49.

47. Forrester Research, "Online Direct Marketing Revenues to Increase to 36% by 2001," 2 April 1997. Available <http://www.forrester.com/pressrel/970402MD.htm>.

2

Domestic Law

The mid-1990s saw radically increased competition among broadcast media, a trend perhaps best illustrated by the proliferation of cable channels available to consumers through traditional providers and satellite networks. While this growth gives consumers many more choices than before, the resulting audience fragmentation poses serious difficulties for advertisers in reaching their target demographic groups. Nielsen ratings boxes, viewer logs, and other tools help derive the information the networks and advertisers need to make informed buying and selling decisions for broadcast advertising. Internet marketers, however, are faced with the much more difficult task of tracking users over what is still a mostly anonymous medium.

Fortunately for WWW hosts, the protocol underlying the Web, the Hypertext Transfer Protocol (HTTP), does request seven basic pieces of information from the browser accessing the site:

- User name (rarely provided, but it is requested).
- Authentication name (requested if the user attempts to view a secure page).
- Host name and/or Internet protocol address of the visitor's computer.
- Time and date of the request.
- Specific HTTP command issued by the visitor's browser.

- Status of the request (such as "404 Not Found").
- Bytes of data transferred.

WWW server software maintains a log of every HTTP request from remote users. As will be seen in Chapter 7, there are ways to derive useful information from those records. This chapter addresses the legal status of information generated by users traversing the Web.

PERSONAL INFORMATION: PRIVACY AND POLICY

The concept of privacy as a legal right first saw the light of day in a famous 1890 *Harvard Law Review* article by Boston lawyer Samuel Warren and his former law partner, future Supreme Court Justice Louis Brandeis. Their conception of a "right to be let alone" allowed an individual to maintain distance from society and "protect the privacy of private life."[1] As William Prosser relates in his landmark 1960 *California Law Review* article, Warren enlisted Brandeis's aid in writing the article after the Boston media, particularly the *Saturday Evening Gazette*, reported events from a series of parties hosted by Mrs. Warren and, as the final straw, when the newspapermen "had a field day" covering the wedding of one of the Warrens' daughters.[2]

The 1890s were marked by rapid advances in photographic technology, allowing reporters to capture images of individuals with an ease not possible before. In a similar vein, the latter half of the twentieth century has seen the advent of computer technologies that allow organizations to gather and correlate massive amounts of information about individuals in ways not possible before. As noted in Chapter 1, opinion polls indicate the public is concerned about the effect information technologies have on their privacy. What is less clear is precisely what "privacy" means.

Defining Privacy

One problem with defining privacy is that the concept means different things to different people at different times. The social distance citizens keep from strangers, acquaintances, friends, business associates, companies, and the government all depend on the context of the interaction, the familiarity with the individual or organization in question, and the value a person places on privacy in each of those situations. Despite these difficulties, it is important to survey the privacy literature to determine how the term is used by itself and in the context of the phrase "informational privacy." This section will draw from several sources for definitions and analyses of privacy:

- Common law.
- Constitutional law.
- Domestic law.

Common Law

William Prosser, dean of the University of California Law School at Berkeley, argued in his 1960 *California Law Review* article that four "torts," or common law principles, had been used in court decisions to protect different aspects of privacy. The torts he specified, which are still accepted as legal canon, protect against

- Intrusion upon an individual's seclusion, solitude, or private affairs.
- Public disclosure of embarassing private facts.
- Publicity placing an individual in a false light.
- Appropriation of an individual's likeness for advantage.[3]

The problem with this analysis, of course, is that the statements of the intrustion and public disclosure torts use the word "private," a term Prosser never properly defines in his article. He does use the words "secret" and "secluded" as part of his discussion of the first two torts, though neither of those terms is particularly helpful in the present context.[4] In practice, it has been left up to the courts to decide which facts are private under the common law and which are not. The same confusion extends to the realm of Constitutional privacy, where a number of U.S. Supreme Court decisions have examined aspects of privacy without forming an overarching framework for the concept.

Constitutional Law

Griswold v. Connecticut

The first United States Supreme Court decision to explicitly name a "right to privacy" was rendered in *Griswold v. Connecticut*, a 1965 case in which a doctor and Planned Parenthood director challenged the constitutionality of a Connecticut law prohibiting the dissemination of birth-control advice to married couples.[5] In the Court's opinion, Justice Douglas wrote that "specific guarantees in the Bill of Rights have penumbras ("shadows"), formed by emanations from those guarantees that help give them life and substance. . . . Various guarantees create zones of privacy." Douglas singled out several amendments as establishing such zones:

- First Amendment guarantees of freedom of association.
- Third Amendment protections against housing troops against one's will during peacetime.
- Fourth Amendment guarantees against unreasonable searches and seizures.
- Fifth Amendment rights against self-incrimination.
- Ninth Amendment provisions that the Constitution did not need to name a right for it to exist.

• Fourteenth Amendment assurances of due process.

So, while privacy is not mentioned directly in the Constitution, the *Griswold* court held that it existed in the "penumbra" of the Amendments listed. Subsequent cases helped refine the concept, starting with the 1967 case *Katz v. United States*.

Katz v. United States

In *Katz*, a California man was convicted of transmitting gambling information across state lines from a Los Angeles pay phone.[6] To secure the conviction, the prosecution relied heavily on recordings federal agents made of Katz's calls from the pay phone by means of a wiretap placed on the line, a wiretap for which the agents had not sought a court order. The question before the Court, then, was whether a wiretap constituted a "search" requiring a judge's approval under Fourth Amendment jurisprudence.

Up to the time of the *Katz* decision, wiretaps were not considered searches for Fourth Amendment purposes; the reigning precedent was a 1928 Supreme Court ruling in *Olmstead v. United States* that a physical trespass needed to occur for a "search" to require a warrant.[7] Justice Stewart's opinion specifically rejected this formulation in *Katz*, however, holding that "the Government's eavesdropping activities violated the privacy upon which petitioner justifiably relied while using the telephone booth and thus constituted a 'search and seizure' within the meaning of the Fourth Amendment."[8]

While the Court did use language indicating that citizens have an expectation of privacy when using a pay phone and taking steps to ensure their words were not overheard (i.e., closing the door), the Court did not extend this analysis to infer a broader Constitutional right to privacy. Instead, Justice Stewart's opinion was reminiscent of the "penumbra" construcution used in *Griswold*:

The Fourth Amendment cannot be translated into a general constitutional "right to privacy." That Amendment protects individual privacy against certain kinds of governmental intrusion, but its protections go further, and often have nothing to do with privacy at all. Other provisions of the Constitution protect personal privacy from other forms of governmental invasion. But the protection of a person's general right to privacy—his right to be let alone by other people—is, like the protection of his property and of his very life, left largely to the law of the individual States.[9]

The policy-making problem with this conception is that it defines privacy interests by negation, specifying what form privacy does not take within the framework of Constitutional law, and then only in part. The issue is clouded even more elsewhere in the opinion, where Stewart writes that "what a person knowingly exposes to the public, even in his own home or office, is not a subject of Fourth Amendment protection. . . . But what he seeks to preserve as private, even in an area accessible to the public, may be constitutionally protected."[10]

Fortunately, Justice Harlan's concurring opinion offers a two-pronged test for determining when Constitutionally implied privacy rights are at issue. The two criteria are as follows:

1. A person must have exhibited an actual (subjective) expectation of privacy.
2. The expectation be one that society is prepared to recognize as "reasonable."[11]

While Justice Harlan's test does not establish a "bright line," it is much more useful for making policy and judicial decisions regarding privacy than the vague penumbral conception found in the main *Katz* opinion. The implications of this test, especially the prong addressing societal expectations, will be examined later in this chapter.

Paul v. Davis

In this case, Davis's name and picture had been included in a flyer distributed to Louisville businesses listing active shoplifters, despite the fact that shoplifting charges brought against him were eventually dismissed.[12] Rather than bring an action in state court under the false-light tort described earlier, Davis chose to challenge the flyer on Constitutional due process and privacy grounds. The court of appeals ruled in Davis's favor on due process grounds (declining to make a finding on the privacy claim), but the Supreme Court ruled that neither Davis's due process nor his privacy rights had been violated.

For a claim under the due process clause of the Fourteenth Amendment to be valid, an individual must have been deprived of "liberty" or "property" without due process of law. In reversing the appeals court's decision, the Supreme Court specified that damage to reputation alone did not constitute a due process violation. Doing so, Justice Rehnquist wrote, would allow individuals to sue if law-enforcement officers were to "announce that they believe such person to be responsible for a particular crime in order to calm the fears of an aroused populace," or, if taken to the extreme, the proposed "construction would seem almost necessarily to result in every legally cognizable injury which may have been inflicted by a state official acting under 'color of law' establishing a violation of the Fourteenth Amendment."[13]

In addressing the privacy question, the Court looked to its precedents to determine if the information disseminated by the Louisville police department violated Davis's constitutional privacy expectations. *Katz* did not apply, as Davis's claim was not about evidence acquired during a search, so Justice Rehnquist used the privacy analysis from *Roe v. Wade*,[14] the decision that invalidated many state laws regulating abortion as violations of personal autonomy guaranteed by the Fourteenth Amendment:

In *Roe* the Court pointed out that the personal rights found in this guarantee of personal privacy must be limited to those which are "fundamental" or "implicit in the concept of ordered liberty" as described in *Palko v. Connecticut*. . . . The activities detailed as being within this definition were ones very different from that for which respondent claims constitutional protection—matters relating to marriage, procreation, contraception, family relationships, and child rearing and education.[15]

The Court's holding in *Paul v. Davis* represents a watershed in privacy law, as it restricts what interests are implied by the Fourteenth Amendment, though it is also significant in that the government had used a data collection to generate a list of undesirable characters that was distributed in the area where Davis lived, worked, and shopped. Though the information-system aspects of the case was minimal, 1976 and 1977 saw two important decisions about privacy rights and record keeping: *United States v. Miller* and *Whalen v. Roe*.

United States v. Miller

This case examined whether bank records were "personal records" for Fourth Amendment purposes.[16] Miller had been arrested for illegally producing and selling liquor and evading paying taxes on the income generated. While building the case against Miller, police subpoenaed records from two banks where he had accounts; the banks complied, but Miller's counsel argued that the records were "private papers," protected from disclosure because they fell within a zone of privacy established by the Bank Secrecy Act. The trial court disallowed the motion, but the court of appeals agreed that the papers were constitutionally protected under the Fourth Amendment. Unfortunately for Miller, the Supreme Court reversed the court of appeals decision by a seven-to-two vote.

The main reason the Supreme Court set forth for reversing the lower court decision was that Miller had no privacy interest in the bank records released to the police. Quoting *Katz*, the Court stated, "What a person knowingly exposes to the public . . . is not a subject of Fourth Amendment protection."[17] The Court interpreted this standard in the prosecution's favor, arguing,

The checks are not confidential communications but negotiable instruments to be used in commercial transactions. All of the documents obtained, including financial statements and deposit slips, contain only information voluntarily conveyed to the banks and exposed to their employees in the ordinary course of business.[18]

The Court also rejected Miller's argument that the Bank Secrecy Act created a constitutional expectation of privacy in bank records, citing Congress's legislative intent when it drafted and passed the act. Though the recent ruling that the Communications Decency Act was unconstitutional indicates that legislative intent is not an absolute guarantee of legitimacy, the Court found in *Miller* that

The lack of any legitimate expectation of privacy concerning the information kept in bank records was assumed by Congress in enacting the Bank Secrecy Act, the expressed purpose of which is to require records to be maintained because they "have a high degree of usefulness in criminal, tax, and regulatory investigations and proceedings."[19]

The *Miller* decision lends at least indirect credence to private third-party database operators' claims that the information they maintain (and certainly the names, addresses, and phone numbers of clients who file a change of address form, fill out warranty cards, or subscribe to magazines) are not "private," as the information has been released voluntarily during the "ordinary course of business."

Through *Miller* the Supreme Court's decisions had been relatively consistent. Unfortunately, the final decision discussed here, *Whalen v. Roe*, has done much to unravel that precedential thread.

Whalen v. Roe

The New York state legislature passed a law in 1972 that required physicians to fill out a form in triplicate every time a patient was prescribed a drug on the state's Schedule II (e.g., methadone, opium and opium derivatives, amphetamines, and others); the forms were to be collected by the New York state government and retained in a central database for five years. The purpose of the law, which was modeled on similar statutes in California and Illinois, was to prevent illegal distribution of legally prescribable controlled substances. Several doctors and patients affected by the law challenged its legitimacy and convinced a New York Federal District Court to enjoin the state from enforcing the law on privacy grounds. Specifically, the lower court ruled that "the doctor–patient relationship is one of the zones of privacy accorded constitutional protection."[20] The Supreme Court disagreed with the district court's analysis, however, and unanimously reversed the decision.

The high court's opinion, written by Justice Stevens, made specific mention of the New York state government's safeguards against unauthorized disclosure of any information contained in the database. Had the controls been less stringent it is possible that the danger of unauthorized disclosure might have tilted the Court's judgment against the law. As it was, Stevens's opinion noted that there was a duty to protect sensitive information and inadvertantly touched off a wave of confusion in privacy jurisprudence. The passage in question reads as follows:

The right to collect and use such data for public purposes is typically accompanied by a concomitant statutory or regulatory duty to avoid unwarranted disclosures. Recognizing that in some circumstances that duty arguably has its roots in the Constitution, nevertheless New York's statutory scheme, and its implementing administrative procedures, evidence a proper concern with, and protection of, the individual's interest in privacy.[21]

This passage has several important aspects. The first is that the decision only refers to "public" information gathering; as will be explored further in this chapter, the United States has chosen to regulate public- and private-sector information gathering separately. Second, as mentioned, the opinion cites New York's procedures to protect the data in their possession as a reason for upholding the statute. The source of the constitutional confusion, however, can be found in the phrase, "In some circumstances that duty arguably has its roots in the Constitution." As Gellman notes, that phrase has caused significant confusion in the lower courts, resulting in privacy decisions all over the constitutional map.[22]

Reno v. Condon

As of January 2000, the most recent Supreme Court case with significant privacy implications is *Reno v. Condon*, a case where South Carolina challenged the constitutionality of the Driver's Privacy Protection Act of 1994 (DPPA).[23] Prior to 1994 there was no federal law requiring state Departments of Motor Vehicles (DMVs) to get affirmative permission from citizens doing business with the DMV to sell the citizens' personal information to direct-marketing firms. The DPPA (as amended in 1999) changed that by mandating that state DMVs needed to adopt an "opt-in" policy: Rather than require clients to check a box if they did not want their information sold, the revised law prevented states from selling an individual's personally identifiable information unless the individual checked a box stating they gave the DMV permission to do so. South Carolina law ran contrary to the federal law, so the state challenged the DPPA on the grounds that the DPPA violated the principle of federalism, which governs the division of power between the federal government and the states.

Since states derive significant revenue from selling DMV information (for example, Wisconsin received more than $8 million annually from such sales), it is not surprising South Carolina's attorney general challenged the law. The Supreme Court ruled unanimously against South Carolina, however, holding that the DPPA did not violate the principle of federalism or make the states the unwilling enforcers of federal law. In part, the Court found as follows:

The United States asserts that the DPPA is a proper exercise of Congress' authority to regulate interstate commerce under the Commerce Clause, U.S. Const., Art. I, §8, cl. 3.2. The United States bases its Commerce Clause argument on the fact that the personal, identifying information that the DPPA regulates is a "thin[g] in interstate commerce," and that the sale or release of that information in interstate commerce is therefore a proper subject of congressional regulation. United States v. Lopez, 514 U.S. 549, 558–559 (1995). We agree with the United States' contention.[24]

Having established that the DPPA was a proper regulation of interstate commerce, the Supreme Court then turned to whether the DPPA encroached on states' sovereignty, as embodied in federalism. Here, the Court found as follows:

Like the statute at issue in Baker, the DPPA does not require the States in their sovereign capacity to regulate their own citizens. The DPPA regulates the States as the owners of databases. It does not require the South Carolina Legislature to enact any laws or regulations, and it does not require state officials to assist in the enforcement of federal statutes regulating private individuals.[25]

The key issue here is that the states were regulated "as the owners of databases." If the DPPA had required the states to pass laws implementing programs similar to the DPPA, then the law might have been unconstitutional on the grounds it violated federalism.

While *Reno v. Condon* may seem like a watershed privacy case, the ruling turns on the separation of powers between the federal government and the states, not privacy. However, the finding that Congress may regulate how the states and private individuals who purchase DMV information from the states may distribute information about motorists "as the owners of databases" raises questions as to the circumstances in which the ruling might be extended to laws regulating how private companies collect and disseminate personally identifiable information.

Domestic Law

Beyond legal theories that create a "right to privacy" where none is clearly enunciated in the U.S. Constitution, Congress has passed a number of laws that explicitly grant individuals privacy protections in specific areas, such as credit reporting, electronic data transmission, and videotape rentals. Unlike the European Union countries, which have created broad laws that restrict private companies and individuals from obtaining, correlating, and disseminating personally identifiable information, the United States has limited its restrictions, for the most part, to how governments may collect and process such information. The following paragraphs summarize U.S. laws that grant citizens privacy protections.

The Fair Credit Reporting Act

One of the first major computer applications in the private sector was collecting and disseminating credit information. Originally passed in 1970, and amended in 1996, the Fair Credit Report Act (FCRA) requires that "consumer reporting agencies adopt reasonable procedures for meeting the needs of commerce for consumer credit, personnel, insurance, and other information in a manner which is fair and equitable to the consumer,with regard to the confidentiality, accuracy, relevancy, and proper utilization of such information."[26] The FCRA was Congress's response to widespread public concerns about the possibility that consumer credit companies could determine individuals' financial prospects without data subjects being able to inspect or challenge the contents of their dossiers. The FCRA restricted what types of information could be kept in the files, established procedures for how the files were to be maintained, limited gatherers' abilities to repackage and re-sell the information, and gave consumers the right to obtain copies of their files and to challenge the files' contents.

From a privacy standpoint, the FCRA is important because it limits who may obtain a credit report about an individual. Even so, its protections are not comprehensive. While the law stipulates that credit reports may only be re-quested by persons (which, by definition in the FCRA, means individuals or organizations) who are considering entering into a financial arrangement with the data subject, those reasons are not checked before the report is issued. Credit reporting bureaus are required to keep detailed records of parties that have requested a copy of an individual's credit report, so there is some pro-tection against frivolous requests, though only after the fact. The problem is that the data subject must take the time to obtain a copy of the report and then check every party that bought a report to ensure each request is legitimate.

Privacy Act of 1974

The first American law that recognized a general right to privacy was the Privacy Act of 1974, which granted American citizens significant protections against misuses of federal government data collections. In particular, Congress found

(1) the privacy of an individual is directly affected by the collection, maintenance, use, and dissemination of personal information by Federal agencies;

(2) the increasing use of computers and sophisticated information technology, while essential to the efficient operations of the Government, has greatly magnified the harm to individual privacy that can occur from any collection, maintenance, use, or dissemination of personal information;

(3) the opportunities for an individual to secure employment, insurance, and credit, and his right to due process, and other legal protections are endangered by the misuse of certain information systems;

(4) the right to privacy is a personal and fundamental right protected by the Constitu-tion of the United States.[27]

While a significant step forward in the formal recognition and protection of individual privacy in the United States, the Privacy Act suffers from a number of limitations. The most significant limitation is that the law only applies to federal agencies—private data collections are left untouched. The second limit is that while the law does prohibit agencies from using records collected for one pur-pose to be used for another incompatible purpose, there is no definition of how one identifies a "compatible" purpose. The closest the bill's drafters came to defining a compatible purpose was to give the definition of a "routine use," which the law defines circularly: "The term 'routine use' means, with respect to the disclosure of a record, the use of such a record for a purpose which is compatible with the purpose for which it was collected."[28] In other words, a federal agency need merely put forward the claim that the matching was done for a compatible purpose to defend against claims it had violated an individual's rights under the Privacy Act. Proving otherwise, especially in the absence of any demonstrable harm from the use, would entail a lengthy court battle, with the plaintiff having to first find out about the use and then convince a jury and appellate courts that the use was not routine.

The second limitation is that the law does nothing to regulate the private collection and correlation of records about individuals. Since the ZAG (zip code, age, and gender) is usually enough information to correlate records about an "unknown" individual with a known individual via a public records search, there have been calls for similar restrictions for private-sector organizations.

Freedom of Information Act

The Freedom of Information Act (FOIA), which became law in 1974, is perhaps the most familiar of the privacy laws in effect. FOIA allows private individuals to request copies of any records federal agencies have about them. While the ability to get copies of records held by federal agencies is an important means of ensuring the agencies are following the law, FOIA's provisions only allow after-the-fact checks on any abuses. There are also a large number of exceptions in the law that allow law enforcement and national security agencies to redact significant portions of any records if they assert those portions are related to an ongoing investigation or impact national security. Requesters can challenge any withheld or redacted records, sometimes causing the withholding agency to release more complete versions of the information.

Right to Financial Privacy Act

The Right to Financial Privacy Act (RFPA) was passed in 1978 to protect bank and other financial account holders from arbitrary government requests for information about their holdings and activities. As with other provisions mentioned in this chapter, the RFPA does not prevent banks from providing private organizations with information about its customers' activities. As might be expected, government agencies can gain access to an individual's records by means of a court order, administrative subpoena, or if the customer authorized the release of those records.

Privacy Protection Act

Like other laws passed in the 1970s and 1980s, the Privacy Protection Act (PPA) offers individuals protections against government searches and seizures. In this case, the 1980 law prohibits government agents from using searches and seizures to seize materials relating to a criminal act that are intended for publication or broadcast. Specifically, the law states,

It shall be unlawful for a government officer or employee, in connection with the investigation or prosecution of a criminal offense, to search for or seize any work product materials possessed by a person reasonably believed to have a purpose to disseminate to the public a newspaper, book, broadcast, or other similar form of public communication, in or affecting interstate commerce.[29]

The law sets out several exceptions, most notably that law-enforcement officials may seize materials relating to a crime if they believe the person controlling the materials committed the crime(s) referred to by the work products or if there is reason to believe not seizing the materials would lead to the death or bodily injury of another person. The most significant loophole in the PPA, however, is its provision for a "good faith defense." Specifically, the law states, "It shall be a complete defense to a civil action brought under . . . this section that the officer or employee had a reasonable good faith belief in the lawfulness of his conduct."[30] The term "reasonable" is the operative word in that sentence: For a judge to find a search and seizure improper under the PPA would require the defense to prove the officer had insufficient reason to believe the information's controller was not the person who had committed the criminal act or that there was no reason to believe anyone was in danger. A tall order, especially since the officer could quite reasonably claim his or her experience provided insights not available to persons who were not law-enforcement officials.

Cable Communications Policy Act

Unlike the laws passed in the 1970s and early 1980s, the Cable Communications Policy Act (CCPA) restricts how private parties handle personally identifable information. Passed in 1984, the CCPA offers cable television subscribers a number of substantial protections against how their personal information can be used and distributed. Despite the limits, the law contains significant exceptions that curtail its effectiveness. The first protection is that of notification. Under the CCPA, cable operators must send their subscribers an annual communication describing the nature of personally identifiable information collected, how the information will be used, to which types of organizations that information will be distributed, the purpose for which the information is disclosed, the period the operator will maintain the information, the times and places where the customer may gain access to their information, and the limitations on collection provided by the CCPA.

The second protection is the requirement that cable operators not use the cable system itself to collect personally identifiable information about subscribers "without the prior written or electronic consent of the subscriber concerned . . . except as necessary to render a cable service or other service provided by the cable operator to the subscriber; or . . . [to] detect unauthorized reception of cable communications."[31] With these provisions, the CCPA establishes an opt-in policy for monitoring viewing habits, a practice that mirrors the physical limitations of broadcast television. For a ratings bureau to be able to determine which channel a household is watching at a given time, the bureau must either ask viewers to keep a log of every program they watch or install a box that records the information automatically. The Cable Communications Policy Act provides similar limitations on what personally identifiable information may be disclosed to other organizations, though subscribers' names and addresses may be disclosed unless the subscriber specifically requests that information not be disclosed. In other words, addresses are treated under an opt-out policy, as opposed to the opt-in policy that governs viewing information.

While the CCPA allows cable operators to disclose the names and addresses of subscribers under an opt-out policy, the law significantly limits the circumstances under which the names and addresses may be disclosed. In particular, the disclosure may not reveal "directly or indirectly, the . . . extent of any viewing or other use by the subscriber of a cable service or other service provided by the cable operator, or . . . the nature of any transaction made by the subscriber over the cable system of the cable operator."[32] This restriction is important, in that if extended to include Internet access providers and Web site managers, companies would not be allowed to correlate information about Web users with independent information sources. As noted earlier, an individual's zip code, age, and gender are usually sufficient to identify an individual from public records. Chapter 6 discusses methods for tracking Web users that are directly analogous to those activities prohibited by the CCPA.

Electronic Communication Privacy Act

Passed in 1986, the Electronic Communcation Privacy Act (ECPA), extended the antiwiretapping provisions of the Omnibus Crime Control and Safe Streets Act of 1968 to the world of the Internet. In short, neither government agents nor private individuals may ever intercept or record an electronic, wire, or oral communication that is not broadcast over the public airwaves for general consumption. The main difference between the ECPA and its 1968 predecessor is that the ECPA allows for "roving wiretaps," or wiretaps without a specific location, if the government can demonstrate a surveillance target is attempting to evade wiretaps by switching telephones.

Video Privacy Protection Act

The Video Privacy Protection Act of 1988 (VPPA) is the clearest example of the American federal legislature's proclivity to extend privacy protections to very specific areas. In this case, the VPPA was passed as a reaction to a reporter's acquisition of Supreme Court Justice nominee Robert Bork's videocassette rental records during the Federal Court of Appeals judge's confirmation hearings. The act allows individuals who have had their videocassette rental records disclosed absent a court order to collect attorney's fees, court costs, a minimum of $2,500 in actual damages, and punitive damages as determined by the court or a jury. An oft-cited quirk of American law is that an individual's videocassette rental records are afforded more extensive protections than that same person's medical records.

Telephone Consumer Protection Act

This law, passed in 1991, sets a number of limits on the technology and practices of telemarketers. Specifically, the Telephone Consumer Protection Act (TCPA) prohibits telemarketing firms (of which there were more than 30,000 when the TCPA was introduced) from using machines that randomly or sequentially generate telephone numbers and from calling individuals to deliver a prerecorded or automated message. The law has the added effect of outlawing the use of "war dialers," which computer hackers used to find access numbers for publicly accessible machines.

While the TCPA has not been extended to junk e-mail on the federal level, it is important to note that the TCPA was passed to fill a gap in similar laws passed by the states. In particular, Congress found that "over half the States now have statutes restricting various uses of the telephone for marketing, but telemarketers can evade their prohibitions through interstate operations; therefore, Federal law is needed to control residential telemarketing practices."[33] That the TCPA was passed to enhance the protections of similar state laws is particularly relevant to the online privacy environment. As will be noted later in this chapter, several states have adopted legislation that limits how businesses may compile and use personally identifiable information derived from the Internet, with more states considering similar laws. Given the precedent of the TCPA, it will be necessary for businesses and organizations making use of the Internet and other online services to consider whether Congress will enact nationwide legislation to mend holes in the patchwork of state laws.

Driver's Privacy Protection Act

As originally passed in 1994, the Driver's Privacy Protection Act (DPPA) required state departments of motor vehicles to give their clients the opportunity to have their names removed from lists rented or sold to advertisers. In 1999 Congress amended the DPPA to require states to implement an opt-in policy, under which customers would need to check a box on a form indicating the department had their permission to sell or rent their personally identifiable information to other parties. As mentioned in the discussion of *Reno v. Condon*, the U.S. Supreme Court unanimously ruled that the law, as amended, was not an undue infringement of the division of power between the federal government and the states.

Children's On-Line Privacy Protection Act

Passed in 1999, the Children's On-Line Privacy Protection Act (COPPA) prevents Web sites from collecting personal information from children, defined as individuals under the age of thirteen, though the statute does not cover some nonprofit entities. The COPPA prevents Web site operators from collecting personally identifiable information about children without parental consent and, if the site offers children the opportunity to participate in a game or activity, prevents the Web site operators from asking for more personally identifiable information than is necessary to participate in the activity. As is typical of Congressional legislation in the privacy area, the bill contains a number of safe harbor defenses Web site operators can call upon to satisfy the requirements of the legislation. In particular, operators may adhere to a self-regulatory regime that implements the protections in the COPPA, provided the regime has previously been made available for public comment and subsequently deemed acceptable by the Federal Trade Commission.

Gramm–Leach–Bliley Act of 1999

As of January 2000, the most recent American legislation affecting personal privacy is the Gramm–Leach–Bliley Act of 1999 (GLBA).[34] The GLBA, signed by the president on November 12, 1999, institutes new regulations for a wide range of financial activities, including repealing parts of the Glass–Steagall Act of 1933 (the "Banking Act") and the Bank Holding Company Act of 1956. (These changes are beyond the scope of this book, but they will be of significant interest to many readers and should be explored independently.) The most relevant provisions of the act for this book are presented in Title V—Privacy.

Prior to the GLBA's introduction, the board of governors of the Federal Reserve System, Federal Deposit Insurance Corporation, Office of the Comptroller of the Currency, and Office of Thrift Supervision had published for public comment a set of proposed "Know Your Customer" regulations.[35] The regulations would have required banks and other financial institutions to

determine the identity of its customers, to determine normal and expected transactions for its customers, to determine its customers' sources of funds, to identify transactions that are not normal or expected transactions for the customer, and to report suspicious transactions under existing suspicious activity reporting requirements.[36]

The goal of the proposed regulations was to deter and uncover money laundering and other illegal activities but, not at all surprisingly, the regulations came under withering fire from privacy-rights advocacy groups. The banks themselves also balked at following the proposed rules, as doing so would require them to build profiles of their customers and, essentially, embark on a fishing expedition to uncover a few lawbreakers. Particularly noisome was the requirement to determine customers' sources of funds, which put banks in an adversarial position vis-à-vis their customers. After the public comment period revealed practically no support and widespread, pointed opposition to the "Know Your Customer" program, the proposed regulations were withdrawn on March 29, 1999.[37]

By contrast, the Gramm–Leach–Bliley Act builds on the premise that "each financial institution has an affirmative and continuing obligation to respect the privacy of its customers and to protect the security and confidentiality of those customers' nonpublic personal information."[38] The law requires the federal banking agencies, the National Credit Union Administration, the secretary of the treasury, the Securities and Exchange Commission, and the Federal Trade Commission to consult with the states and promulgate regulations that enact policies that insure the security and confidentiality of customer information, anticipate threats to that information, and guards against unauthorized access and use of the information.[39] It is interesting to note that the agencies that would have been responsible for carrying out the mandates of the "Know Your Customer" policy are the same ones charged with creating policies to protect that same information.

This is how the act defines its key terms, in particular "nonpublic personal information." The act offers a minimal standard, but (in sec. 504) allows the rule-making agencies leeway in defining "publicly available information." With that in mind, sec. 509(4) of the act offers the following definition of "nonpublic personal information":

(A) The term "nonpublic personal information" means personally identifiable financial information—

(i) provided by a consumer to a financial institution;

(ii) resulting from any transaction with the consumer or any service performed for the consumer; or

(iii) otherwise obtained by the financial institution.

(B) Such term does not include publicly available information, as such term is defined by the regulations prescribed under section 504.

(C) Notwithstanding subparagraph (B), such term—

(i) shall include any list, description, or other grouping of consumers (and publicly available information pertaining to them) that is derived using any nonpublic personal information other than publicly available information; but

(ii) shall not include any list, description, or other grouping of consumers (and publicly available information pertaining to them) that is derived without using any nonpublic personal information.[40]

The apparent intent of this definition and its attendant regulations is to allow consumers to preclude financial institutions from building and disseminating profiles based on consumers' transactions, such as credit card purchases, either by itself or in combination records from other sources. As will be seen later in this book, these regulations could have a significant impact on the online advertising and marketing industry, though the act's control regime is based on an opt-out policy instead of an opt-in policy. Indeed, the title of sec. 502(b) is "OPT OUT."[41] That portion of the act prohibits financial institutions disclosing nonpublic personal information to an unaffiliated third party unless

(A) such financial institution clearly and conspicuously discloses to the consumer, in writing or in electronic form or other form permitted by the regulations prescribed under section 504, that such information may be disclosed to such third party;

(B) the consumer is given the opportunity, before the time that such information is initially disclosed, to direct that such information not be disclosed to such third party; and

(C) the consumer is given an explanation of how the consumer can exercise that nondisclosure option.[42]

The act goes on to require financial institutions to provide a "clear and conspicuous disclosure" to consumers on an annual basis.[43]

Health Privacy

The most visible area where privacy protections were lacking in American life until very recently was with regard to health and medical information. Unlike an individual's video rental records, which were protected from scrutiny by the Video Privacy Protection Act, medical records were only protected by a weak mesh of state and local laws that protected certain types of information more than others.[44] In fact, as the White House's Office of the Press Secretary noted in a background document,

Today, even amidst a boom in the collection and dissemination of personal data, patients do not have the right under Federal law to see their own health files or to know who is receiving their health information. Nor do they have basic protections to ensure that sensitive information is not inappropriately used or disclosed. Indeed, under the current loose patchwork of state laws, personal health information can be distributed—without consent—for reasons that have nothing to do with a patient's medical treatment. Patient information held by an insurer can in many cases be passed on to a lender who may then deny the patient's application for a home mortgage or a credit card, or to an employer who may use it in personnel decisions. Moreover, patients wishing to access or control the release of such information may be subject to the whim of their insurance company or health care provider.[45]

The new regulations, which the president was allowed to put forth after Congress failed to pass laws governing health privacy in the three years leading up to October 1999, set significant restrictions on how health information may be used and disseminated. In particular, the regulations do the following:

- Limit the release of health information without consent. Rather than allow medical information to be released to marketers or corporations for use in hiring and promotion decisions, the new regulations prohibit releases for purposes other than treatment, payment, or use in setting policy.
- Require health care providers to inform individuals of how their information is being used.
- Allow patients access to their own files, which was not guaranteed under previous laws.
- Restrict the information requested to the minimum necessary.
- Require the establishment of privacy-conscious business practices.
- Require that information released for research purposes only be handled responsibly.
- Enact new civil and criminal penalties for mishandling medical information.[46]

CONCLUSIONS

Action in the area of health information has closed a significant privacy gap in the American legal framework, but American privacy regulations can best be described as a set of laws that limits what the government can do with personally identifiable information but puts practically no limitations on what private enterprise can do with the same information. There have been some signs of change, with a few new regulations put in place to prevent private organizations from gathering information about individuals' television and video viewing habits and the new health privacy standards, but the overall trend remains the same: Personally identifiable information can be traded in the United States with few restrictions. As will be seen in the next chapter, such is not the case in Europe.

NOTES

1. Samuel Warren and Louis Brandeis, "The Right to Privacy," *Harvard Law Review* 4, no. 5 (1890): 193, 215.
2. William Prosser, "Privacy," *California Law Review* 48, no. 3 (1960): 383.
3. Ibid., 389.
4. Ibid., 407.
5. *Griswold v. Connecticut*, 381 U.S. 479, 484 (1965).
6. *Katz v. United States*, 389 U.S. 347 (1967).
7. *Olmstead v. United States*, 277 U.S. 438, 457, 464, 466 (1928).
8. *Katz v. United States*, 351.
9. Ibid. Internal citations and footnotes omitted.
10. Ibid., 352.
11. Ibid., Justice Harlan (concurring), 361.
12. *Paul v. Davis*, 424 U.S. 693 (1976).

13. Ibid.

14. *Roe v. Wade*, 410 U.S. 113, 152–153 (1973).

15. *Paul v. Davis*, 714. Internal citations omitted.

16. *United States v. Miller*, 425 U.S. 435 (1976), 442.

17. *Katz v. United States*, 351.

18. *United States v. Miller*, 441.

19. Ibid., 442.

20. As quoted in *Whalen v. Roe*, 429 U.S. 589 (1977).

21. Ibid., 606.

22. Robert Gellman, "Does Privacy Law Work?" In *Technology and Privacy: The New Landscape*, ed. Philip E. Agre and Marc Rotenberg (Cambridge, Mass.: MIT Press, 1999), 204.

23. *Reno v. Condon*, 155 F.3d 453, reversed (2000). Awaiting formal publication. Available <http://supct.law.cornell.edu/supct/html/98-1464.ZO.html>.

24. Ibid.

25. Ibid.

26. *Fair Credit Reporting Act, U.S. Code*, vol. 15, secs. 1681 et seq. (1970).

27. *Privacy Act of 1974, U.S. Code*, vol. 5, secs. 552 et seq. (1974).

28. Ibid.

29. *Privacy Protection Act, U.S. Code*, vol. 42, sec. 2000a (1980).

30. Ibid.

31. *Cable Communications Policy Act, Public Law 98-549, U.S. Code*, vol. 47, sec. 551 (1984).

32. Ibid.

33. *Telephone Consumer Protection Act, Public Law 102-243, U.S. Code*, vol. 47, sec. 227 et seq. (1991).

34. *Gramm–Leach–Bliley Act of 1999, Public Law 106-102, U.S. Code*, vol. 12, sec. 1811 et seq. (1999).

35. U.S. Department of the Treasury, Office of Thrift Supervision, "Know Your Customer," *Federal Register* 63, no. 234 (1998): 67536–67542. Available <http://www.ots.treas.gov/docs/73062.html>.

36. Ibid.

37. Iowa's Community Bankers, "'Know Your Customer' Rules Withdrawn," 2 June 1999. Available <http://www.iacb.org/customer.html>.

38. *Gramm–Leach–Bliley Act of 1999, Public Law 106-102, U.S. Code*, vol. 12, sec. 501(a) (1999).

39. Ibid., sec. 501(b).

40. Ibid., sec. 509(4).

41. Ibid., sec. 502(b).

42. Ibid., sec. 502(b)(1).

43. Ibid., sec. 503(a).

44. Ann Cavoukian, "Applications in Health Information Networks," In *Visions of Privacy: Policy Choices for the Digital Age*, ed. Colin J. Bennett and Rebecca Grant (Toronto: University of Toronto Press, 1999), 116.

45. The White House, Office of the Press Secretary, "President Clinton Takes Strong New Steps to Protect the Privacy of Personal Health Information," 29 October 1999. Available <http://www.pub.whitehouse.gov/uri-res/I2R?urn:pdi://oma.eop.gov.us/1999/10/29/4.text.1>.

46. Ibid.

The European Union
and Other Nations

As seen in the court decisions and laws described in the last chapter, the U.S. government has chosen to regulate privacy only in specific areas where significant public concern has arisen. The most extreme case of this approach is the Video Privacy Protection Act of 1988, passed in the wake of public disclosure of Supreme Court Justice nominee Robert Bork's videotape rental records. The European Union approaches regulation differently: Rather than carve out specific privacy protections, the EU has chosen to enact sweeping laws regulating the collection of personally identifiable information, limiting how that information can be processed, and restricting the collector's ability to pass the information to third parties without the data subject's consent. In particular, the European Union Data Protection Directive prohibits the transfer of personally identifiable information from an EU country to a country, business sector, or business lacking equivalent restrictions on the use and transfer of personally identifiable information.

The Data Directive, which served as the base of legislation enacted in every EU country, is based on a set of guidelines developed by the Organization for Economic Cooperation and Development (OECD), of which the United States is a member. This chapter presents the OECD guidelines and the EU's Data Protection Directive, analyzes the directive with an eye to its impact on

U.S. businesses, and examines the state of U.S.–EU negotiations to resolve the regulatory differences between the two political units. Finally, this chapter looks at how relevant Canadian laws, passed on both the national and provincial level as a response to the Data Directive, will impact Canadian businesses' ability to transfer data to and from EU member countries.

OECD GUIDELINES

In 1980 the Organization for Economic Cooperation and Development promulgated a set of principles to serve as a minimum standard for the protection of personally identifiable information.[1] Though put forth in the form of a nonbinding resolution, the OECD principles have served as the basis for EU regulation since they were issued. The OECD has issued subsequent guidelines regarding electronic commerce, which will be discussed later in this chapter.

Goal of the Guidelines

According to the comments attached to the OECD guidelines, the group had several goals in mind when they created the guidelines. In particular, the OECD wanted to achieve minimum privacy and individual liberty protections, minimize the difference among national privacy laws, remove any hindrances from moving personal data among member countries, and eliminate the risk of nations raising barriers to transborder data flows because of a difference in data protection policies.[2] Differences in national policies regarding personal data, such as the United States' preference to allow industry to self-regulate and the United Kingdom's distinction between paper-based and automated information storage and retrieval systems. The following paragraphs discuss the guidelines' limitations on personal data processing.[3]

Collection Limitation

There should be limits to the collection of personal data and any such data should be obtained by lawful and fair means and, where appropriate, with the knowledge or consent of the data subject. At its most basic, this limitation seeks to protect citizens of OECD countries from being constantly probed for information about their persons and activities. It also encourages notifying the subjects that data are being collected about them and to only use "lawful and fair" means to gain that information. On the Web, of course, it is easier to collect information about a user and his or her activities than it would be to physically surveil a person throughout a shopping trip, but the notion of fairness and when it would be appropriate to require the knowledge or consent of a data subject is largely dependent on culture.

Data Quality

Personal data should be relevant to the purposes for which they are to be used, and, to the extent necessary for those purposes, should be accurate, complete and kept up-to-date. This limitation speaks to data accuracy, the bane of database marketers and credit applicants. U.S. citizens often receive junk mail or telephone calls for persons years removed from that address or number. It is more rare, though much more damaging, for individuals to be denied credit or employment because a routine credit history or criminal background check included erroneous derogatory information.

Purpose Specification

The purposes for which personal data are collected should be specified not later than at the time of data collection and the subsequent use limited to the fulfillment of those purposes or such others as are not incompatible with those purposes and as are specified on each occasion of change of purpose. Again, different cultures will interpret this requirement differently. American businesses, with their tradition of aggressive direct marketing, will have a much broader interpretation of what represents a compatible purpose. Most U.S. businesses regard providing consumers notice whenever their data are to be used for a new purpose as a costly and unnecessary restriction.

Use Limitation

Personal data should not be disclosed, made available or otherwise used for purposes other than those specified except with the consent of the data subject or by the authority of law. In the United States it is common practice to sell mailing lists to anyone who believes a given list might contain contacts in a desired demographic group, so selling subscriber lists to third parties is usually considered part of the original purpose for collecting the data. Organizations in EU countries have a different perspective on the matter (as evidenced by past data protection laws, which are summarized later in this chapter). Most commercial and fundraising organizations in the United States view requiring U.S. data subjects to affirmatively opt in for any additional use of their personal information as a completely unwarranted and unnecessary restriction.

Security Safeguards

Personal data should be protected by reasonable security safeguards against such risks as loss or unauthorised access, destruction, use, modification or disclosure of data. This principle is followed scrupulously in both the EU and the United States: A good mailing list is worth many times its printed weight in gold, and while a company might sell its lists for a fair price, it is loath to give that information away. Discovering which lists a company subscribes to and how that buying pattern has changed can also be a valuable competitive intelligence find, so companies are loath to divulge that information.

Openness

There should be a general policy of openness about developments, practices and policies with respect to personal data. Means should be readily available of establishing the existence and nature of personal data, and the main purposes of their use, as well as the identity and usual residence of the data controller. Many Americans know that private companies record their credit and employment histories, though they have comparatively little knowledge of the technologies companies can use to relate consumers' purchase histories to their demographic information.

Individual Participation

An individual should have the right to obtain from a data controller, or otherwise, confirmation of whether or not the data controller has data relating to him; to have communicated to him data relating to him within a reasonable time, at a reasonable charge, in a reasonable manner, and in an intelligible form; to be given reasons if a request is denied; to be able to challenge the denial to challenge data relating to him; and, if the challenge is successful to have the data erased, rectified, completed or amended. Under the Fair Credit Reporting Act, credit reporting agencies are required to provide a consumer with a copy of his or her credit report if requested. There are mechanisms for challenging derogatory credit information, though the derogatory information usually stays on the report along with the challenge.

Accountability

A data controller should be accountable for complying with measures which give effect to the principles stated above. This seemingly simple requirement is at the center of the U.S.–EU debate: How should U.S. businesses be brought to account for violations of privacy policies? The EU favors government regulation, while the United States favors self-regulation.

History of Privacy Regulation in Europe

Viktor Mayer-Schönberger's chapter "Generational Development of Data Protection in Europe" in Agre and Rotenberg's *Technology and Privacy: The New Landscape* provides a comprehensive overview of the history of data protection laws in the EU. Mayer-Schönberger divided European data protection laws into four generations, the first of which occurred in the early and mid-1970s.

First-Generation European Data Protection

The first generation of data protection laws in Europe were promulgated as a reaction to proposals for large government and corporate databases, though at that time the intention was to create national data banks consisting of a single database, as opposed to the distributed nature of contemporary data storage and combination.[4] Several laws passed in German state legislatures and Sweden, proposed laws in Austria, and the 1977 German Federal Data Protection Act are all examples of laws comprising this first generation.

The specific proposals that gave rise to these data protection laws were based on the widening of many European countries' social welfare systems, which shifted many responsibilities from the individual to the state. As Mayer-Schönberger notes,

This shift in responsibilities required a sophisticated system of government planning, and planning requires data. Thus, government bureaucracies had to constantly collect increasing amounts of information from the citizens to adequately fulfill its tasks and to appropriately plan for the future. But the gathering of data alone is not sufficient. Data must be processed and linked together to create the necessary planning instruments, and so that complex social legislation can be applied to the demands of individual citizens.[5]

Because the phenomenon of large-scale data processing was new when these first generation laws were passed, legislators looked to design laws to establish data processing's place in society. Indeed, Mayer-Schönberger cites several analyses which concluded that "the use of computers itself endangers humane information processing."[6] Notably absent from those early laws are words like "privacy," "information," and "protection of intimate affairs."[7]

Second-Generation Laws

While the first generation of European data protection laws were intended to establish data processing's place in society, the advancement of computer technology presented lawmakers with a new set of circumstances to address. Rather than regulating a few easily identified and controlled national data banks, the advent of the minicomputer and increasingly affordable storage space made the regulators' job a matter of controlling the spread of personally identifiable information throughout their countries. Mayer-Schönberger notes that while Austria, Spain, and Portugal included a right of informational privacy in their constitutions, the majority of European states gave citizens a say in the information collection and handling process. The first-generation laws had not given individuals a say in whether their personally identifiable information was collected and processed; the second-generation laws sometimes required an individual's consent before their information could be processed.[8]

The problem with these second-generation laws is that the general presumption against collecting and processing individuals' personally identifiable information flies in the face of the information requirements of the welfare society. European governments had not changed their social policies, so their need for comprehensive information about their citizens had not disappeared. As Mayer-Schönberger notes, "In real life the individual rarely had the chance to decide between taking part and remaining outside society."[9] This contradiction gave rise to the third generation of information privacy laws in Europe.

Third-Generation Laws

Under the second generation of information privacy laws in Europe, individuals were able to shield their information from outside collectors, but it was an all-or-nothing affair: Either the individual participated in society by sharing his or her information, or he or she remained cut off from society. The third generation of laws allowed individuals to selectively participate in society by choosing when and where they released their personally identifiable information. In West Germany the Constitutional Court decided in 1983 that there was a constitutional right to informational self-determination and that the right applied to all stages of information gathering and processing. Rather than force individuals to make a one-time decision on whether to allow access to their data, the court found that the "principle of informational self-determination forces data processing to bring the individual human being back into the loop."[10]

As with the previous generations of European privacy laws, however, there were problems implementing the ideals embodied in the laws. As with the second generation of laws, the cost of not participating was extremely high. Even worse, Mayer-Schönberger points out, "They routinely and unknowingly contracted away their right to informational self-determination as part and parcel of a business deal, in which the right itself was not even a 'bargaining chip' during negotiations."[11] Thus, only individuals who could afford to insulate themselves from society were able to take advantage of the third-generation privacy laws in Europe.

Fourth-Generation Laws

The current generation of laws, the fourth, represents a hybrid approach to protecting personally identifiable information. Like the third-generation laws, these regulations give individuals the right to restrict how their personally identifiable information can be collected and processed while simultaneously establishing classes of information that cannot be bargained away. Mayer-Schönberger cites a number of laws, including the Norwegian Data Protection Act, the Finnish Persons Register Act, the Belgian Data Protection Act, the French Data Protection Act, and the British Data Protection Act, as examples of laws that preclude the processing of certain types of sensitive personal information.[12] The 1995 European Union Directive on Data Protection codifies these principles into an overarching framework designed to homogenize data protection in European Union nations and to ensure nations to which personally identifiable information might be transferred have adequate protections as well.

THE EUROPEAN UNION DATA DIRECTIVE

As part of the trend toward a more unified Europe, the European Parliament has passed a number of directives that call for standardized laws throughout the European Union's member countries. Directive 95/46/EC of the European Parliament and EU Council, passed October 24, 1995, establishes such a standard for regulations about the collection and processing of personally identifiable information. The European Commission proposed the Data Protection Directive in 1990 as a response to incomplete and inconsistent adoption of laws based on the 1981 Council of Europe Convention Number 108, which dealt with the automated processing of personal data.[13] Specifically, Convention 108 did not prohibit transfers of personally identifiable information to countries that were not party to the convention, allowing parties to circumvent the regulations by purchasing data from organizations within the protected region. Neither did the convention require subscribing nations to establish any kind of a national infrastructure to investigate complaints.[14]

These inconsistencies led to the possibility that some transfers of personally identifiable information could be prohibited between EU member nations and provided an impetus for an overarching standard by which laws in the fifteen member nations (Austria, Belgium, Denmark, Finland, France, Germany, Greece, Ireland, Italy, Luxembourg, the Netherlands, Portugal, Spain, Sweden, and the United Kingdom) could be judged. Realizing that member nations would need time to formulate regulations that met the directive's requirements while staying within national law, the EU set October 24, 1998, as the date on which the regulations were to be in place. As of January 11, 2000, France, Ireland, Germany, Luxembourg, and the Netherlands had yet to implement adequate regulations, though none of those countries have made public any resistance to the requirements of the EU's directive.[15] Indeed, as noted earlier in this chapter, Germany has often been the vanguard of data protection legislation. Scott Blackmer of the Washington, D.C., law firm Wilmer, Cutler, and Pickering also noted that many other European nations had put directive-compliant legislation in place: the Czech

Republic, Hungary, Iceland, Liechtenstein, Lithuania, Monaco, Norway, Poland, Russia, Slovakia, Slovenia, and Switzerland.[16]

The remainder of this section looks at the provisions of the Data Protection Directive in some detail, with the aim of giving decision makers a thorough understanding of the directive's goals and requirements. While every country's implementation of the directive will be slightly different, and perhaps more restrictive in some areas, the information here will provide a solid framework for policy analysis. The full text of the directive is included in Appendix A.

Definitions

Though the directive contains a number of definitions, four are particularly germane to this discussion: the definitions of "personal data," "processing," "controller," and "the data subject's consent." The first definition, of "personal data," sets the tone of the directive as a document meant to encompass a wide range of information. The definition is as follows:

Any information relating to an identified or identifiable natural person ("data subject"); an identifiable person is one who can be identified, directly or indirectly, in particular by reference to an identification number or to one or more factors specific to his physical, physiological, mental, economic, cultural or social identity.[17]

In other words, the directive comprehends any data that relate to an individual, regardless of whether the data in question can be used to identify the individual to which the data relate. The definition of "processing" is similarly broad:

Any operation or set of operations which is performed upon personal data, whether or not by automatic means, such as collection, recording, organization, storage, adaptation or alteration, retrieval, consultation, use, disclosure by transmission, dissemination or otherwise making available, alignment or combination, blocking, erasure or destruction.[18]

Though quite complete, the definition's inclusion of the term "use" operates as a catch-all to extend the directive's influence to anything that can be done with data. The next definition, that of a "controller," illustrates one of the major differences between American and European data protection laws:

The natural or legal person, public authority, agency or any other body which alone or jointly with others determines the purposes and means of the processing of personal data.[19]

With a few notable exceptions, such as the Cable Communications Policy Act and the Video Privacy Protection Act, U.S. laws only regulate how public authorities can process data. Under the directive, any natural or legal person (e.g., a corporation) must be bound by the national laws implementing the directive's mandates, though Swire and Litan point out that the directive contains a number of exceptions for government operations, national security, criminal proceedings, and the like.[20]

The final definition, that of "the data subject's consent," underscores another significant difference between the directive and U.S. policy toward data collection and processing:

Any freely given specific and informed indication of his wishes by which the data subject signifies his agreement to personal data relating to him being processed.[21]

As written the definition seems to allow, especially in the American context, data controllers to argue that an individual was given the opportunity to indicate they did not wish their data to be processed (i.e., opt out). The legislative intent behind this definition comes out in Section 7(a), however; that section contains language that requires data subjects to consent "unambiguously" to having their data processed. Leaving a box unchecked is at best an ambiguous statement of an individual's intent, so the directive may be read as requiring an opt-in system.

Scope

Article 3 of the directive defines the types of information processing systems the directive regulates. The definition is quite broad, extending the directive's coverage to include any information collected and processed, in whole or in part, by automatic means. The directive also includes manual records, so long as the records are part of a "filing system, or are intended to form part of a filing system."[22] Colin Bennett, then of the University of Victoria in British Columbia, Canada, notes that the United Kingdom objected to including purely manual filing systems under the directive. The United Kingdom's 1984 Data Protection Act only regulates automated data processing systems and, the United Kingdom's representatives to the EU argued manual filing systems are not capable of finding and correlating records with the speed and efficiency of automated systems. The other representatives refused to concede the larger point, but the British were given extra time to implement the directive with regard to manual filing systems. Only after being granted the extension was the British government willing to abstain from the final Council of Ministers vote to adopt the directive.[23]

The directive does have a number of exceptions. The first broad exception noted in Article 3(2) is that the directive does not comprehend "public security, defence, State security (including the economic well-being of the State when the processing operation is bound up with questions of State security) and the activities of the State in areas of criminal law."[24] The "economic security" element of this exception could present EU member countries with a way to circumvent the directive (in some cases) if it could be argued that the use of personally identifiable information was required to protect the economic security of the state. One such example would be the case of a firm deemed part of the critical economic infrastructure of a country. If the firm were engaged in a bidding or negotiation process that would have a profound impact on the firm for good or ill, it could be argued that the personally identifiable information processed as part of the information gathering process for the negotiations would not fall within the directive's purview because of the exception. The second exception, when the information is used for a "purely personal or household activity," indicates that EU citizens can maintain address books of friends and relatives, but that a similar collection for business purposes would probably be regulated.[25]

Principles

Articles 6 and 7 of the Data Directive enumerates the guiding principles for the national legislatures and data protection establishments in compliant nations. Like the Organization for Economic Cooperation and Development guidelines presented earlier in this chapter, the Data Directive guidelines set the context for the regulations found elsewhere in the document. With regard to data quality (Article 6), the directive requires EU nations to uphold the following general principles in their data protection legislation:

- Data must be processed fairly and lawfully, which Blackmer notes is a "catch-all" principle that sets the tone for the directive.[26]
- Data must be collected and processed for specific purposes and not for other, incompatible purposes, though that restriction is not taken to disallow historical, statistical, or scientific processing by the state so long as safeguards are in place.
- Data collection and processing must not be excessive; that is, a data controller may not collect more data than are necessary for their purpose.
- Data must be kept current and accurate. If the data controller cannot keep the data up-to-date or verify their accuracy, the controller must either delete or update the data.
- Data may not be stored in a manner that allows viewers to identify data subjects for any longer than absolutely necessary.[27]

Article 7 of the directive contains the principles governing legitimate causes for data collection. The directive's guidelines only allow processing personally identifiable information if the following conditions are met:

- The data subject has given unambiguous consent to the processing.
- The data are necessary to fulfill a contract with the data subject or for the data subject to enter into such a contract.
- The controller is legally obligated to process the data.

- The processing is required to safeguard the vital interests of the data subject.
- The data are processed in the performance of a public duty or by a third party at the request of a government institution (essentially, subcontracting public functions).
- The controller and/or processor have a legitimate interest in processing the data and that interest is not outweighed by the individual's rights as expressed in Article 1(1).[28]

While Articles 6 and 7 offer general principles for the nation states to embody in their laws, Article 8 of the Data Directive specifically prohibits data controllers from processing data about a data subject's "racial or ethnic origin, political opinions, religious or philosophical beliefs, trade-union membership, and the processing of data concerning health or sex life."[29] Paragraph 2 of Article 8 offers a number of exceptions, such as when the individual has given his or her unambiguous consent to have their data processed, or if a trade union or other organization processes information about its members, but the memory of oppressive regimes using data collections to remove political and ideological enemies certainly informs these restrictions.

Notifying Data Subjects

Another significant restriction the Data Directive places on collection and processing personally identifiable information is that data controllers must identify themselves and their agents to data subjects. Article 10 requires data controllers to inform data subjects of the following facts *at a minimum*: the identity of the controller and their representatives, the purpose of the processing, the parties that will receive the data, whether the data subjects responses are optional or obligatory, the consequences of refusing to answer the questions, and that the data subject has the right to examine and correct any personally identifiable information collected by the controller.[30] Article 11 extends similar protections for data that have been transferred to a third party, but grants exceptions for statistical or historical processing or where providing the information to data subjects "proves impossible or involves a disproportionate effort or if recording or disclosure is expressly laid down by law."[31] This exception seems to be intended to permit public and academic institutions (or their agents) to process data without needing to inform each data subject that the data are being used for such a purpose, but there is some room for argument as to what circumstances would constitute "a disproportionate effort."

Rights of the Data Subject

Articles 12, 14, and 15 of the Data Directive enumerate specific rights to be granted data subjects under the national legislation implementing the directive. Article 12 grants data subjects the right of access to their personally identifiable information without unreasonable cost or delay. Inherent to this right are the ability of the data subject to find out whether a controller has any information about them, the data maintained, what type of processing is done with the data, and to what, if any, third parties the data have been or will be disclosed. The nature of the personally identifiable information and of the processing is to be communicated in a readable form, as is information about the source of the data.[32] Article 12 also grants the data subject the right to correct the information held by the controller, or, if the data are incomplete or inaccurate, to insist that the controller erase or block the transfer of that subject's personally identifiable information. The controller is also obligated to inform any third parties to whom the data have been divulged of any erasure or blocking, but again provides an exception if the notification would involve undue effort or expense.[33]

Article 14 grants data subjects the right to object to having their personally identifiable information processed. Subsection (a) grants the right to object even if the data are being processed for a state function or to fulfill a legitimate obligation on the part of the data controller. In these cases, if the controller finds that an EU citizen's objection is legitimate, they must continue the processing without that individual's personally identifiable information. Subsection (b) is potentially very important for American businesses: It gives every data subject the right to object to "the processing of personal data relating to him which the controller anticipates being processed for the purposes of direct marketing . . . or . . . to be informed before personal data are disclosed for the first time to third parties or used on their behalf for the purposes of direct marketing, and to be expressly offered the right to object free of charge to such disclosures or uses."[34] The directive also mandates that EU nations make their citizens aware of their ability to object to such processing. Blackmer argues that the language in Article 7(f) does not prohibit firms from pursuing a commercial relationship with consumers, which is a "legitimate interest" of the firm, "so long as those are not overridden by the data subject's privacy rights."[35]

Article 15 extends the data subject's rights by requiring EU member nations to ensure that no one has an employment or creditworthiness decision made entirely on the basis of an automated process, though the individual countries may mandate that individuals could be subjected to such a process if the citizen were given adequate means to dispute the finding or if the state created safeguards that met their citizens' legitimate interests. Articles 16 and 17, while they do not deal directly with data-subject rights, do compel data controllers and processors to implement strong confidentiality and security measures to prevent unauthorized disclosure of or access to personally identifiable information.

National Authorities

Articles 28 to 30 of the Data Directive require each EU member nation to establish a national authority in charge of administering data privacy issues.

In particular, Article 28(3) requires the member nations to endow the supervisory authority with at least the following powers:

- investigative powers, such as powers of access to data forming the subject-matter of processing operations and powers to collect all the information necessary for the performance of its supervisory duties;
- effective powers of intervention, such as, for example, that of delivering opinions in accordance with Article 20, before processing operations are carried out and ensuring appropriate publication of such opinions, or that of ordering the blocking, erasure or destruction of data, or of imposing a temporary or definitive ban on processing, or that of warning or admonishing the controller or that of referring the matter to national parliaments or other political institutions;
- the power to engage in legal proceedings where the national provisions adopted pursuant to this directive have been violated or to bring these violations to the attention of the judicial authorities.[36]

Every supervising authority is to be independent, much like the Federal Communications Commission and other executive agencies in the United States. Blackmer points out that some European data protection establishments have the power to investigate and render opinions on data control and processing practices, but that they do not have the power to enforce their decisions independently.[37] The directive requires member nations to endow the supervisory authorities with such powers, while providing that all decisions rendered by the national authority may be appealed to the member nation's courts.

As noted earlier in this chapter, Article 10 of the Data Directive requires data controllers to notify data subjects that the controller has information about the subject, the controller's identify, and so forth. In a similar vein, Articles 18 and 19 require data controllers to register with the national authority and disclose the nature of the processing they undertake. Specifically, Article 19 requires data controllers to provide the state with at least the following information:

(a) the name and address of the controller and of his representative, if any;
(b) the purpose or purposes of the processing;
(c) a description of the category or categories of data subject and of the data or categories of data relating to them;
(d) the recipients or categories of recipient to whom the data might be disclosed;
(e) proposed transfers of data to third countries;
(f) a general description allowing a preliminary assessment to be made of the appropriateness of the measures taken pursuant to Article 17 to ensure security of processing.[38]

This provision was put in place to standardize the licensing and notification requirements across member states. Blackmer notes that Austria had required licensing, and the United Kingdom, the Netherlands, and France registration, for quite a few years before the Data Directive was put in place. Article 19 also makes use of a German practice that made registration optional "so long as the company appoints a legally responsible individual as the 'data controller.'"[39]

Under Article 18, any data controller or processor must register with the national supervisory authority before "carrying out any wholly or partly automatic processing operation or set of such operations intended to serve a single purpose or several related purposes."[40] That the article comprehends partly automated processing is an important subtlety, in that it prevents processors from adding a human to the processing loop and maintaining their process should not be covered by the directive. The directive does offer member states a number of ways the notification process can be simplified or eliminated for data controllers and processors who take steps to ensure the data they maintain are stored and processed in manners consistent with the directive. Those exceptions come into play under the following conditions:

For categories of processing operations which are unlikely, taking account of the data to be processed, to affect adversely the rights and freedoms of data subjects, they specify the purposes of the processing, the data or categories of data undergoing processing, the category or categories of data subject, the recipients or categories of recipient to whom the data are to be disclosed and the length of time the data are to be stored and/or . . . the controller appoints, in compliance with the national law which governs him, a data protection official, responsible in particular . . . for ensuring in an independent manner the internal application of the national provisions taken pursuant to this Directive [and] for keeping the register of processing operations carried out by the controller . . . thereby ensuring that the rights and freedoms of the data subjects are unlikely to be adversely affected by the processing operations.[41]

Article 20 extends the notification requirement by mandating that member states identify processing operations that the national legislature deems could pose significant risks to individual privacy. In such cases, the data controllers and processors must register *before* processing the data. Member states do have the option of performing such checks on an industrywide basis before passing the legislation.[42] Article 21 further requires member states to publicize the nature of the processing by maintaining and making publicly available a list of data controllers and their agents.[43]

Transfers to Third Countries

Articles 25 and 26 of the Data Directive, which define the circumstances under which personally identifiable information can be transferred to non-EU member states, have generated much discussion in the United States and abroad. The discussion here focuses on the language of the articles, while Chapter 6 will delve into the EU's statements regarding how the articles will be applied and U.S. proposals to meet the EU's requirements for transferring personally identifiable information to third countries.

The central idea behind Article 25 is that personally identifiable information may only be transferred to third countries that provide an "adequate level of protection" for that information.[44] Rather than lay out a set criteria by which the data protection regimes of third countries will be judged, the directive allows the EU member nations to determine whether a third country provides adequate protection in light of the overall legal environment in that third country. Where the data transfer is specific to an economic sector or industry, the member nations may address themselves to the legal environment concerning that industry. The nature of the data, the purpose and duration of the processing, and any professional codes adhered to by the industry to which the personally identifiable information is transferred also factor into the decision.[45] If a member nation determines that a third country does not have adequate protections in place, the directive requires that nation to begin negotiations with that third country in an attempt to bring that country's policies into compliance with the directive.[46] The United States and the EU reached a preliminary agreement on May 31, 2000.

Article 26 provides a number of exceptions ("derogations") under which personally identifiable information may be transferred to third countries that lack adequate protections. Paragraph 1 lists a number of derogations, allowing EU member nations to transfer personally identifiable information to third parties without adequate data protection laws if

1) the data subject has given his consent unambiguously to the proposed transfer, or

2) the transfer is necessary for the performance of a contract between the data subject and the controller or the implementation of precontractual measures taken in response to the data subject's request, or

3) the transfer is necessary for the conclusion or for the performance of a contract concluded in the interest of the data subject between the controller and a third party, or

4) the transfer is necessary or legally required on important public interest grounds, or for the establishment, exercise or defence of legal claims, or

5) the transfer is necessary in order to protect the vital interests of the data subject, or

6) the transfer is made from a register which according to laws or regulations is intended to provide information to the public and which is open to consultation either by the public in general or by any person who can demonstrate legitimate interest, to the extent that the conditions laid down in law for consultation are fulfilled in the particular case.[47]

The first derogation, that personally identifiable information may be transferred to any third country if the data subject has unambiguously consented to the transfer, faces the same definitional problem as the similar provision regarding processing in Article 7(a). The definition of "the data subject's consent" requires the subject's "freely given specific and informed indication" that the processing may take place.[48] The ambiguity of that statement and the potential for differing interpretations, even among EU member nations, means there is room for significant disagreement over what constitutes consent. Because the United States has no history of requiring data-subject approval before processing personally identifiable information, the definition of consent in the United States would likely be quite different than that put forward by EU member nations. Chapter 6 examines in some depth this and other issues regarding applying the Data Directive in the United States.

Paragraphs 2 to 4 of Article 26 provide another important derogation: Individual data controllers in third countries may enter into contractual agreements with EU data controllers that specify how the controller in the third country will safeguard the personally identifiable information transferred there. If the contractual terms are deemed adequate by the member country and the European Union's Commission, the EU controller may transfer the data to the third party.

Working Party on the Protection of Individuals with Regard to the Processing of Personal Data

An important part of the support infrastructure for the Data Directive is the Working Party on the Protection of Individuals with Regard to the Processing of Personal Data, also known as the "Working Party" or, more usually, the "Article 29 Working Party." The Working Party, established by Article 29 of the Data Directive, is an independent advisory body with a mandate to

(a) examine any question covering the application of the national measures adopted under this Directive in order to contribute to the uniform application of such measures;

(b) give the Commission an opinion on the level of protection in the Community and in third countries;

(c) advise the Commission on any proposed amendment of this Directive, on any additional or specific measures to safeguard the rights and freedoms of natural persons with regard to the processing of personal data and on any other proposed Community measures affecting such rights and freedoms;

(d) give an opinion on codes of conduct drawn up at Community level.[49]

Another of the Working Party's charges is to generate an annual report on data protection in the European Union's member states and in third states, though the Working Party is free to investigate and render opinions on any matter relating to the control and processing of personally identifiable information.[50] The Working Party issued an important report on proposed U.S. measures to comply with the Data Directive's restrictions: the proposal, and the Working Party's response, are considered in the next chapter.

Data Directive and International Commerce

The cost of complying with the EU Data Directive and similar data protection laws is not insignificant, especially for companies that derive their livelihood from collecting and processing personally identifiable information. However, Swire and Litan note,

Foreign firms ordinarily expect to comply with local laws. U.S. companies that have chosen to operate in Europe, for example, expect to comply with the local minimum wage or antipollution laws. These local regulations are not an attack on U.S. interests, except where there is evidence that they are discriminatory or otherwise have international repercussions.[51]

That most U.S. and other non-European firms will need to devote significant time and effort to complying with the Data Directive does put a different burden on the non-European firms than on the companies that have already come into compliance with the laws, but that difference is mitigated somewhat by the fact that the European firms have lacked the advantage of unrestricted access to personally identifiable information that most non-European firms have had since the 1970s, when most EU member nations passed their initial privacy laws.

Swire and Litan conclude that there is the possibility that the regulations could very well cause an overall decrease in commerce due to the cost of compliance and restraint of trade, but that any decrease could be offset by increased consumer confidence and the normative value of enhanced privacy for consumers.[52]

PRIVACY LEGISLATION IN CANADA

For a number of years privacy legislation in Canada followed a model similar to that of the United States: regulate what the government may do with personally identifiable information, but not the private sector. The Canadian Human Rights Act established a limited set of privacy rights which the Privacy Act, passed in 1983, extended significantly. Like the U.S. Privacy Act of 1974, the Canadian legislation requires the government to do the following:

- Limit its collection of personal information to the minimum details needed to operate programs or activities.
- Collect the information, whenever possible, directly from the person concerned.
- Tell the person why the information is being collected and how it will be used.
- Not use the information for other purposes, unless allowed by law.
- Keep the information for long enough to allow the person a reasonable opportunity to obtain access.
- Ensure the information is as accurate, up-to-date, and complete as possible.
- Not disclose personal information unless specifically allowed by the Privacy Act or another law.[53]

The Privacy Act also allows Canadians to examine personally identifiable information about themselves held by more than 100 government agencies and, if they find the data to be inaccurate, to request a correction. Even if the government declines to make the correction, the request for the change must still be included with the record.[54] The Privacy Act also established the office of the privacy commissioner of Canada. The privacy commissioner acts as an ombudsman with regard to individual privacy in Canada, meaning that while the commissioner has no powers of enforcement, the office can conduct investigations, administer oaths, and, if circumstances warrant, bring complaints to the Canadian court system on behalf of citizens who believe their privacy rights have been violated by the government.

While these protections were important, they did not bring Canada in line with the vanguard of data protection laws. Recently, the Canadian Parliament passed a sweeping new privacy law to bring Canada's data protection regime in line with the strictures of the European Union's Data Directive. This law, known as the Personal Information Protection and Electronic Documents Act, enacted protections required by the Data Directive.

The Personal Information Protection and Electronic Documents Act

The Personal Information Protection and Electronic Documents Act was introduced in the Canadian Parliament on October 1, 1998, but did not progress beyond the second reading and died when the Parliament took their summer break. The bill was reintroduced at the beginning of the next parliamentary session and became law on April 13, 2000, going into effect January 1, 2001.

The text of the Personal Information Protection and Electronic Documents Act is based on a model code promulgated by the Canadian Standards Association, which emphasizes ten dimensions of privacy protection:

1. Accountability.
2. Identifying Purposes.
3. Consent.
4. Limiting Collection.
5. Limiting Use, Disclosure, and Retention.
6. Accuracy.
7. Safeguards.
8. Openness.
9. Individual Access.
10. Challenging Compliance.[55]

These principles are functionally equivalent to the general principles listed in the OECD Principles, the EU Data Directive, and the Privacy Act. Bruce

Phillips, Canada's privacy commissioner, emphasized during a December 10, 1999, speech that "this bill therefore does not constitute the heavy-handed imposition on an unwilling business community of principles foreign to their thinking. Rather, perhaps more so than almost any other piece of federal legislation in recent years, it reflects the consensus of significant sectors of Canada's business community."[56] Be that as it may, earlier language in the commissioner's presentation indicated there was significant disgruntlement within the business community to having previously voluntary practices imposed by law, which is to be expected whenever new restrictions on doing business are introduced.

A major difference between the Senate and House of Commons versions of the Personal Information Protection and Electronic Documents Act was that the Senate version contains a one-year delay in implementing the act's provisions in the health care field. The health care sector's primary reason for requesting additional time to comply with the act is that the new policy would require them to get a patient's consent for every use of their information. Canada's minister of industry, the Honorable John Manley, felt the exception was unnecessary because the noncommercial or research use of patient information is protected under the act:

Following the CSA Standard, express consent is not required where an individual would reasonably expect a collection, use or disclosure of their personal information to be part of a transaction. For example when patients request a pharmacy service, they are implicitly consenting to collection, use or disclosure of their personal information, as necessary to render that service. It is only for secondary uses and disclosures, not reasonably expected by patients in the context of the transaction, that express consent is required. Consent doesn't have to be given at each step and each time for the same purpose, and there are a variety of ways to obtain it. But the Standard insists on the knowledge and consent of the individual.[57]

Other important provisions of the Personal Information Protection and Electronic Documents Act include a primacy clause, which places the restrictions embodied in the act above those of other laws unless Parliament includes language that gives the new law precedence. Also, the act allows the provinces to pass their own "substantially similar" laws during the first four years the act is in force. Once a province has passed a similar law, then any organizations governed by the provincial law would no longer be governed by the federal law.[58] So far, the only province with a personally identifiable information protection regime that meets the European Union's standards is Quebec.

Privacy Protection in Quebec

The province of Quebec has two laws governing personally identifiable information. The first law, the *Loi sur l'accès aux documents des organismes publics et sur la protection des renseignements personnels* (Law on access to

publicly held documents and the protection of personal data), deals with government control of personal information. The second law, the *Loi sur la protection des renseignements personnels dans le secteur privé* (Law on personal
data protection in the private sector), offers similar protections for information controlled by private organizations.[59] These laws embody many of the
protections in the European Union's Data Directive, but critics point out that
the effect of the laws in practice is quite different than intimated by the titles
of the laws. In "The 'Quebec Model' of Data Protection," Rene Laperriere
argues that there are significant loopholes in Quebec's provincial privacy stat-
ues that allow virtually unfettered transfer of personally identifiable information between public and private bodies.[60]

The first loophole LaPerrière identifies is that there are a number of circumstances under which personally identifiable information may be exchanged
without running afoul of the law. One exception is that the private-sector law
allows public and private investigators to exchange data without restriction;
the same condition exists between debt collectors and marketers. The law
also suffers from overbroad language, allowing personal data to be collected
and exchanged for verification purposes, a term defined nowhere in the law.
Data exchanged under these exceptions does not need to meet the law's accuracy provisions, has no limit on the amount of time the information may be
kept, and may be collected without informing the subject either of the
controller's identity or the subject's rights under the law.[61] The second loophole is bureaucratic in nature: When the Commission a l'access d'information
(CAI) was given the new responsibility of overseeing privacy protections in
the private sector, its funding was not increased to match the new workload.
Laperriere notes that the CAI must now neglect important functions, including "audit and investigation, on-site visits, and surveys, all of which enable
the commission to probe the systems, assess their compliance with the law,
and explore future developments."[62] The third and potentially most significant limitation is that the private-sector law did not include stakeholders in
establishing the privacy practices for their sectors. While the law does set
general guidelines for the type of conduct that is permitted, in Laperriere's
opinion it does not go far enough in specifying which types of personally
identifiable information are so sensitive as to warrant a prohibition on their
collection. This lack of definition, plus the use of vague terms like "relevance"
and "necessity,"

grant permission to act without the data subject's consent and expropriate informational self-determination. Thus, despite Quebec's privacy statutes applying to both
the public and the private sectors, one can still hear official proposals to sell entire
public information banks to the private sector or to use the information superhighway
to allow any government official to amalgamate and retrieve all data on a given individual from the data banks of private bodies. One wonders if the next step would be
to link this virtual information bank to those of private institutions . . . to obtain a

more extensive profile. That is just what the Quebec government resolved to do by amending the Social Welfare Act in 1996 to allow extensive data searches to check the eligibility of welfare applicants or recipients. Permission is thus officially granted to extend surveillance on whole sectors of the population.[63]

CONCLUSION

Privacy protections have evolved significantly in Europe, but less so in the United States and, absent the passage of the Personal Information Protection and Electronic Documents Act, in Canada. In Europe the transition has gone from regulation of large, centralized databases that posed a threat in the 1970s to a human rights approach, where the interests of the data subject are put ahead of commercial interests. Data subjects can consent to having their personally identifiable information used for commercial purposes, but the default is to protect that information and not allow it to be used indiscriminately for marketing purposes. By contrast, data protection in the United States is reminiscent of the second generation of data protection laws in Europe, passed during the early 1980s. Rather than place the rights of the data subject over that of commercial and other interests that could gain economic benefit from collecting and processing an individual's personally identifiable information, the U.S. Congress has chosen to cordon off sections of personally identifiable information, often in response to "crises of the moment," such as the Video Privacy Protection Act, passed as a result of journalists obtaining Supreme Court Justice nominee Robert Bork's videocassette rental records. The next chapter examines attempts to resolve the differences between U.S. and European law.

NOTES

1. Organization for Economic Cooperation and Development, "Guidelines on the Protection of Privacy and Transborder Flows of Personal Data," 1980. Available <http://www.oecd.org//dsti/sti/it/secur/prod/PRIV-EN.HTM>.
2. Ibid.
3. Ibid.
4. Viktor Mayer-Schönberger, "Generational Development of Data Protection in Europe," In *Technology and Privacy: The New Landscape*, ed. Phil Agre and Marc Rotenberg (Cambridge: MIT Press, 1999), 221.
5. Ibid., 222.
6. Ibid., 223, note 23.
7. Ibid., 224.
8. Ibid., 227.
9. Ibid., 228.
10. Ibid., 230.
11. Ibid., 232.

12. Ibid., 233.

13. Scott Blackmer, "The European Union Data Protection Directive" (paper presented at the Privacy & American Business Meeting on Model Data Protection Contracts and Laws, 24–25 February 1998). Available <http://www.privacyexchange.org/tbdi/EU_PDR/blackmerdirective.html>.

14. Working Party of EU Data Protection Commissioners, "Transfers of Personal Data to Third Countries: Applying Articles 25 and 26 of the EU Data Protection Directive," working paper, 24 July 1998. Available <http://www.europa.eu.int/comm/dg15/en/media/dataprot/wpdocs/wp12en.htm>.

15. Linda Harrison, "EC Busts Five States Over Data Protection," 11 January 2000. Available <http://www.theregister.co.uk/000111-000013.html>.

16. Blackmer, "The European Union Data Protection Directive."

17. "Directive 95/EC of the European Parliament and of the Council: On the Protection of Individuals With Regard to the Processing of Personal Data and on the Free Movement of Such Data" (hereafter, Data Directive), *Official Journal of the European Communities* L281 (23 November 1995): Article 2(a).

18. Ibid., Article 2(b).

19. Ibid., Article 2(d).

20. Peter P. Swire and Robert E. Litan, *None of Your Business: World Data Flows, Electronic Commerce, and the European Privacy Directive* (Washington, D.C.: Brookings Institution Press, 1998), 27.

21. Data Directive, Article 2(h).

22. Ibid., Article 3(1).

23. Colin Bennett, "Convergence Revisited," in *Technology and Privacy: The New Landscape*, ed. Phil Agre and Marc Rotenberg (Cambridge: MIT Press, 1997), 107.

24. Data Directive, Article 3(2).

25. Ibid.

26. Blackmer, "The European Union Data Protection Directive."

27. Data Directive, Article 6(1).

28. Ibid., Article 7(1).

29. Ibid., Article 8(1).

30. Ibid., Article 10(1).

31. Ibid., Article 11(2).

32. Ibid., Article 12(1).

33. Ibid., Article 12(2)–(3).

34. Ibid., Article 14(b).

35. Blackmer, "The European Union Data Protection Directive."

36. Data Directive, Article 28(3).

37. Blackmer, "The European Union Data Protection Directive."

38. Data Directive, Article 19(1).

39. Blackmer, "The European Union Data Protection Directive."

40. Data Directive, Article 18(1).

41. Ibid., Article 18(2).

42. Ibid., Article 20.

43. Ibid., Article 21.

44. Ibid., Article 25(1).

45. Ibid., Article 25(2).

46. Ibid., Article 25(5).

47. Ibid., Article 26(1).

48. Ibid., Article 2(h).

49. Ibid., Article 30(1).

50. Ibid., Article 30(2) and (6).

51. Swire and Litan, *None of Your Business*, 42.

52. Ibid., 44.

53. Privacy Commissioner of Canada, *The Privacy Act: A Preamble*, 7 February 1999. Available <http://www.privcom.gc.ca/english/02_07_e.htm>.

54. Ibid.

55. Canadian Standards Association, *Model Code for the Protection of Personal Information*. Available <http://gov.mb.ca/mihac/eng/csa.html>.

56. Bruce Phillips, "Bill C-6, the Personal Information Protection and Electronic Documents Act" (remarks to the CENTRUM Conference, Toronto, Ontario, 10 December 1999). Available <http://www.privcom.gc.ca/english/02_05_a_991210_e.htm>.

57. John Manley, *Presentation to the Senate Committee Studying Bill C-6*, 2 December 1999. Available <http://strategis.ic.gc.ca/virtual_hosts/e-com/english/speeches/42d8.html>.

58. Ibid.

59. Commission d'Acces a l'Information, *Une Commission, Deux Lois*, 8 March 1999. Available <http://www.cai.gouv.qc.ca/commiss.htm>.

60. René LaPerrière, "The 'Quebec Model' of Data Protection," in *Visions of Privacy: Policy Choices for the Digital Age*, ed. Colin J. Bennett and Rebecca Grant (Toronto: University of Toronto Press, 1999).

61. Ibid., 188.

62. Ibid., 189.

63. Ibid., 191.

4

Differences Between U.S. and European Law

As has been seen in the last two chapters, the United States and Europe approach privacy regulation very differently. U.S. governments have a strong tendency to prefer industry self-regulation and, as part of that approach, to treat personally identifiable information as a commodity to be traded. The U.S. Congress has identified a number of specific types of information to be protected—videotape rental records, cable television viewing information, and so forth—but has not extended those protections to many sectors of an individual's life. The most significant arena where personally identifiable information lacked protection was in the health sector, though executive rule-making at the end of 1999 and into 2000 closed some of those gaps. The European Union's Data Directive, by contrast, takes a human rights approach with regard to the balance between business and government functions in relation to an individual's right to privacy. By requiring organizations to obtain a data subject's unambiguous consent before processing or passing on a subject's personally identifiable information, the European regime shifts the balance of power from the organization to the individual.

The difference between the two approaches has led to a series of negotiation sessions between the United States and the European Union, with the goal of creating an informational privacy regime in the United States that the EU Commission determines would offer sufficient protection for personally identifiable information. Once the protections are in place, the EU would encourage its member nations to allow the free flow of data to and from the United States. American proposals have centered on the creation of a "Safe Harbor"; essentially a self-regulatory regime under which companies would indicate their willingness to follow a set of information practices that would protect personally identifiable information in a manner acceptable to the EU. There have been a number of stumbling blocks in the negotiations, not in the least the American insistence that the Safe Harbor provisions take the form of a self-regulatory scheme and not legislation. This chapter looks at American proposals to institute acceptable data protection policies (vis-à-vis Europe) and examines the differences between the American and European positions. Later chapters will build on this factual base to detail the most likely legislative and policy scenarios for American businesses.

THE AMERICAN POSITION

Throughout the negotiations between the United States and the European Union, the U.S. position has been that the best regulatory structure to follow in the United States would be self-regulation, where organizations develop in-house policies and self-certify that they are following the edicts of the European Union's Data Directive. The document which contains the U.S. Department of Commerce's proposal is the Draft International Safe Harbor Privacy Principles; as of July 2000 the most recent version of those principles was released on June 9, 2000. The principles, in concert with a number of Frequently Asked Questions (abbreviated "FAQs," a term that originated among ARPANET users), offer U.S. data controllers an outline of the procedures they would need to follow to receive transfers of personally identifiable information from the EU. Organizations may either comply with the principles as stated or "by developing their own self regulatory privacy policies provided that they conform with the principles."[1] If an organization fails to comply with an internally developed privacy policy, that organization could be pursued by the Federal Trade Commission for using unfair and deceptive advertising practices.

The Principles

At first glance, the Safe Harbor principles bear a strong resemblance to the OECD Guidelines and the EU Data Directive (described in Chapter 5):

Notice: An organization must inform individuals about the purposes for which it collects and uses information about them, how to contact the organization with any inquiries or complains, the types of third parties to which it discloses the information, and the choices and means the organization offers individuals for limiting its use and disclosure, where the organization is using or disclosing it for a purpose other than that for which it was originally collected or for a purpose which it was processed by the transferring organization. . . .

Choice: An organization must offer individuals the opportunity to choose (opt out) whether and how personal information they provide is used or disclosed to third parties, where such use or disclosure is incompatible with the purpose(s) for which it was originally collected, or subsequently authorized by the individual. . . . For sensitive information (i.e., personal information specifying medical or health conditions, racial or ethnic origin, political opinions, religious or philosophical beliefs, trade union membership or information specifying the sex life of the individual) they must be given an affirmative or explicit (opt in) choice. . . .

Onward Transfer: An organization may only disclose personal information to third parties consistent with the principles of notice and choice. . . . If the organization complies with these requirements, it shall not be held responsible when a third party to which it transfers such information processes it in a way contrary to any restrictions or representations.

Security: Organizations creating, maintaining, using or disseminating personal information must take reasonable precautions to protect it from loss, misuse and unauthorized access, disclosure, alteration and destruction.

Data Integrity: Consistent with the principles, an organization may not process personal information in a way that is incompatible with the purposes for which it has been collected or subsequently authorized by the individual. To the extent necessary for those purposes, an organization should take reasonable steps to ensure that data is reliable for its intended use, accurate, complete, and current.

Access: Individuals must have access to personal information about them that an organization holds and be able to correct, amend, or delete that information where it is inaccurate, except where the burden or expense of providing access would be disproportionate to the risks to the individual's privacy in the case in question, or where the rights of persons other than the individual would be violated.

Enforcement: Effective privacy protection must include mechanisms for assuring compliance with the principles, recourse for individuals to whom the data relate affected by non-compliance with the principles, and consequences for the organization when the principles are not followed. At a minimum, such mechanisms must include (a) readily available and affordable independent recourse mechanisms by which each individual's complaints and disputes are investigated and resolved by reference to the principles and damages awarded where the applicable law or private sector initiatives so provide; (b) follow up procedures for verifying that the attestations and assertions businesses make about their privacy practices are true and that privacy practices have been implemented as presented; and (c) obligations to remedy problems arising out of failure to comply with the principles by organizations announcing their adherence to them and consequences for such organizations. Sanctions must be sufficiently rigorous to ensure compliance by organizations.[2]

As might be expected, the voluntary nature of the principles and the differences in language between the Safe Harbor principles and the Data Directive have given rise to a number of significant objections to the principles from the Article 29 Working Group.

European Opinion on the Safe Harbor Principles

The European Union, as represented by the Data Protection Working Party established under Article 29 of the Data Directive, has published several working papers evaluating the adequacy of the American Safe Harbor proposals. The basis for the Working Party's evaluation is a working paper entitled "Transfers of Personal Data to Third Countries: Applying Articles 25 and 26 of the EU Data Protection Directive." This document sets forth the Working Party's methodology for evaluating a third country's data protection regime, beginning with an overall look at what, in the Working Party's opinion, constitutes "adequate protection"; lists situations where the methodology could be applied (differentiated by ratification of treaties, preference for self-regulation, etc.); the role of contractual provisions; and under what circumstances a third country could be exempted from fulfilling the adequacy requirement.

Assessing Adequacy

The first element of assessing the adequacy of any national regulatory scheme dealing with data protection concerns that country's ratification and adherence to international conventions, such as the 1981 Council of Europe Convention Number 108 and the 1980 OECD Guidelines. From the number of countries that ratified these agreements, the Working Party infers a general, international consensus as to the scope and application of data protection rules.[3] The Working Party document does, however, acknowledge that the standard practice of embodying data protection standards in law is not necessarily shared by third countries with which organizations in EU member nations transact personally identifiable information.[4] As one example of the range of policies available to third countries that subscribe to international charters, the Working Party notes that Convention 108 of the Council of Europe does not require a national supervisory body to oversee the data protection regime within a country. While the directive does put such a requirement in place, the Working Party does allow for the possibility that a nation could offer personally identifiable information adequate protection without such a body.

As a starting point for evaluating a country's data protection regime, the Working Party identified a set of minimum conditions that would need to be met for an analysis to proceed:

- Purpose limitation, meaning data are gathered for a specific purpose and not reprocessed or transferred for uses incompatible with the original use.

- Data quality and proportionality, meaning that data should be accurate, timely, and not excessive.

- Transparency, meaning data subjects should know who is collecting their data and for what purpose.

- Security, meaning that the processor is responsible for ensuring there are no unauthorized transfers or disclosures.

- Access, rectification, and opposition, meaning data subjects should be able to view, challenge, and correct their files.

- Restrictions on onward transfers, meaning the data may only be transferred to third parties that are also subject to a regime ensuring adequate protection.[5]

The Working Paper also lists areas where third countries might invoke stronger protections, such as in the collection and processing of sensitive data (i.e., ethnic, political, or health-related data), for direct marketing, and in automated decision making. While the Working Party realizes that no regime guarantees perfect compliance with data protection rules, the commission should look for a good level of compliance, support, and help for data subjects, and the opportunity to gain redress for harms resulting from improper data collection or processing.[6] It is important to note that the American Safe Harbor proposal is designed to meet this bare minimum standard of adequacy.

Evaluating Self-Regulation

The Working Party recognizes a number of valid self-regulatory schemes, ranging from an industry body developing a code for its members on one extreme to a professional organization, such as a medical or legal association that has significant certification and disciplinary authority, on the other. In industries where a number of standards bodies are competing, the Working Party would be much less likely to advise the commission that it should find the industry or sector's self-regulatory scheme affords adequate protection. The Working Party also notes that, in the case of direct marketing, organizations in different industrial sectors exchange data as a matter of course, meaning that a transaction could easily occur between organizations governed by differing (or no) privacy principles.[7] In such a case, the presence of an overarching legal instrument, such as the Canadian data privacy law or Quebec's provincial data privacy statute, would offer the Working Party firmer ground on which to make their evaluation.

In evaluating a self-regulatory regime, the Working Party would take several specific factors into account. The first factor is the content of the self-regulatory code itself. The Working Party would examine what practices are allowed and disallowed and what duties member organizations have with regard to personally identifiable information, and prohibit the transfer of data to organizations lacking an adequate level of protection. The second factor is the potential effectiveness of the code. For instance, if the standards body has taken no action to publicize the code to the organization's members, it is highly unlikely there would be adequate protection provided. Other considerations include efforts to make the industry's code known to data subjects, an external system for verifying compliance, and the nature of enforcement actions and penalties taken in response to noncompliance. In particular, the Working Party recommends that an evaluation of a self-regulatory scheme ask the following questions:

- What efforts does the representative body make to ensure that its members are aware of the code?
- Does the representative body require evidence from its members that it has put the provisions of the code into practice? How often?
- Is such evidence provided by the member company itself or does it come from an external source (such as an accredited auditor)?
- Does the representative body investigate alleged or suspected breaches of the code?
- Is compliance with the code a condition of membership of the representative body or is compliance purely "voluntary"? Where a member has been shown to breach the code, what forms of disciplinary sanction are available to the representative body (expulsion or other)?
- Is it possible for an individual or company to continue working in the particular profession or industry even after expulsion from the representative body?[8]

The Working Party notes in particular that the lack of "genuinely dissuasive and punitive sanctions" represent a significant weakness; indeed, their lack is a weakness that probably cannot be overcome when attempting to establish a self-regulatory scheme that provides adequate protection for personally identifiable information.[9]

EUROPEAN POSITION ON THE SAFE HARBOR PRINCIPLES

Negotiations between the EU and the United States in an attempt to establish an American data protection scheme that would offer adequate protection for personally identifiable information have gone on since mid-1998 with neither side changing their position significantly. The American team, lead by Ambassador David Aaron, undersecretary of commerce for international trade, has consistently maintained that the Safe Harbor principles would offer adequate protection for personally identifiable information transferred from the EU to the United States. The European position, as might be expected, is that the Safe Harbor principles are significantly flawed and that the United States has made little effort to change its position to meet legitimate objections raised by the EU. The Working Party goes so far to state in a December 3, 1999, working paper that it "deplores that most of the comments made in its previous position papers do not seem to be addressed in the latest version of the US documents."[10]

The first objection to the Safe Harbor principles is that the self-certification principles, as explained by FAQs 6 and 11, are inadequate for several reasons.[11] The primary reason that these provisions are inadequate is that the Department of Commerce, or its designee, is under no obligation to verify whether an organization is eligible to apply for protection under the Safe Harbor principles, such as by being subject to a binding privacy policy or under Federal Trade Commission (FTC) jurisdiction for unfair and deceptive practices. The Working Party also finds fault with the requirement that organizations renew their self-certification on an annual basis, arguing that this restriction is not sufficient to prevent companies from adhering to the rules for one year and then choosing to end compliance even if they are still in possession of personally identifiable information transferred from an EU member nation. Finally, the Working Party notes that mergers and acquisitions are increasingly common "in the course of business in general and in the on-line business in particular," which could lead to an organization adhering to the principles being taken over by an organization that does not, removing prior protections from the personally identifiable information of European Union data subjects.[12] The second area of objection lies in the voluntary nature of the Safe Harbor provisions and the reliance on self-certification. Because the only threat of legal action comes from the FTC's ability to investigate and sanction unfair and deceptive practices, the Working Party notes that unless a data subject files a complaint, it is possible for organizations to be on the list who have no intention of complying with the Safe Harbor principles.[13] Once again, the problem lies with the lack of an up-front check into the status of an organization's compliance with the principles.

A third problem lies with the scope of organizations and types of data covered by the principles. In the case of employment and human resources data, two letters from Ambassador Aaron to the EU Commission indicated that the FTC only has jurisdiction over actions "in or affecting commerce,"[14] which means that nonprofit or research enterprises could argue they were not subject to the principles.[15] A similar EU complaint addresses the provision in FAQ 6 that organizations may choose which of their activities will be covered by the Safe Harbor principles and which will not. The Working Party argues that such uneven coverage, especially in light of intracompany data transfers, is much too vague and that companies could use the legal uncertainty generated by the inconsistencies to sidestep the Data Directive.[16] The Working Party also expressed concern that the Safe Harbor principles exclude entire categories of data, including "publicly available" data, without regard to the manner in which the data was collected, the purpose of the collection, or the intended uses beyond that for which the data was originally collected.[17]

The Working Party lists a number of other objections, such as places where the Safe Harbor principles fall short of providing data protection consistent with the OECD Guidelines, let alone the Data Directive, and that the principles seem to deal exclusively with online information practices by emphasizing the oversight role to be played by private-sector organizations like TRUSTe, BBB Online, and Web Trust. The Working Party specifically noted that the enforcement provisions listed in the principles and amended in FAQ 11 offer a confusing picture of what rights a data subject has under the principles. In its conclusion, the Working Party asked the Department of Commerce to make the following improvements to the Safe Harbor principles:

- to clarify the scope of the "Safe Harbor" and in particular to remove any possible misunderstanding that US organisations can choose to rely on the "Safe Harbor" principles in circumstances when the Directive itself applies;
- to provide more reliable arrangements allowing "Safe Harbor" participants to be identified with certainty and avoiding the risk that "Safe Harbor" benefits will continue to be accorded after "Safe Harbor" status has, for one reason or another, been lost;
- to make it absolutely clear that enforcement by an appropriately empowered public body is in place for all participants in the "Safe Harbor";
- to make it the rule that private sector dispute resolution bodies must refer unresolved complaints to such a public body;
- to make the allowed exceptions and exemptions less sweeping and less open-ended, so that exceptions are precisely that—that is, they apply only where and to the extent necessary, and are not general invitations to override the principles; this is particularly important as regards the right of access;
- to strengthen the Choice principle, which is the lynchpin of the US approach.[18]

CONCLUSION

The United States and the EU came to an agreement on language for the Safe Harbor Principles on May 31, 2000, with the changed language reflecting the EU's concern over the lack of a strong enforcement mechanism in FAQ 11. After approval by the EU member nations, the principles were passed on to the European Parliament for its recommendation on the agreement. While the European Parliament has no power to void the deal, it did vote against accepting the principles as presented by a count of 279 to 259, and asked the EU to renegotiate provisions to allow EU citizens to sue companies that breach the principles and appeal Federal Trade Commission decisions to an independent body. The EU's negotiators and the United States have both said insisting on those positions would negate any chance of agreement, so now the European Commission must choose between the Parliament's stance or maintaining the deal in its current form.[19]

NOTES

1. U.S. Department of Commerce, *Draft International Safe Harbor Privacy Principles*, 15 November 1999. Available <http://www.ita.doc.gov/td/ecom/Principles1199.htm>.

2. Ibid.

3. Data Protection Working Party, "Transfers of Personal Data to Third Countries: Applying Articles 25 and 26 of the EU Data Protection Directive," Working paper, p. 5, 24 July 1998. Available <http://www.europa.eu.int/comm/dg15/en/media/dataprot/wpdocs/wp12en.htm>.

4. Ibid.

5. Ibid., 6.

6. Ibid., 7.

7. Ibid., 10.

8. Ibid., 12.

9. Ibid.

10. Article 29 Working Party, "Opinion 7/99 on the Level of Data Protection Provided by the "Safe Harbor" Principles as Published Together with the Frequently Asked Questions (FAQs) and Other Related Documents on 15 and 16 November 1999 by the US Department of Commerce," p. 3, December 1999. Available <http://www.europa.eu.int/comm/dg15/en/media/dataprot/wpdocs/wp27en.htm>.

11. For FAQ 6, see <http://www.ita.doc.gov/td/ecom/FAQ6Self-cert1199.htm>. For FAQ 11, see <http://www.ita.doc.gov/td/ecom/FAQ11DisputeRes1199.htm>.

12. Article 29 Working Party, "Opinion 7/99," p. 4.

13. Ibid.

14. Ambassador David Aaron, "Data Protection: Draft of the U.S. Side of the Exchange of Letters with the European Commission," November 1999. Available <http://www.ita.doc.gov/td/ecom/USletter1199.html>.

15. Article 29 Working Party, "Opinion 7/99," p. 5.

16. Ibid.

17. Ibid.

18. Ibid., 14.

19. Keith Perine, "U.S.–EU Data Privacy Deal Panned," *The Industry Standard*, 6 July 2000. Available <http://www.thestandard.com/article/display/1,1151,16637,00.html>.

5

Internet Economics

The American public has long been willing to purchase goods from catalogs, calling stores using toll-free numbers and giving their credit card numbers to total strangers. The telephone is a familiar tool, however, and the cost of producing and distributing a catalog is quite a bit higher than that of creating an equivalent Web site. When consumers have something tangible in their hands, they tend to have a much better feeling about doing business with a company. Another consideration is that mail-order catalogs are often easier to use than Web sites. A *Consumer Reports* study conducted between May and July 1999 found that Web sites were often poorly organized, contained no information on how to return products, did not spell out what security measures were in place to protect the consumer, and explained shipping options poorly. One retailer, L.L. Bean, changed their site to meet customer concerns.[1]

As the public becomes more comfortable with the Internet and the concept of making purchases online, the preference to conduct business with "brick and mortar" stores will lessen. Recent surveys from a number of research firms indicate that online shopping is indeed gaining momentum, though their estimates of the number of households with members that have made a purchase online differ significantly. One estimate, released on September 29, 1999, by Forrester Research, indicated that 17 million U.S. households will shop online by the end of 1999, for total online retail sales of $20.2 billion.

The survey further notes that approximately 7 million consumers will make their first online purchase in 1999.[2] Forrester also predicted that 49 million U.S. households would shop online by 2004, for total sales of $184 billion, with the average annual expenditure by each household to rise from its current average of $1,167 to $3,638 in 2004.[3]

A competing study from NFO Interactive, entitled *Online Retail Monitor: Branding, Segmentation & Web Sites*, indicated that the actual number of U.S. households with a member who has shopped online is closer to 27 million, with 3 million of those shoppers making their first purchase in the 1999 holiday season.[4] The study also found that the 3 million new online buyers were typically female (56%) and that 55 percent of the new buyers came from households with annual incomes above $50,000. The substantial majority of the respondents (80%) said that price discounts would lead them to make an online purchase, while 67 percent said that privacy assurances would encourage them to buy online as well. The ability to return a purchase to a physical location and the promise of immediate customer support were also listed as incentives.

While the exact size of the Internet economy is open to question, researchers agree that the number of households that shop online and the total amount of purchases made over the Internet will increase. Investigations into the nature of online commerce have discovered a number of principles that can inform companies looking to establish an Internet business presence. One of those principles is *increasing returns*.

TRADITIONAL ECONOMICS AND INCREASING RETURNS

In *The Competitive Advantage of Nations*, Michael Porter lays out four determinants of national advantage:

1. *Factor conditions.* Factor endowments can include the presence of skilled labor or natural resources.
2. *Demand conditions.* If a nation's domestic market is advanced and demands high quality, that nation's firms will become stronger.
3. *Related and supporting industries.* The number and quality of suppliers and internationally competitive related industries.
4. *Firm strategy, structure, and rivalry.* How companies are organized, managed, and compete.[5]

The most important of these elements in traditional markets is a nation's factor endowments. It is possible for a firm to overcome a shortfall in one area, such as Japanese automobile manufacturers have overcome their need to import steel, though the firms must excel in all other areas to compete with companies located in countries that are rich in natural resources. Regardless of how effectively a company can marshal its technology in a traditional manufacturing environment, however, the firm can only manufacture a given amount of a product before inefficiencies increase the cost of producing each additional unit until it is greater than the profit derived from that unit. This principle is known as *diminishing* (or *decreasing*) *returns*.

A central characteristic of diminishing returns is *equilibrium*, or the tendency of competing economic forces to find the optimal mix of two technologies or approaches. One example of how competing companies can reach an equilibrium is in the electricity-generation industry. Suppose competing firms use dams and coal-burning plants to generate electricity. While some dams will produce electricity at a lower cost than coal-burning plants, if a utilities region relies exclusively on dams, they will need to build dams on less productive (that is, more expensive) sites. At some point, electricity produced by coal-fired plants will be less expensive than electricity produced by less-efficient dams. The electricity-generation industry for that region will then settle into a relatively stable equilibrium, with the price-optimal amount of electricity generated by all available sources. This type of equilibrium describes commodity-based industries quite well: The companies produce undifferentiated products (in this case, electricity) and are separated only by their production costs. Diminishing returns do not adequately describe the digital realm, however, where products are differentiated by function, adherence to standards, and quality.

When products are not fully substitutable for one another because of function, standards adherence, or quality, the industry may evince increasing returns, where profitability rises more quickly than production costs increase. Increasing returns were first introduced by Allyn A. Young in 1928, and while they were not fully accepted by the academic community until the mid-1980s, they do accurately represent the digital economy.[6] Jeremy Maselko of Susquehanna University describes a system evincing increasing returns as a system with many equilibria, where a single small event can change the dynamics of an industry. Maselko offers the competition between the VHS and Beta videocassette formats as an example of increasing returns.[7] In the early days of the videocassette recorder (VCR) industry, consumers purchased machines in both formats at about the same rate. More consumers began to purchase VHS machines, so video-store owners began to purchase more tapes in the VHS format to meet the demand. As the number of tapes available in the VHS format that were not available in the Beta format increased, consumers increasingly disdained the technologically equal Beta standard in favor of VCRs that offered them a greater variety of movies. This type of increasing return is known as a *network effect*: the more consumers who use a particular technology, the more value that technology has. A recent example of a new technology that benefited from network effects is the fax machine. In the early 1980s, when few businesses and private individuals had fax machines, only consumers who saw an immediate and specific need for the machines bought them. As time went by prices came down, more organizations bought fax machines, and companies and private individuals began to expect to be able to communicate with each other via fax machines. Unlike VHS and Beta videocassettes, a clear example of *lock-in*, where a technology acquires such a lead over its competitors that consumers are unwilling to switch to other technologies, transmission standards mean it is simple to send a fax to a machine made by a different manufacturer.

In *Net Gain*, Hagel and Armstrong identify two other scenarios where increasing returns come into play. In one form, increasing returns result "when a business incurs large up-front expenditures to develop a new product or service and the incremental cost of producing each incremental unit of the product or service is minimal."[8] The authors point to the software industry as a prime example of where producing the first copy of a product (such as a word processor or database program) is huge and the cost of producing additional copies is negligible, though the online bookseller Amazon has followed a similar strategy. The third form of increasing returns comes from one company being farther up the *learning curve* for a given technology than its customers. That is, as a firm gains experience with products, it is better able to create those products and to innovate. One example of direct relevance to electronic commerce is RSA Data Security (http://www.rsasecurity.com). RSA Data Security was founded by three Massachusetts Institute of Technology faculty members (Ron Rivest, Adi Shamir, and Len Adleman) to take commercial advantage of the encryption technologies they had developed. Since the late 1970s RSA Data Security has been a leader in encryption technology, and even though the patent the company holds on its mainstay encryption algorithm (also named RSA, after the inventors and company founders) is due to expire on September 20, 2000, the company is banking on its experience working with encryption solutions to see it through after the patent expires.

Artificially Created Increasing Returns Fail

One aspect of increasing returns that has been reinforced in recent years is the importance that the market establish which technologies will win the battle for market share. On April 16, 1993, newly elected President Bill Clinton announced the Escrowed Encryption Initiative, a federal standard designed to "improve security and privacy of telephone communications."[9] Government engineers had created an encryption device called the Clipper Chip that could be used to encrypt voice, fax, and computer communications. The stated goal of the chip was to balance law-enforcement demands to access communications via wiretaps with consumer and business privacy concerns. To that end, the Clipper Chip used a government-developed encryption algorithm with a password of sufficient length to foil any unauthorized party from decrypting the message. To meet the law-enforcement community's need to intercept and decrypt communications made with a Clipper-enabled device, each chip would have a fixed, unique identifier built into it. That identifier, which the chip would use to encrypt and decrypt its messages, would be split into two pieces and stored securely by separate government agencies. The only way law-enforcement agents could access messages encrypted with a particular Clipper Chip would be to get a court order and present that order to both escrow agencies, which would then release that chip's identifier.

To encourage the market to support the Escrowed Encryption Initiative in general and the Clipper Chip in particular, the U.S. government ordered 9,000 Clipper-enabled phones and proposed the Escrowed Encryption Standard, which would require any organization that needed to communicate with any government agency over an encrypted phone line to use a Clipper-enabled phone. The National Institute of Standards and Technology (NIST) solicited public comments on the proposed standard. Despite only 2 positive letters out of 320 and numerous negative letters from sources including the Department of Energy, the U.S. Agency for International Development, and the Nuclear Regulatory Commission, NIST adopted the Escrowed Encryption Standard in February 1994. Much as happened with the Lotus and P-Trak examples, the Escrowed Encryption Standard elicited strong negative reactions from Internet users and security professionals. In *Privacy On the Line*, Whitfield Diffie (a cryptography pioneer) and Susan Landau enumerate a number of objections to the standard.[10] First, one element of a secure cryptographic regime is to constantly change passwords. Every Clipper Chip would have a single password, albeit one that is broken into two parts, which means that any message sent with a Clipper-enabled device could be decrypted if the key were ever released. Second, although dividing the chip's identifier into two pieces under control of separate agencies would greatly reduce the likelihood that a foreign government or nongovernmental organization could compromise a user's key, introducing the human element into an otherwise technical process creates a weakness that did not exist before. Third, even though the computing power required to decrypt a message by trying all possible keys (a *brute force* attack) is out of reach today, Diffie and Landau note that the steady increase in computer processor power means that it is not inconceivable that, in ten years, an organization might be able to find a Clipper Chip's identifier and gain access to every message ever sent from that machine.[11] Finally, Diffie and Landau note that escrowed encryption violates individuals' privacy *"even if the escrowed keys are never accessed"*[12] (italics in original). Since the government could record any encrypted conversation at any time and only afterward get a court order to decrypt it, even law-abiding users would have to assume the government was listening to their conversations.

In the end, the Escrowed Encryption Standard never took hold. AT&T, the phone's manufacturer, sold less than 20,000 Clipper-enabled devices, many of which were made-for-export editions of the device that were sold to organizations in Venezuela and the Middle East.[13]

DIGITAL PRODUCTS

Choi, Stahl, and Whinston argue that while the Internet can certainly be used to sell traditional products, the future of electronic commerce will be dominated by digital products and services more inherently suited to the online environment.[14] Information-based services, such as product reviews and information and software packages, are easily distributed via electronic networks and are prototypical digital products. Some characteristics that make digital products unique are indestructibility, transmutability, and reproducibility.[15]

Indestructibility

Unlike durable goods such as cars or household appliances, which wear down and need replacing, digital products are practically impervious to time and wear. While the magnetic media used to store a program or data will fail over time, the information itself will remain in its original condition so long as the storage medium remains intact. One tremendous advantage of practically infinitely durable products is that the consumer will never need to return the product under a warranty claim. While it is certainly possible that the software might not meet a user's needs and could be returned (licensing terms associated with the package notwithstanding), once the consumer has taken delivery of the product it is unlikely they will need to replace it for the useful life of the product. Enhanced product durability is certainly a boon for the consumer, but it requires constant innovation on the part of manufacturers to maintain a revenue stream from the product's customer base.

Transmutability

In addition to being practically indestructible, digital information is also transmutable, meaning it can be changed from one form to another readily. One example of how digital information can be transmuted from one product to another is the success of the open-source software movement. Software packages released under an open-source license allow anyone to modify or add to the program's source code to create new packages. Open-source licenses usually require that programs derived from existing open-source code also be released under an open-source license, though companies are finding ways to profit from open-source software. Red Hat, a software company that distributes a version of the Linux operating system, has added installation tools and collections of Linux tools that add value to the baseline operating system. The risk of producing transmutable products is that users can reverse engineer the products and use the knowledge they gain to create competing products without investing in the research and development performed by the creator. Most end-user licenses prohibit the purchaser from decompiling (extracting the source code from executable files) or reverse engineering the programs, though enforcing those provisions against competitors doing research in secured facilities is problematic.

One offshoot of product transmutability is that digital products are almost infinitely customizable. For example, assume a consumer wanted to purchase an integrated office product suite but did not want to pay for a spreadsheet program, a presentation-creation package, or spell-checking dictionaries in languages other than American English. Alternatively, a consumer might be willing to purchase an accounting package if the vendor could add on certain functions, such as the ability to link directly to the customer's point-of-sale system and keep a real-time inventory of products on hand. The software manufacturer could adjust its pricing based on the elements taken away or added, but it might also be possible for the manufacturer to charge its customers the maximum amount they would be willing to pay for the package instead of setting a single price that is calculated to generate the most revenue. Setting prices based on what a consumer is willing to pay is referred to as discriminatory pricing.

Discriminatory Pricing

Although the term "discriminatory pricing" makes it sound like a seller is doing something unsavory, charging users what they are willing to pay for a product is a time-honored business practice. One simple form of discriminatory pricing is to charge early adopters of a technology a premium price. For instance, every new generation of computer central processing units (CPUs) is marketed to the public for approximately $350. After a few weeks or months at that price, depending on demand, manufacturers will drop the price to attract consumers who are willing to purchase the faster chips, though not at a premium. Once the chip has become common currency, which usually means that the company has released an even faster chip, or when following companies release similar chips of their own, prices begin to drop more precipitously. Shapiro and Varian identify three different types of discriminatory pricing: personalized pricing, in which the manufacturer sells its products to each user at a different price; versioning, in which the manufacturer offers a product line and allows users to choose the version of the product most appropriate for their needs; and group pricing, where the manufacturer sets different prices for different groups, such as students.[16] Indeed, the authors note that it is possible to learn quite a bit about one's customers by offering a series of products for sale and seeing which customers purchase which package.

Choi, Stahl, and Whinston, all of whom are professors at the University of Texas at Austin, note that three characteristics of the electronic commerce environment make it possible to price products based on information gathered from user registration information and online behavior patterns: the ability to gain definite information about consumer tastes, the potential to customize products with little marginal cost, and the ability to bill consumers independently.[17] As those authors note, detailed data on consumer preferences are more abundant in computerized market environments. As a result, consumers derive greater satisfaction from customized products that are tailored to meet their needs, instead of needing to make do with average quality products that, while adequate, are not the best solution to their needs.[18]

Reproducibility

A final defining characteristic of digital products is reproducibility. As the name implies, it is often trivially easy to reproduce a digital product, whether it is information or an executable program. One way to limit the impact of unauthorized copying is to distribute time- and feature-limited versions of a software package and only offer full functionality to users who register their copy of the software. It is possible to derive a unique product registration code for each computer from the identification number for the machine's operating system and information about the computer's physical configuration (memory, hard drive space, central processing unit, etc.), though many software manufacturers now rely on their customers' good will to register their products. One such product is the SnagIt screen capture program from TechSmith (http://www.techsmith.com). TechSmith offers a free thirty-day evaluation version of SnagIt that can be downloaded from the company's Web site. The evaluation version of the software is fully functional, though a reminder (or "nag") screen appears after every two or three captures to remind the user to register the product and so receive technical support, free upgrades to the next two versions of SnagIt, and the end of the reminders to register. It is possible to delete the evaluation version of the program and reinstall it for another thirty days, but TechSmith is betting users of the program will be willing to pay the $39.95 price to gain the benefits of registration.

COMPETITION AND DIGITAL PRODUCTS

One aspect of the online economy is that the value of "pure" information products, such as phone books and encyclopedias, tend to go down in value. In *Information Rules*, Shapiro and Varian offer two examples of what happens to pure information products in a digital environment. One example is paper versus electronic phone books. Shapiro and Varian relate that in 1986 Nynex (the New York Regional Bell Operating System following the breakup of AT&T) released the first CD directory for the New York area. The disk, which sold for $10,000 per copy, was purchased by the Federal Bureau of Investigation, the Internal Revenue Service, and other organizations with an interest in easy access to phone listings and the money to purchase the product. James Bryant, who had overseen the project for Nynex, started ProCD with the goal of producing a national phone directory available on CD. After the phone companies refused to rent their lists at an affordable price, ProCD hired Chinese workers to key in every listing in every U.S. phone book (twice, to catch mistakes). Those CDs were then sold for a few hundred dollars apiece, netting ProCD a substantial profit.[19]

Now, of course, there are a number of online services where you can look up business and personal phone listings for free, with the cost of providing the service covered by advertising revenues. USWest Dex (http://www.uswestdex.com), WhoWhere (http://www.whowhere.lycos.com), and Big Yellow (http://www.bigyellow.com) are just a few of the sites where you can look up listed numbers across the country at no charge.

Shapiro and Varian's second example is the battle between the *Encyclopedia Britannica* and Microsoft's *Encarta*. As recently as the early 1990s a hardback set of the *Encyclopedia Britannica* would cost on the order of $1,600. Then, in 1992, Microsoft purchased *Funk & Wagnalls*, a competitor of the *Britannica* that had lost almost all of its customer base. Microsoft programmers combined a multimedia interface with the information in the encyclopedia and sold the resulting product for $49.95, with even better prices for original equipment manufacturers (OEMs). By 1996, price competition from *Encarta* had cut the *Britannica*'s sales in half. A Swiss investor bought the company that year and moved to a purely electronic strategy, reducing the cost of a yearly subscription to the encyclopedia from $120 to $85 (by comparison, in 1992 it cost $2,000 to subscribe to an electronic version of the *Britannica*), though that effort only resulted in 11,000 subscribers.[20]

On October 19, 1999, the company took the revolutionary step of putting the entire encyclopedia on the Internet for free (http://www.britannica.com).[21] The new site includes the complete, updated *Encyclopedia Britannica*, as well as selected articles from more than seventy of the world's top magazines—including *Newsweek*, *Discover*, *Sports Illustrated*, and *The Economist*—and daily news from the *Washington Post* (http://www.washingtonpost.com). The site's editors have chosen more than 125,000 Web sites, consisting of more than 100 million Web pages, for visitors to search for more information on topics in the encyclopedia or related articles. Another welcome feature of the site is access to the *Books in Print* database, a handy research tool for finding out whether books are still available through the standard retail channels.[22] It will be interesting to see how Britannica's competitors react to the move and whether the company, which will still produce value-added CD print versions of their encyclopedia, can generate enough advertising revenue to make the venture worthwhile.

SIGNALING QUALITY AND AVOIDING LEMONS

A significant element of succeeding at online commerce involves convincing customers that your products are worth the purchase price. TechSmith's approach to the problem, offering free versions of their product and encouraging registration by offering technical support and other benefits, has two benefits. The first benefit is that it gives consumers a chance to use the company's screen capture software before making a purchase decision. Rather than rely exclusively on a third party's opinion of the software, consumers can form their own opinion over the course of the thirty-day trial period. The second benefit comes from the company's including the next two versions of the software in the base purchase price. By demonstrating that SnagIt is a "living" product, one that is being continually upgraded and supported, TechSmith engenders consumer confidence while encouraging SnagIt users to purchase upgrades beyond those included in the original purchase.

Traditional Methods for Signaling Quality

In the event a company would prefer not to release its software to the general public, even on a trial basis, there are several ways consumers can determine the quality of its product. Those methods include paying attention to informative advertising, keeping abreast of industry and third-party quality standards (and how given products stack up against those standards), reading the results of third-party brand comparisons, and monitoring the resale market for the product in question.[23] As an example of how these forces work for advertising traditional products, consider the automotive industry. Car manufacturer commercials often use a *feature-benefit* presentation in an effort to convince consumers to buy that company's cars, mentioning amenities like air bags, antilock brakes, leather interiors, and a plethora of cup holders a driver might look for in a new vehicle. Automobile manufacturers are also quick to point out when their vehicles have met or exceeded government safety or fuel efficiency standards. Commercials for Volvo played up that company's reputation for producing cars that were "boxy but safe," though Volvo's recent campaigns emphasize the new models' attractive styling as well as their safety. Third-party product comparisons play a significant role in the automotive industry: Any vehicle mentioned favorably in a J.D. Power survey or that makes *Car and Driver* magazine's Ten Best list has that distinction prominently featured in ads for that model. Other magazines that publish the results of product comparisons, such as *Consumer Reports*, are also well-known and respected indicators of product quality. Finally, it is relatively easy to watch the newspaper classified advertisements and online auto-sales sites like AutoByTel (http://www.autobytel.com) to see which makes and models consumers are attempting to unload via the used car market.

A Web Site for Rating Web Sites

Consumer Reports is a well-established source of information for the durable-goods industry, offering trusted reviews of televisions, appliances, automobiles, and other common products. The magazine's companion Web site (http://www.consumerreports.com) has reviewed the privacy policies of numerous electronic commerce sites, though the publishers do charge a $3.95 monthly fee (or $24 annually) to access those ratings. Another site, BizRate.com (http://www.bizrate.com), takes a different approach to signaling quality. Instead of charging users a fee to view the rating of online shopping sites, BizRate.com, like Yahoo! and the *New York Times*, makes money by aggregating consumer information and selling the results to the sites it rates and other interested parties.

For example, when a user makes a purchase from Egghead.com, an online hardware and software vendor, the purchaser is invited to complete a survey rating the shopping experience. The survey asks the user about how easy it was to navigate the site, whether the prices were in the expected range, and about their overall experience at the site. As an incentive to complete the survey, users are given the opportunity to win up to $5,000 instantly if they can match three symbols on an electronic "scratch and win" card. The survey also includes a question asking if the consumer would be willing to complete a follow-up survey after the merchandise arrives. That survey, which also gives the consumer another chance to win a price via the scratch and win contest, asks if the merchandise arrived on time, whether it was in the advertised condition, whether the consumer contacted the vendor's customer service department, and, if so, whether they were able to do so without undue delay and get a satisfactory response from the company. Visitors to the site can then search the results of those surveys, complete with satisfaction ratings (on a scale of one to five stars) and on-time delivery percentages, by business type.

The online bookseller Amazon (http://www.amazon.com) offers a related service, though in this case readers review books sold through the company's Web site. Reviewers can rate a book from zero to five stars and write a lengthy review of the book's contents. Amazon also provides marked slots for the publisher and author to offer their own opinions on the book, though the company does have a policy of not allowing electronic mail or Web site addresses in the reviews. The intent is to prevent visitors from exiting Amazon's Web site easily, thus encouraging them to see a potential purchase through. This "black hole" approach means that Amazon's site does not allow visitors to offer resources for other visitors, cutting down unrelated commercial advertising but also preventing users from offering useful links to related sites as part of their reviews.

VIRTUAL COMMUNITIES

A contrasting approach to the black hole model is to open up a site to all manner of user contributions, even if those contributions take site visitors away from the primary site temporarily. The Internet and online service providers offer organizers a unique opportunity to bring consumers together by creating *virtual communities*. The philosophical basis for virtual communities is as a "third place" (that is, a place other than where someone lives and works) for people to gather and interact on an informal basis, what Rheingold calls "conviviality."[24] Rheingold quotes a lengthy passage from Ray Oldenberg's *The Great Good Place*, which emphasizes the informal nature of locations outside home or work. In these third places the main form of interaction is through conversation. Conversations take place in the home and at work, but they are tempered by the expectations of family or colleagues and are either quite personal (as at home with one's family) or formal (as at work).

Rheingold describes the online discussion areas of the WELL, a San Francisco Bay area BBS that grew into an Internet Service Provider, as such communities. He notes that "logging into the WELL for just a minute or two, dozens of times a day, is very similar to the feeling of peeking into the café, the pub, the common room, to see who's there, and whether you want to stay around for a chat."[25] One of the benefits of online discussion areas is that they remove a significant barrier to forming relationships: establishing a common interest. For someone to log into a discussion group named "gardening" implies that person has at least a passing interest in gardening and would like to read others' thoughts on the subject and, in many cases, contribute their own thoughts or answer questions if they have the appropriate information or experience. Since the WELL started out as a local provider, with its members hailing from the San Francisco area, the feeling of community was even stronger based on members' geographic proximity. It is possible for members of virtual communities to establish virtual friendships with other participants even if they do not live in the same area, but the common frame of reference from living in the same physical community makes the bonds that much stronger.

Virtual Communities as Business Phenomena

In *Net Gain: Expanding Markets Through Virtual Communities*, Hagel and Armstrong advocate establishing virtual communities to create value in online markets.[26] Such communities would have five important characteristics: distinctive focus, integrated content and communication, appreciation of member-generated content, access to competing publishers and vendors, and commercial orientation.[27]

Distinctive Focus

One of the hallmarks of any virtual community, whether it is a Usenet newsgroup or an AOL discussion forum, is that conversations in the group center on a specific topic. Among the more than 25,000 Usenet newsgroups are groups that discuss gardening, specific makes of automobiles, computers, travel, and gaming on the personal computer. Groups can also host discussions about particular geographic areas, such as Scandinavia or Brazil. A commercial Web site can focus on a company's products, or even a single product, but that focus should be obvious to users when they enter the site. If a visitor understands that the site they are viewing focuses on the Chevrolet Corvette, they will not be surprised when advertisements for automobile customization services appear at strategic locations on the page.

Capacity to Integrate Content and Communication

A virtual community should have a distinctive focus, but it should not be a static site to which its visitors cannot contribute. Instead, Hagel and Armstrong stress that the site hosting the community must balance published content (such as articles, product information, and advertisements) with communication. That is, site visitors must feel they have the freedom to voice opinions, debate issues, and generally interact with other consumers and representatives of the hosting organization. Community organizers must allow for this freedom of interaction, but they must also establish a clear policy of what types of behavior and communication are acceptable. Just as coffee shops ask their guests to refrain from shouting and other uncivilized behavior, virtual community visitors should understand that constructive criticism is welcome, but that known falsehoods, threats, and other antisocial behavior that destroy group cohesion will not be tolerated.

Appreciation of Member-Generated Content

Ongoing discussions on a range of topics are a vital element of a thriving virtual community, though some visitors might want to publish their opinions as a distinct page on the site. Reasons for doing so can include using Web presentation features not supported by online chat software and setting their document apart as something that has had a bit more thought put into it than the typically off-the-cuff comments found in discussion areas. Community organizers could allow users to establish their own Web pages within the site, with the proviso that any page so established is clearly marked as a personal page and might not reflect the views of the organizers. Then, within reasonable limits, guests could publicize their pages in the discussion areas, perhaps with the result of the pages becoming the topic of one or more discussions within the groups.

Access to Competing Publishers and Vendors

While any virtual community will attempt to meets its members' needs, there is the strong likelihood that other virtual communities and organizations will exist and try to attract the attention of virtual community members. Rather than wall the community off from competing views, Hagel and Armstrong argue that the community should "seek to aggregate the broadest range of high-quality resources possible, including competing publishers and vendors" as part of fulfilling the community's role as an agent of its members.[28] That last consideration is extremely important and bears repeating: Virtual communities exist to serve their members, not the reverse. If members feel they are being railroaded or that they are being prevented from accessing pertinent information, they may very well seek another virtual community that does not restrict their access to information.

Commercial Orientation

Consumers understand that creating a virtual community is a business proposition. No organization is likely to put up the capital to establish a technologically robust virtual community, which Hagel and Armstrong estimated at $2 million in 1997, unless the community was a potential source of profit.[29] As Anne Wells Branscomb noted in *Who Owns Information?* however, users are increasingly demanding that they receive fair value for the information they provide, either explicitly or implicitly.[30] An early example of how Web site owners could collect consumer information is Yahoo! (http://www.yahoo.com). The first major search engine on the World Wide Web, Yahoo! makes money from selling advertising, but a substantial portion of its income comes from selling data about which search terms users enter. For instance, Intel might be very interested in finding out how many users search for information on Pentium III or Celeron microchips. Of course, Intel market researchers might also be interested in how many users search for chips from other sources, such as Advanced Micro Devices (http://www.amd.com) and Via, an independent microprocessor manufacturer based in Taiwan.

Virtual Communities and Reverse Markets

The World Wide Web gives companies unprecedented abilities to gather information about their present and potential customers by tracking the pages they visit on their Web sites and determining how the user arrived at the site in the first place. Those technologies are described in detail later in this book, but there is another important aspect of the Web in general and virtual communities in particular: Users can take advantage of Internet-based communications channels to trade information about manufacturers and products. Hagel and Armstrong refer to this change in dynamics as a "reverse market," where customers are able to locate the vendor offering the best combination of price, quality, and product features that meets their needs.[31] Until the Internet, organizations were able to control the information released about themselves and their products by relying on the fact that consumers would need to use relatively expensive and time-consuming methods, such as newsletters or monthly magazines, to spread information about a substandard product. Now that the Internet allows consumers to find like-minded individuals, accumulate significant stores of information, and disseminate that information, companies no longer have that advantage. Some companies may view reverse markets as a threat, especially if that company tries to skim by with substandard products or poor customer service, but attempting to prevent virtual community participation is all but impossible. As Hagel and Armstrong note, if even one company (probably a newcomer or a smaller vendor) breaks ranks and develops a virtual community, companies that do not immediately trump the leader's effort at community building will face a significant competitive disadvantage as the leader's community grows and that company generates goodwill from interested consumers.[32]

Encouraging Virtual Community Participation

Rather than discourage participation in virtual communities, companies should look for ways to allow users to gain from their relationship with the company, regardless of whether that gain comes from taking advantage of information about that company's products or by engaging in dialog with other consumers. Of course, as with any other economic activity, participating in a virtual community is voluntary. For consumers to join a virtual community, they must realize some sort of benefit from joining and contributing to the community. For a user to perceive that participating in a virtual community is valuable, that consumer must be convinced that they are getting equal value for the information they are giving up by registering in a community and allowing the community's organizers to record and track their demographic information and usage habits within the community. In a word, users must *trust* a community to join, provide truthful information about themselves, and engage in forthright dialog with other users and the community's sponsors.

There are several requirements for community organizers to earn that trust. First, consumers must be able to gain sufficient information about the company organizing the community, and its products, for them to find the best offer for a given product. For example, if Intel created a virtual community dedicated to providing information on their own products exclusively, the site would not attract consumers seeking information about available processors and existing community members would be inclined to defect to another virtual community which offered more evenhanded comparisons of available computer systems. While Intel would certainly feature its own products, the company would need to hold a delicate balance between promoting the Pentium III and Celeron processors and driving away customers with one-sided advertising and product comparisons.

Second, community organizers must be willing to respect the interest community members have in keeping their personally identifiable information private. The GVU study cited earlier found that 75 percent of users would not provide personal information while registering at a site if the site did not disclose how the information would be used. A similar percentage (73.1%) said they refused to register at a site because they did not perceive the value offered in exchange for their personal information as being worth the risk of having that information misused. In addition, 67.3 percent of respondents noted that they have refused to register at a site because they did not trust the entity collecting the data. On two questions that approached the issue from the opposite direction, respondents were equally emphatic about whether they considered it acceptable for information gatherers to pass their personal information on to third parties and whether users should control their own information. The study found that 84.3 percent of survey participants disagreed (65.1% strongly) with the proposition that it was acceptable for companies to sell magazine subscription information to third parties. In a similar vein, 90.5 percent of respondents agreed (72.9% strongly) that users should control their own personal information.[33]

Finally, to earn members' trust virtual communities must exhibit the five characteristics of a viable virtual community; most important, the capacity to integrate content and communication, an appreciation of member-generated content, and access to information from competing publishers and vendors. Unless users are able to participate in a meaningful dialog with other consumers and the community's organizers, they will not get full value in exchange for the information they allow the community's organizers to collect about themselves. As Peppers and Rogers stress in *The One to One Future*, a "marketer's relationship with any individual customer must be built on trust. Your own company's share-of-customer objective can only be realized if you concentrate on developing a long, flourishing relationship with your customer, and you must build this relationship gradually, through increasing levels of dialogue and interaction."[34]

Handling User Profile Information

A significant part of the value virtual community organizers receive for their investment is accurate demographic information about community members, their stated preferences, and their usage patterns. This information can be gathered in several ways, such as by requiring users to register when they enter a site, by placing a marker on their computer to identify them when they visit the site (a *cookie*), or, more passively, by examining the usage logs for the community Web site. The *New York Times* Web site (http://www.nytimes.com) offers users free access to the information on the site, but requires that each user register on their first visit to the site and to sign in every visit thereafter. Shapiro and Varian wrote in *Information Rules* that the registration requirement allows the *Times* to collect information on the demographics and reading habits of 2.1 million users, which can then be used to set advertising rates. When Shapiro and Varian wrote their book, the *Times* only asked for three pieces of information, which they referred to as the "classic information used in the paper-based subscription business, the ZAG: zip code, age, gender."[35] As of January 2000, the *Times* Web site asks for three additional pieces of information: the user's country, e-mail address, and annual income. The registration process also allows users to choose whether or not they want to receive additional mailings from the *Times* and from the site's advertisers. The default choice for receiving these messages is "yes," so users must make an effort to opt out of the mailing lists. The other questions reflect the increasingly international nature of the Internet and the desire of the *Times* to gather additional demographic data to establish ad rates for the site. The *Times* maintains a separate site, which does not require registration, for persons under the age of eighteen. That site targets students in grades six to twelve, and complies with Federal guidelines prohibiting Web sites from collecting information about children.

Once registered, the *Times* site places a cookie on the visitor's computer that can be used to track the visitor's movement through the site. In addition to accessing news articles, the site allows users to engage in moderated discussions in the site's forums. Forums are message boards the *New York Times* staff created as a way of allowing users to contribute to the site by offering their own opinions and discussing views presented by other visitors. Participating in the forums, however, requires users to disclose their e-mail addresses to other users on the site. This additional disclosure is necessary because if a user were to make defamatory or demonstrably untrue statements about another party, the *Times* would need that user's contact information to respond affirmatively to a court order seeking the identity of the person who made the actionable remarks.

How the *New York Times* addresses user concerns over personal privacy can serve as a model for other organizations seeking to offer similar services to their visitors. The *Times* has a detailed privacy policy (published on the site at http://www.nytimes.com/subscribe/help/privacy.html and easily located from any page within the site), that spells out what information the *Times* collects, why the information is collected, how the information is collected (e.g., through registration or via cookies), how the information is processed, and what information is shared with third parties. The privacy policy also instructs users how to withdraw their registration and remove their personal information from the site database.

The primary purpose of publishing a privacy policy is to gain user trust and encourage visitors to register and provide complete, accurate demographic information. The GVU study cited earlier in this book demonstrated that Internet users are wary of providing their information to sites where they are unsure about how their information will be used and, potentially, reused by other organizations. In *Information Rules*, Shapiro and Varian cite a similar study by Donna Hoffman, Tom Novak, and Marcos Peralta of Vanderbilt University, which states that 94 percent of Web users have refused to provide registration information to a site at least once, and 40 percent have given false information.[36] No business can survive with any appreciable amount of known false information in its database, so it is imperative that sites win user trust by being completely open and truthful about what information is collected and how it will be used. An alternative to collecting information directly from consumers, where consumers interact with Web sites through third parties called *infomediaries*, is explored later in this book.

Integrating Customer Concerns into a Business Model

Certainly satisfying customers is a goal for any business, but how should a company weigh that satisfaction? One methodology for weighing customer satisfaction as part of a broader set of measures is to use the Balanced Scorecard approach, developed by Kaplan and Norton.[37] The Balanced Scorecard allows a business to create a matrix in which it tracks the various measures to be included in an overall evaluation of the firm. The authors note the following:

In the customer perspective of the Balanced Scorecard, managers identify the customer and market segments in which the business unit will compete and the measures of the business unit's performance in those targeted segments. This perspective typically includes several core or generic measures of the successful outcomes from a well-formulated and -implemented strategy. The core outcome measures include customer satisfaction, customer retention, new customer acquisition, customer profitability, and market and account share in targeted segments. But the customer pespective should also include specific measures of the value propositions that the company will deliver to customers in targeted market segments. The segment-specific drivers of core customer outcomes represent those factors that are critical for customers to switch or remain loyal to their suppliers. For example, customers could value short lead times and on-time delivery. Or a constant stream of innovative products and services. Or a supplier able to anticipate their emerging needs and capable of developing new products and approaches to satisfy those needs. The customer perspective allows business unit managers to articulate the customer and market-based strategy that will deliver superior future financial returns.[38]

For companies whose customers use the Internet, and specifically the World Wide Web, this type of information can be obtained through online tracking and surveys. Infomediaries, which allow in-depth tracking while maintaining user privacy, can help establish profiles for users that would normally not be available. The process of tracking is explained in Chapter 7, while infomediaries are described in Chapter 8.

NOTES

1. NUA Internet Surveys, "Nando Times: Catalog Shopping Beats Online Shopping," 27 October 1999. Available <http://www.nua.ie/surveys/index.cgi?f=VS&art_id=905355366&rel=true>.

2. NUA Internet Surveys, "Forrester Research: 17 Million U.S. Households to Shop Online in '99," 29 September 1999. Available <http://www.nua.ie/surveys/index.cgi?f=VS&art_id=905355307&rel=true>.

3. Ibid.

4. NFO Interactive, *Online Retail Monitor: Branding, Segmentation & Web Sites*, 29 October 1999. Available from NUA Internet Surveys <http://www.nua.ie/surveys/index.cgi?f=VS&art_id=905355373&rel=true>.

5. Michael E. Porter, *The Competitive Advantage of Nations* (New York: Free Press, 1990), 71.

6. Allyn A. Young, "Increasing Returns and Economic Progress," *The Economic Journal* 38 (1928): 527–542.

7. Ken Brakke, "Increasing Returns," 16 May 1996. Available <http://www.susqu.edu/facstaff/b/brakke/complexity/maselko/increase.htm>.

8. John Hagel, III and Arthur G. Armstrong, *Net Gain* (Boston: Harvard Business School Press, 1997), 43.

9. <http://www.epic.org/crypto/clipper/white_house_statement_4_93.html>.

10. Whitfield Diffie and Susan Landau, *Privacy On the Line* (Cambridge: MIT Press, 1998).

11. Ibid., 212–213.

12. Ibid., 212.

13. Ibid., 215.

14. Soo-Yong Choi, Dale O. Stahl, and Andrew B. Whinston, *The Economics of Electronic Commerce* (Indianapolis: Macmillan Technical Publishing, 1997), 21.

15. Ibid., 69.

16. Carl Shapiro and Hal Varian, *Information Rules* (Boston: Harvard Business School Press, 1999), 39.

17. Choi, Stahl, and Whinston, *The Economics of Electronic Commerce*, 321.

18. Ibid., 313.

19. Shapiro and Varian, *Information Rules*, 23.

20. Ibid., 19–20.

21. Reuters, "Britannica.com takes mammoth reference online." *C|Net News.com.* 19 October 1999. Available <http://news.cnet.com/news/0-1005-200-919486.html>.

22. Britannica.com Editors, "About Britannica.com," 1999. Available <http://www.britannica.com/bcom/about/>.

23. Choi, Stahl, and Whinston, *The Economics of Electronic Commerce*, 143–144.

24. Howard Rheingold, *The Virtual Community* (Reading, Mass.: Addison-Wesley, 1993), 25.

25. Ibid., 26.

26. John Hagel and Arthur Armstrong, *Net Gain*, 5.

27. Ibid., 8–9.

28. Ibid., 9.

29. Ibid., 63.

30. Anne Wells Branscomb, *Who Owns Information? From Privacy to Public Access* (New York: Basic Books, 1994), 49.

31. Hagel and Armstrong, *Net Gain*, 17.

32. Ibid., 35.

33. Georgia Tech Research Corporation, *GVU Tenth Annual Survey*, October 1998. Available <http://www.gvu.gatech.edu/user_surveys/survey-1998-10/graphs/privacy/>.

34. Don Peppers and Martha Rogers, *The One to One Future* (New York: Doubleday, 1996), 305.

35. Shapiro and Varian, *Information Rules*, 34.

36. Ibid., 35.

37. Robert S. Kaplan and David P. Norton, *The Balanced Scorecard: Translating Strategy Into Action* (Boston: Harvard Business School Press, 1996).

38. Ibid., 26.

6

Internet Advertising

As the Internet became more commercialized, the importance of advertising, both as a means of supporting Web sites and promoting products and services, increased rapidly. Where users would once have balked at any hint of Internet-based advertising, most visitors to a Web site will think nothing of seeing an advertisement at the top of the screen. Advertising on the Internet offers companies several unique advantages over traditional methods like billboards and television commercials. The most important advantage is that the linked nature of the Internet, especially the World Wide Web, means that in most circumstances advertisers can tell exactly which ad caused the user to visit their site. While some users will write down a Web site address and visit it later, the majority of site visitors that respond to an ad will do so by clicking it, immediately moving the user to the sponsor's site. As will be seen later in this book, the sponsoring site records the exact time of the visit, the user's progression through the site, and (with the use of additional software) whether or not the user made any purchases on that visit. A second advantage of online advertising is that users are automatically segmented by interest. Web sites tend to have fairly specific focuses, such as ESPN's concentration on sports (http://espn.go.com) and Priceline's concentration on discount travel (http://www.priceline.com). Unlike advertising in a mass medium like broadcast television, companies can target their ads toward a particular audience with a demonstrated interest in the subject matter of the Web site. Finally, advertising on the Web means the company can change its ads at a moment's notice, whether to try different ads on a given site or to update its ads to reflect new products or offers.

Although Internet-based advertising takes up a relatively small amount of most firms' advertising budgets, the online community has seen a constant growth in advertising revenues. A June 2000 report from Jupiter Communications said that global online advertising expenditures for the 2000 calendar year would exceed $7 billion, with that total to rise to $28 billion by the year 2005. The report also predicted another growth spurt for the Internet user population, with the number of people online globally to increase from its current level of 300 million to 800 million in 2005.[1]

This chapter begins with a general discussion of Web advertising, defines important terms used to describe Internet advertising, examines different online advertising models, and then looks at online advertising standards. After that discussion, the chapter examines different pricing schemes, such as paying by number of times an ad is viewed, the number of visitors an ad generates, or as a commission on sales resulting from the ad. The chapter concludes with a look at resources available to advertisers, such as ad management services, rating programs, and banner exchange programs.

GOALS OF ONLINE ADVERTISING

While the Internet and online services are relatively new forums for advertisers, advertising in any medium should follow a few basic guidelines. In *The Economics of Electronic Commerce*, Choi, Stahl, and Whinston enumerate a number of well-established principles for all types of advertising:

- Ads should be visually appealing.
- Ads should be persuasive.
- Ads must emphasize brands and a firm's image.
- Ads must be part of an overall marketing strategy.
- Content should be valuable to consumers.
- Ads must be targeted to specific consumers.[2]

The first consideration, visual appeal, is an area where the Internet, in particular the World Wide Web, has some advantages over traditional media. One advantage of online advertising is that advertisers can try a variety of designs in rapid succession and get immediate feedback by tracking which ads generate user responses. While a relatively small (seven inches long by one inch high) graphic on a Web site does not provide nearly as much room as a full-page magazine ad, designers can add motion and interactivity to the ads to enhance their visual appeal. Persuasiveness, the second criteria, complements visual appeal—a viewer must be given a call to action, usually an invitation to click an advertisement and visit a Web site with information about the company, product, or service mentioned in the ad. The third consideration, that ads must emphasize a brand or a firm's identity, is absolutely vital to building any kind of corporate or product recognition on the Internet. With literally millions of Web sites available, many of which carry advertising of one form or another, it is absolutely imperative that an organization's ads make it easy for viewers to recognize the firm sponsoring the message and remember the product, service, or at the very least the company making the offer. In *The Caring Economy*, Gerry McGovern argues that in the physical world brands exist in a context; online, there is very little context to support a new brand, so the burden of creating and maintaining brand identification falls on the firm's advertising and relationship-building skills.[3] That such advertising would be part of a comprehensive plan (the fourth principle) is obvious, though it bears mention.

The final two principles of successful advertising, that an ad must contain information that is useful to consumers and that ads must be targeted to specific consumers, are areas where advertising on the Internet, especially the World Wide Web, has the potential to greatly surpass advertising in traditional media. Before the Internet, a company that wanted to provide useful information to potential customers was limited to doing so through print advertising and offering some means of communicating directly with the company, such as by a reader response card or a phone number the potential customer could send back or call to receive more extensive printed information. Printing and production costs, determining which customers to send materials to (or printing enough for everyone that might request a brochure or report), and space limitations all significantly curtailed how much information an organization could send out. On the Web, however, space limitations are all but irrelevant. Businesses can create Web sites that contain all of their corporate information, product fact sheets, press releases, comparisons, reviews, and even advertisements for potential customers to browse when they want and at their own pace.

The Holy Grail of Internet advertising, however, is the potential to *personalize* a Web site to fit each user's needs. One site that allows users to personalize their interface is Yahoo. Users can choose what type of news story they want to appear when they log onto Yahoo, decide whether or not to have their horoscope (or another specific item) appear, and change the layout of the page as a whole. There are a variety of technologies sites can use to track user preferences and movements—some of those technologies are discussed briefly in this chapter, but there is a more complete discussion later in the book.

ONLINE ADVERTISING STANDARDS

Online advertising is a relatively new phenomenon, so it is not surprising that it took some time for companies to begin to agree on any standards. Until the middle of 1998, for example, there were not even general guidelines for ad sizes. A number of organizations, including the Internet Advertising Bureau and the Coalition for Advertising Supported Information and Entertainment (CASIE) (http://www.casie.org) were formed in an effort to build a consensus on advertising issues. While those groups have been mostly successful in helping the industry come to agreement on issues like ad sizes, there has been ongoing disagreement over how to measure the effectiveness of online ads. In an attempt to establish a standard measurement regime, many of the major players in online advertising (including 24/7 Media, AdForce, Adsmart, BURST! Media, DoubleClick, Engage, Flycast Communications, Microsoft bCentral, Real Media, Sabela Media, SmartAge.com, Teknosurf. com, and ValueClick formed the Advertising Standards Alliance (http:// www.adstandard.org).[4] Ad-response measurement techniques and technologies are discussed later in this chapter.

Definitions

One of the benefits standards organizations like the IAB brought to the online advertising industry is a standard set of definitions for terms describing the World Wide Web, advertising, and ad performance measurement. These definitions are derived from definitions presented in Allen, Kania, and Yaeckel; Zeff and Aronson; and *The Marketing Manager's Plain English Internet Glossary* (http://www.jaderiver.com/gloss1.htm).[5]

Ad request A message sent by a Web site asking an *ad server* to supply an advertisement for the requesting site.

Ad server A Web site or online database containing advertisements which can be parceled out to other Web sites.

Ad view The presentation of an advertisement on a Web site.

Auditor A third party that verifies the accuracy of advertising or Web site log files.

Bandwidth The capacity of a communications channel, as measured in volume (such as bytes) per unit of time (usually seconds).

Banner An advertisement that appears at the top or bottom of a Web page. While there are different "standard" banner sizes, the most common is 468 × 60 pixels.

Bookmark A record of a Web site address a user stores in his or her Web *browser*. This term is sometimes used to refer to a *link* on a page with a list of interesting Web addresses.

Browser A software program, such as Netscape Navigator, Internet Explorer, or Lynx, which is used to view Web sites.

Button A small ad, ranging anywhere from 120 × 90 pixels to 88 × 31 pixels.

Click-through A visit to an advertiser's Web site resulting from a user clicking on an advertisement.

Click-through rate The percentage of users who visit a site as the result of a particular advertisement, derived by dividing total *click-throughs* by total *ad views*.

Cookie A text file placed on a user's computer by a Web site. Cookies can contain user identification codes and records of user activity on different Web sites, though only the originating site for a specific cookie can read that cookie later.

Cost per click The average cost of persuading each user to accept an ad's invitation to visit a site, calculated by dividing the total dollars spent on an ad by the number of *click-throughs*.

Cost per lead The average cost of persuading a potential customer to submit information to a company as a result of viewing a Web ad, calculated by dividing the total dollars spent on an ad by the number of leads generated by that ad.

Cost per sale The average cost of generating a sale from an advertisement, calculated by dividing the total dollars spent on an ad by the number of sales generated by that ad.

CPM (cost per thousand) The amount charged by a Web site for each thousand *ad views* for a given advertisement.

Domain name The human-readable name assigned to one or more computers owned by the same organization. For instance, amazon.com is a domain name, while www.amazon.com is a particular computer within that domain.

Exposures The number of times an ad is displayed for site *visitors*.

Flame A "verbal" attack on another Internet user or organization, originally through e-mail but now in any medium. A *flame war* is a continuing exchange of flames in a given forum, such as on an e-mail list or in a Usenet newsgroup.

Hit An attempt to access a given Web page.

HTML (Hypertext Markup Language) The coding system used to create Web pages.

Hypertext Text which can be navigated nonlinearly by means of *links*.

Impression The number of time an ad is displayed for site *visitors*.

Interstitial An advertisement that appears while a user is engaged in an activity and requires the user to dismiss the advertisement by closing its window.

Java A programming language designed with the goal of promoting cross-platform compatibility (allowing programmers to write a single program that could be used on different operating systems and computer architectures).

JavaScript An interpreted language Web designers can use to enhance Web site functionality.

Keyword A term entered into a *search engine* that is used to generate a list of relevant Web sites. A search can look for more than one keyword. Some search engine companies sell keywords to advertisers so that company's site will appear at the top of the list for searches on a given term. For example, Amazon might purchase "book."

Link A *hypertext* object that allows users to move from one part of a document to another without viewing any intervening contents.

Page view A page view occurs when a browser downloads a Web page from a site.

Pay per click An advertising model where advertisers only pay a site for the number of times an advertisement is clicked by a user.

Pay per lead An advertising model where advertisers only pay a site for the number of leads generated by an ad.

Pay per transaction An advertising model where advertisers pay a site based on the number of sales generated by an ad.

Pixel A colored dot on a computer screen. The number of dots per inch is a screen's resolution.

Response rate The percentage of site visitors who click on an ad, calculated by dividing the number of *click-throughs* by the number of *impressions*.

Search engine A Web site that catalogs other Web sites and allows users to search for Web pages by entering *keywords*.

URL Web address, such as http://www.amazon.com.

Visitor An individual who accesses a Web site.

TYPES OF ONLINE ADVERTISING

The first order of business in creating an online advertising campaign is to determine which online advertising channels to use. The majority of online advertising is done on the World Wide Web, either through an entire Web site or with banner ads at the top and bottom of every page in the most popular Web sites. Many companies also advertise by sponsoring e-mail lists.

Web Sites

One of the most direct ways to advertise on the Internet is to create a Web site with information about a company or product. As an example, consider the Web site for Derek Daly's Performance Driving Academy (http://www.derekdaly.com)—the home page for the driving school is displayed in Figure 6.1. From the main page, site visitors can get information about the academy, its instructors, the courses offered, the cars used by the school, and its host track and facilities. Users can also page through an online version of the school's brochure or get information about the companies sponsoring the school. The site is an integrated whole, designed to appeal to the visitor's sense of adventure, willingness to stretch their personal limits, and desire to live the fantasy of becoming a race driver, even if only for a few days. Most other companies will not be able to conjure up the visceral thrills promised by the driving school's Web site, but they can still present their products and services in the best possible light, create brand awareness among their target audience, and offer in-depth information about products' features and benefits that convince consumers to purchase their products or services.

Banners, Buttons, and Text Links

In addition to creating a complete Web site to promote a product or company, an organization can also place banner ads on other Web sites. Banner ads are rectangular advertisements, usually placed at the top or bottom of a Web page. The Internet Advertising Bureau and the Center for Advertising Supported Information and Entertainment have established a set of standard

Figure 6.1
Home Page of the Derek Daly Performance Driving Academy

Source: <http://www.derekdaly.com>.

banner sizes, ranging from 468 × 60 pixels (approximately 7 inches long by 1 inch high) to 234 × 60 pixels (about 3.5 inches long by 1 inch high). As the first attempt at Internet-based advertising, banner ads have been criticized for not taking enough advantage of the Internet's technical possibilities. There are a number of different types of banner ads, some of which do more than rest comfortably on a Web page, though a simple message users can download quickly and read easily can still be an effective way to advertise. A banner ad that does not change is a *static* banner. *Dynamic* banners, which do change from the original image, can be divided into two categories: *animated* and *interactive*. Small banner ads are usually referred to as buttons, though it is also possible to advertise on a site using a text-only link.

Static Banners

A static banner is an unchanging image that resides on a Web site. Static banners were the original form of Internet advertising and, since every Web site is able to handle simple graphics, they can be placed on any Web site. Also, as a single image, a static banner downloads very quickly and minimizes the disruption caused by the ad. The disadvantage of static banners is that they may not be disruptive enough—the spread of other types of banners that offer movement or interactivity means that static banners can look staid and unattractive. In the *Internet World Guide to One-to-One Marketing*, Allen, Kania, and Yaeckel note that banner ads typically achieve around a 2-percent click-through rate, though there are techniques that can be applied to the banner design to increase the response.[6]

Animated Banners

Unlike static banners, animated banners use a series of images to simulate movement within the banner. Like cartoon animation, which uses a series of slightly different drawings to create motion, animated banners use a series of between two and twenty banners to create motion and display much more information than a simple static banner. Animated banners also generate a higher click-through rate than static banners. Allen, Kania, and Yaeckel cite a ZDNet study (http://www.zdnet.com) that found that animated banners improved click-through rates by 15 to 40 percent over static banners.[7] At a base click-through rate of 2 percent, that means an extra impression for every 200 people that see the ad. As with most practices on the Web, however, there is a resource trade-off. The down side to animated banners is that they require more time to download than static banners, but compression techniques and good design can keep the individual images small and the overall wait tolerable.

Interactive Banners

The next step beyond animated banners is the interactive banner. As the name suggests, an interactive banner allows the user to interact with the banner, making choices among products, companies, or preferences and then click a button to submit their choice to the ad server and have the server respond with a page or site related to their choice. Zeff and Aronson divide these interactive banners into two subcategories: HTML banners and rich media banners.[8] An HTML banner includes HTML code in the commands to display the banner on the page that allows the user to interact with Web entities that can be created using the markup language, such as drop-down lists, radio buttons, and control buttons. Rich media banners utilize advanced technologies, including audio and video clips, to draw the user's attention and entice them to click the ad. Some examples of items that can be created using rich media include games, news tickers, and video displays. While rich media banners can generate the highest click-through rates of all banners, they also require the most bandwidth and take the most time to download, interrupting the user's browsing experience.

Buttons

A button is a smaller version of a banner, ranging in size from 125 × 125 pixels to 88 × 31 pixels. Because there is less space for a message, buttons tend to be very simple, usually naming a company or a product, or a brief message encouraging users to click the button to visit the site it links to. The most common buttons on the Internet are the Internet Explorer and Netscape Now buttons, which allow users to download Microsoft's and Netscape's Web browsers, respectively.

Text Links

The simplest and least intrusive way to advertise on a Web site is through a text link. Text links download very quickly and can convey quite a bit of information to site visitors, but they are not nearly as eye catching as graphics. They also have the benefit of being less expensive than graphical ads.

Electronic Mail

Advertising via e-mail is a somewhat dicey proposition, though it can be done responsibly and without generating consumer ire. Chapter 1 described the wrong way to go about advertising through e-mail: spam, or unsolicited commercial e-mail (UCE). Sending out unwanted e-mail ads, which shifts the cost of the ads from the sender to the message recipients, will at the very least result in the message's deletion, at the worst consumer complaints that could lead to an ISP cutting off the sender's account. There are two established methods for advertising via e-mail: sponsoring e-mail discussion lists and purchasing opt-in lists of users who have agreed to receive offers via electronic mail.

Sponsoring E-Mail Discussion Lists

In the days before the Internet, companies could keep in touch with their customers by sending out printed newsletters. Many companies still do so, but sending out printed newsletters is a one-way communication channel that does not afford consumers the interactivity they have come to expect in the digital economy. Sending out the same newsletters by e-mail has exactly the same problem, though the transmission costs are much lower, as the sender does not need to pay for printing, supplies, labor, and postage. The next step in creating a dialog with a company's customers is to create an e-mail discussion list, where subscribers can send messages to a central address and a software package distributes the message to every list subscriber. Like Usenet newsgroups, e-mail discussion lists are focused on a particular topic. E-mail discussion lists can be *moderated* or *unmoderated*. On a moderated e-mail discussion list, a human list manager must approve every message before it is forwarded to the list members. List managers often choose to moderate their list so they can keep relatively tight control over what messages are distributed to the list, culling out spam, off-topic messages, or messages that, in the moderator's opinion, use inappropriate language or contain personal attacks.

An unmoderated list lacks those controls and is much more freewheeling. While a spammer may occasionally join a list, send one advertisement, and be removed by the list manager, some managers choose to run unmoderated lists so their subscribers will not feel constrained to stay strictly on topic or afraid to voice strong opinions. Users can still be removed from these lists for violating the code of conduct set by the list manager, but subscribers have much more room to critique each others' arguments and express honest opinions about companies, products, services, and issues related to the list's topic.

There are literally thousands of lists available to sponsor. There is information about mailing lists at a number of sites, including Yahoo (http://dir.yahoo.com/Computers_and_Internet/MailingLists/Web_Directories), Liszt (http://www.liszt.com), and The List of Lists (http://tile.net/lists). There are also Web services that run mailing list software and allow users to run lists for free, with the service paid for by brief advertisements placed in each list message. One such site is egroups (http://www.egroups.com), where visitors can create a mailing list for free, though if they would prefer to run a list without advertising they can do so for a $4.95 monthly fee, paid for a year at a time.

Zeff and Aronson offer a number of suggestions for advertising with sponsored e-mail lists.[9] The first recommendation is to only sponsor moderated mailing lists. Since every post to the list will need to be approved by a human moderator, there is much less chance the ad will be included with an irrelevant, profane, or unwanted commercial e-mail. Their second recommendation, which they attribute to Richard Hoy, moderator of the Online Advertising discussion list (http://www.o-a.com), is to ask the list's moderator to introduce you by sending out an e-mail message announcing your sponsorship. Third, if your organization is the only sponsor for a given list, Zeff and Aronson recommend you request multiple placements in each message. By running different versions of an ad at the beginning, middle, and end of a message, users will see your organization's name at least three times and will have that many opportunities to respond to the ad. Finally, make list members an offer. Remember that the reason subscribers join a list is to read its messages, not to read advertisements. By making readers an offer, such as a discount or a giveaway, you give them a compelling reason to respond to the ad.

Purchasing Opt-In E-Mail Lists

Another way to market effectively using e-mail is to purchase lists of consumers who have agreed to receive marketing messages. While you should still be wary of anonymous e-mail offers for CDs containing millions of e-mail addresses for $99.95, there are a number of companies that compile lists of users who have agreed to receive e-mail solicitations for specific types of products or services. Software manufacturers and Web sites that require users to answer demographic questions while registering their products or as part of the sign-up process to receive free services (like a Web-based e-mail account) ask users if they are willing to receive e-mail advertisements from companies that have established a marketing partnership with the host. One such company, NetCreations (http://w3.netcreations.com), has built a database of more than 5 million e-mail addresses by placing its sign-up forms on more than 190 partner sites, including Rolling Stone (http://RollingStone.com), TechRepublic (http://www.TechRepublic.com), and FastCEO (http://www.FastCEO.com).[10] The first page of the registration form for TechRepublic asks the user to enter his or her position and role in making information technology purchase decisions, and the size of the company. On the next screen the site asks users to enter their address and phone number, but providing that information is optional.

Like the *New York Times*, NetCreations publishes a comprehensive explanation of how it does business on its Web site. The page explains how the company gets the names for its mailing lists and how users can view and modify their personal information, reassures participants they can remove their names from the lists at any time, and tells users their personal information will not be shared with any third party (except in aggregate form) unless authorized by the user. Representing the lists NetCreations accumulates and manages as opt-in lists is not strictly accurate, however. The default choice for the check boxes indicates a user would look to receive offers from companies that partner with a Web site (that is, purchase e-mail address lists from NetCreations), so users need to take an affirmative action to decline the ads. This procedure is more correctly described as opt-out—if users were presented with a check box where the default choice was not to receive advertisements, then the process could properly be called opt-in. There is also no obvious link from the TechRepublic site to NetCreations, so while a user can remove their personal information from the NetCreations database, they would need to find out where the information was stored and then visit that site to take the steps required to remove (or correct) their information.

Establishing a Campaign Strategy

As Choi, Stahl, and Whinston noted in *The Economics of Electronic Commerce*, every element of an online advertising campaign must be part of a well thought-out strategy. The first element of forming a strategy is deciding what impact you want your ads to have on viewers. Do you want the ad to cause users to visit your site, purchase a product or service, or become aware of your brand? Zeff and Aronson note that it is quite possible for an ad with a high click-through rate to produce a negative impact on consumers if the Web site consumers arrive at is substandard. They ask,

What if 50 percent of the people who click on your ad leave your site after they get to the home page? You may have a great click-through rate, but we'd argue that 50 percent of the people who clicked may actually be getting a negative brand impact. They're clicking on an advertisement because they expect something. When they get to the jump page they don't see what they expected and may even feel deceived, so they leave.[11]

The question, then, is how you reward consumers for visiting your site.

Maximizing Click-Through

If you do choose to create an ad campaign with the goal of causing users to click the ad and visit the accompanying Web site, you can work toward that goal in several ways. First, you should place your ads on sites with the highest traffic you can afford. Remember that users do not necessarily need to click on an ad when they see it to become visitors—if the ad makes them aware of your site and they type the address in manually or decide to visit the next time they see the site's name in an ad or news piece, the advertisement has done its job. The second element, which should be part of any advertisement, is the call to action. A user should have a reason to visit a site, be it compelling news stories, the opportunity to buy books at a discount and have them shipped overnight, or to engage in leisure or fantasy activities such as planning travel or playing games. Third, if appropriate, you can extol the virtues of your site as a source of more than plain information. Numerous Web sites, including the free *Encyclopedia Britannica* site, offer visitors free e-mail accounts. The *Britannica* site also runs headlines from the online edition of the *Washington Post*, giving visitors a single site to meet many of their information needs. Finally, you can use advertisements to encourage repeat visitors. If a user has visited your site more than once and discovered that its contents are updated regularly, seeing an ad might cause them to visit the site to see what's new. Suck.com, a satirical news and culture commentary site, often runs small banners or button ads that mention the newest feature on the site.

Making Sales

If your goal is to sell products or services, you should not set out to attract the most visitors possible. Instead, you should run ads that create a want, need, or fear in the mind of the consumer on reputable sites with favorable demographics. As an example, the owners of FastCEO have positioned the site as a portal for executives, with links to daily news sources, business magazines, news feeds, technology magazines, search engines, company research sites, health information, government agencies, small business resources, and so forth. As of January 2000, the interactive banner ad at the top of the main page is for SeniorSite (http://www.seniorsite.com). The ad allows the user to click to get information about travel packages, prescriptions, vitamins, senior's gifts, toys for grandkids, and electronics that can be bought at the SeniorSite mall, reflecting the generally older demographics of corporate officers.

Establishing a Brand

Building brand recognition is at once vitally important and hard to measure, even online, where users leave electronic trails of their activities. While establishing a brand identity in traditional media involves displaying a message to as many viewers as possible, brand building online requires a bit more subtlety. Thomas E. Miller, a vice president at the Internet database marketing firm Cyber Dialogue (http://www.cyberdialogue.com), explains:

The tricks of the trade in building a brand online have to do with mastering the A,B,Cs of interaction with prospects and customers, not just "image building." Moreover, brand impressions are built online in smaller batches. It's not so much a game of reaching as many eyeballs as possible—though that is still a valid kind of goal online— as it is of making sure that each interaction with a potential customer impresses them of your sincerity, willingness to listen, and responsiveness to whatever needs that person may have.[12]

Purchasing Online Advertising Space

There are several pricing models for online advertising, though the most common models are to charge based on the total number of impressions (CPM, or cost per thousand impressions), by performance (a percentage of sales resulting directly from click-throughs), or a hybrid of the two, where an advertiser pays a lower CPM but adds a bonus for any sales resulting from ad clicks on a given site. In the executive summary of the *IAB Internet Advertising Revenue Report: 1999 Second-Quarter Results*, PriceWaterhouseCoopers' New Media Group noted that the hybrid approach of charging for advertising accounted for 52 percent of the $934 million spent on online advertising in the second quarter of 1999. Impression-based price schemes made up 41 percent of the total, while performance-based pricing made up the remaining 7 percent.[13]

Choosing which sites to advertise on requires a bit more research—remember that SeniorSite chose to advertise on FastCEO because the latter site served an upscale audience in the demographic group (older Americans with significant disposable income), which was very attractive to the senior-oriented mall. If you are simply looking for a site that will generate the most impressions, you can turn to MediaMetrix (http://www.mediametrix.com), which offers monthly statistics on the number of visitors for the 500 most popular Web sites and the top fifty or ten in a variety of categories, or NetRatings (http://www.nielsen-netratings.com), which offers daily, weekly, and monthly statistics in categories including the most-viewed banner ads, the top advertisers, and the most popular properties. If you would like to target your ads a bit more closely but do not have the time to do original research into available sites, you could turn to an advertising broker like DoubleClick (http://www.doubleclick.com), Burst! (http://www.burstmedia.com), or FlyCast (http://www.flycast.com). You can find a more comprehensive list of online advertising brokers at the end of this chapter or by searching Yahoo! (http://

dir.yahoo.com/Business_and_Economy/Companies/Computers/Business_to_
Business/Software/Internet/World_Wide_Web/Advertising_Management).

Information Consolidation and Consumer Privacy

Like Internet search engines and virtual communities, advertising firms
make money by selling information about users' habits. In most cases the
information is only maintained in aggregate form, but some observers have
some reservations about how much information a single firm or group of
firms should be allowed to collect. In comments to the Federal Trade Commission filed October 18, 1999, Jason Catlett, the president of Junkbusters
Corp. (http://www.junkbusters.com), a staunch pro-privacy group that views
corporate information gathering with deep suspicion, outlined how the online-
user profiling industry has consolidated into three main groups and how those
groups operate in conjunction with the offline database marketing industry.

According to Catlett, the online advertising and consumer profile industry
underwent significant consolidation in 1999, resulting in three major groups
of companies:

- DoubleClick, which has announced but not consummated mergers with Abacus
  Direct and Netgravity. . . . Privacy advocates have opposed the merger with Abacus
  Direct on the grounds that the companies intend to merge their massive databases
  of online and offline behavior.
- The CMGI group of companies, includes Engage Technologies, Accipiter, and to
  include after mergers AdForce (ADFC), Flycast (FCST), and I/Pro. Also in this
  stable are many others in only somewhat related businesses, such as the Altavista
  and Lycos portals/search engines.
- Excite, Matchlogic, Enliven, @Home and others, related by ownership with AT&T
  and TCI.[14]

Catlett argues that the problem with merging online and offline databases
is the ability to correlate records from an "anonymous" online profile with an
offline database record. The familiar, paper-based publishing request for the
ZAG, he says, is usually enough to identify an individual in a public record.[15]
While he is quick to point out that "consensual relationships" between customers and merchants are highly beneficial to both the consumer and the
company, such as book notification services provided by Amazon.com, "that
kind of profiling is a considerable distance from the surreptitious profiling of
ad networks."[16] Indeed, a public outcry following DoubleClick's announce-
ment it would tie offline personally identifiable information with user identification codes in cookies forced the company to agree not to do so until the
government issued standards for the industry.[17]

As for self-regulation and privacy-protection organizations like TRUSTe
(http://www.truste.org) and the Better Business Bureau Online (http://www.

bbbonline.org), Catlett quotes a Forrester Research report which says that "because independent privacy groups like TRUSTe and BBBOnline earn their money from e-commerce organizations, they become more of a privacy advocate for the industry—rather than for consumers. The FTC should call for a consumer-based organization to provide principles and redress."[18]

Unchallenged, Catlett's arguments seem like a damning indictment of the online advertising and profiling industry, though it should be noted that he was quite willing to admit that consumers and companies both benefit from targeted advertisements. His disagreement with representatives of the advertising management firms is whether or not the current regime of self-regulation is sufficient to meet privacy concerns. With the number of users who have provided false information to a Web site at 40 percent, as noted in the Vanderbilt University study in Chapter 1, the perception among consumers is that the current scheme is insufficient to meet their privacy expectations. The idea of online marketers, then, should be to conduct business in a way that encourages consumers to share their information, safe in the knowledge that it will not be combined with other records that could be used to turn an anonymous profile into a secret dossier. The infomediary is a business model that allows consumers to function anonymously while still allowing the infomediary to capture their movements and establish anonymous contact between vendors and consumers with a demonstrated interest in that vendor's products or services. Infomediaries are described in some detail in Chapter 8.

RESOURCES

This final section of the chapter lists the Web sites of companies and services of interest to Internet marketers. The companies and software packages were current as of July 2000, are listed in alphabetical order, and are for information only. No endorsement is implied.

Ad Management

- Accipiter (http://www.accipiter.com)
- Ad Café (http://www.infohiway.com/adcafe)
- Adfinity (http://www.247media.com/techno/te_adfin.htm)
- AdForce (http://www.adforce.com)
- Ad Juggler (http://www.adjuggler.com)
- AdKnowledge (http://www.adknowledge.com)
- AdServer (http://www.netgravity.com)
- Campaign Management (http://www.matchlogic.com)
- Direct Media (http://www.directmedia.com)
- DoubleClick (http://www.doubleclick.com)
- MatchLogic (http://www.matchlogic.com)

Auditing Services

- ABC Interactive (http://www.abcinteractiveaudits.com)
- BPA International (http://www.bpai.com)
- I/AUDIT (http://www.ipro.com)

Banner Exchange Programs

- Click2Net (http://www.click2net.com)
- HyperBanner (http://www.hyperbanner.com)
- Internet Banner Network (http://www.banner-net.com)
- LinkExchange (http://www.linkexchange.com)
- SmarkClicks (http://www.smartclicks.com)
- TradeBanners (http://www.resource-marketing.com/banner.shtml)

Infomediaries

- Privaseek (http://www.privaseek.com)
- VerticalOne (http://www.verticalone.com)

Measurement Technologies

- Accesswatch (http://www.accesswatch.com)
- ARIA (http://www.andromedia.com)
- FlashStats (http://www.maximized.com/products/flashstats)
- Hit List (http://www.marketwave.com)
- LandscapE (http://www.matchlogic.com)
- Net.Analysis (http://www.netgen.com)
- NetLine (http://www.ipro.com)
- SurfReport (http://www.netrics.com/SurfReport)
- TrueCount (http://www.matchlogic.com)
- WebTrends (http://www.webtrends.com)

Personalization Technologies

- Art Technology Group (http://www.atg.com)
- BroadVision (http://www.broadvision.com)
- Firefly (http://www.firefly.com)
- GuestTrack (http://www.guesttrack.com)
- Net Perceptions (http://www.netperceptions.com)

Rating Firms

* Media Metrix (http://www.mediametrix.com)
* NetRatings (http://www.nielsen-netratings.com)

NOTES

1. NUA Internet Surveys, "Jupiter Communications: Global Online Ad Revenues to Skyrocket," 19 June 2000. Available <http://www.nua.ie/surveys/?f=VS&art_id= 905355850&rel=true>.

2. Soo-Yong Choi, Dale O. Stahl, and Andrew B. Whinston, *The Economics of Electronic Commerce* (Indianapolis: Macmillan Technical Publishing, 1997), 245.

3. Gerry McGovern, *The Caring Economy* (Dublin: Blackhall, 1999), 329.

4. Beth Cox, "Measurement Standards Still Dog Online Ad Industry," 24 November 1999. Available <http://www.internetnews.com/IAR/print/0,1089,12_244141, 00.html>.

5. Cliff Allen, Deborah Kania, and Beth Yaeckel, *Internet World Guide to One-to-One Web Marketing* (New York: John Wiley & Sons, 1998); Robbin Zeff and Brad Aronson, *Advertising on the Internet*, 2d ed. (New York: John Wiley & Sons, 1999).

6. Allen, Kania, and Yaeckel, *Internet World Guide*, 242.

7. Ibid., 245.

8. Zeff and Aronson, *Advertising on the Internet*, 34–35.

9. Ibid., 29.

10. Netcreations Press Office, "Netcreations Tops 5 Million Email Address Mark," 22 November 1999. Available <http://www.netcreations.com/main?page=press2& article=19991122.mhtml>.

11. Zeff and Aronson, *Advertising on the Internet*, 204.

12. Thomas E. Miller, *Online Branding*, 28 March 1998. Available <http://www. cyberdialogue.com/resource/data/articles/branding2.html>.

13. PriceWaterhouseCoopers New Media Group, *IAB Internet Advertising*, 2.

14. Jason Catlett, Re: Online Profiling Project—Comment, P994809/Docket No. 990811219-9219-01. 18 October 1999. Available <http://www.ftc.gov/bcp/profiling/ comments/catlett.htm>.

15. Ibid.

16. Ibid.

17. Chris Oakes, "A Turning Point for E-Privacy," *Wired News*, 4 March 2000. Available <http://www.wired.com/news/politics/0,1283,34734,00.html>.

18. Catlett, Re: Online Profiling Project.

7

User Tracking Technologies

The Internet is at the center of a seeming contradiction in public opinion. On the one hand, there is the popular sentiment that users are secure in their privacy and are able to surf the Web without fear of having a record of their movements end up on another computer. This outlook is often summed up by the now-famous, "On the Internet, no one knows you're a dog" cartoon in the *New Yorker*. The opposite view is the one used by privacy advocacy groups, such as the Electronic Privacy Information Center (EPIC), to argue for legislation restricting how Internet marketers and other third parties gather information about individuals visiting Web sites. EPIC and other information-privacy groups cite studies that indicate that over half of non-Internet users (53%) are staying off the Internet because of privacy concerns, not cost or other factors.[1] So which outlook better reflects reality? The answer depends on the technology used to track visitors at specific sites and the countermeasures the users take to foil the tracking. As in the legislative arena, the technological struggle for information privacy is fought on a complex battlefield; companies use a variety of mechanisms to ensure they are able to determine who, or at least what type of user, accesses their Web sites and what they do when they are there.

This chapter introduces the Internet as a largely pseudonymous entity, going into a bit of technical detail about how computers on the Internet are assigned addresses and how those addresses are translated into human-readable form. After that introduction, the chapter discusses tracking visitors at a single site by using the log files available to the site administrator; many companies produce software or provide services that make those analyses easier. After that section comes an in-depth look at cookies, which are text strings Web sites place on a user's machine to track that user's movements. The chapter notes what cookies are designed to do, what they are not capable of doing by themselves, and how they can be used in cooperation with other technologies. The chapter continues the discussion of visitor tracking by looking at the issue of software and hardware identification numbers, such as those used by RealNetworks, Microsoft, and, in the hardware realm, by Intel in its Pentium III processor. The last section of the chapter looks at three companies that came under fire for issues surrounding personally identifiable information: Yahoo, Intel, and DoubleClick (the last being one of the premier Web advertising firms).

ADDRESSING ON THE INTERNET

Computers are wonderful at dealing with numbers, but are less adept at handling names. Humans are exactly the opposite: They work well with names but can lose track of numbers quickly. To resolve these differing capabilities, Internet addressing uses a combination of the two schemes. Every computer connected to the Internet is given a unique numerical address and every numerical address is represented by a human-readable name. From a purely technical standpoint, including humans in the addressing loop slows the process of locating other machines, but the alternative of requiring humans to either remember or look up machines' numerical addresses on their own would be an even greater inefficiency.

Internet Addresses

The numerical address of an Internet-connected computer is composed of four numbers within the range of 0–255, with each number separated by a period. For instance, a computer could have the numerical address of 206.168.99.131. This address is usually referred to as an *Internet Protocol*, or *IP* address. To make the example simple, imagine that a single, fairly large company hosts a number of Web sites for its customers. If the company never foresaw hosting more than 256 sites (actually more like 252, as some of the numbers are reserved and access providers usually hold one or two addresses in reserve out of every group), then the authority in charge of doling out portions of the address space, the Network Information Center (NIC), would only need to assign the company IP addresses beginning with 206.168.99.*. If a company needed more than 256 addresses, they could request a larger chunk of the address space. Assigning the company two sets of address blocks, such as 206.168.99.* and 206.168.98.* would allow the company to give out

512 addresses. If the company could make a case that it needed many thousands of addresses, like for a multinational corporation with a computer on every employee's desk and many more Internet-connected machines in labs, then the NIC might grant it the entire block of addresses in the 206.16.*.* range. In that case, the company would have the use of 256×256, or 65,536 IP addresses. There are, however, options in between. If an organization could make the case for 2,500 IP addresses, the NIC could assign it addresses in the range from 206.16.101.* to 206.16.110.*.

Of course, humans would find it impossible to memorize all of the IP addresses corresponding to their favorite Web sites, so the creators of the Internet's addressing system allowed system administrators to create human-readable aliases for their computers. This type of address is familiar to anyone who has used the Internet for e-mail or to surf the Web: Examples include yahoo.com, amazon.com, epic.org, and internic.net. The combination of a word or phrase, a period, and an extension is referred to as a *domain name*, because it represents a specific area or "domain" of computers on the network. The extension, such as .com or .org, in theory represents the type of organization that owns the domain name:

- .com: Commercial organizations.
- .edu: Educational institutions.
- .gov: Government organizations.
- .mil: Military organizations.
- .net: Network resources.
- .org: Non- and not-for-profit organizations.
- .int: International organizations.[2]

These addresses are decidedly U.S.–centric—the .gov extension only refers to offices within the American government, for instance. In response to this limitation, other countries have established their own domain naming systems. The United Kingdom, for example, ends all of its addresses with .uk; Australia ends its addresses with .au. A complete list of all approved country extensions is available from a number of sources.[3]

Network administrators are not limited to simple two-part names for their computers. Instead, the naming system is flexible enough to allow administrators to create *subdomains*, or smaller groups of computers. For instance, the company Technology & Society, LLC, which owns the domain name techsoc.com, could create subdomains for each of its functions, like consulting.techsoc.com, documentation.techsoc.com, and ecommerce.techsoc.com. If the administrator so desired, he or she could name each computer that belonged to an employee working within a department. The convention is to use the subdomain "www" for Web servers—hence, addresses like www.yahoo.com—but administrators often choose a theme for the names within a domain or subdomain. A subdomain with a "cats" theme might have machines with names like tabby.ecommerce.techsoc.com, feral.ecommerce.techsoc.com, and siamese.ecommerce.techsoc.com. Human-readable addresses generally exist in a one-to-one relationship with their numerical counterparts. That is, a particular IP address, such as 206.168.99.131, corresponds to a single machine on the Internet. It is possible to have more than one IP address pointing to the same machine, but having records assigning the same IP address to two or more machines causes address-resolution inconsistencies that make packet routing unreliable.

Dynamic and Static IP Addresses

Another aspect of Internet addressing that makes it difficult to pin down a particular user from their network address is the practice of an Internet Service Provider assigning IP addresses to its subscribers randomly whenever they call in. For example, a user might connect to a their ISP at 3:00 PM and be assigned the IP address of 206.191.31.42. The user checks e-mail, visits a Web site to find the price of a stock, and logs off. If that same user calls back at 4:00 PM, it is very unlikely they will be assigned the same IP address as they were when they called at 3:00 PM. The reason is that most ISPs will reserve a block of IP addresses, usually one for each incoming phone line, and assign the user the IP address associated with the line they use to connect (users almost always dial a single number, but are then rotated through the ISPs collection of lines until the dial-up manager finds one that is open). Because users are not associated with specific IP addresses under the standard dial-up scheme, it is impossible to track them accurately. There is a similar problem in tracking users that share a single machine.

Recent changes in the way Internet Service Providers offer connectivity, particularly the advent of Digital Subscriber Line (DSL) technology has made it a bit easier to track user movements throughout the Internet. DSL is a technology that allows computers to be connected to the Internet full-time, rather than the part-time connections allowed under a standard dial-up plan. In addition to being about twenty times faster than the standard modem connection, home computers connected to an ISP via a DSL connection are usually assigned a permanent IP address. When that happens, their address appears consistently in site Web logs, allowing the site administrators to analyze the logs and discover that a user on a particular machine is a frequent visitor to their site and prefers to visit certain pages or has purchased specific products.

TRACKING USERS

As mentioned in the previous section, there are a number of ways to track the activities of Web site visitors. There are quite a few confounding factors, however. Users could access the Internet through a service provider that randomly assigns them an IP address from a pool of addresses controlled by the

ISP, for example. Another problem is that a user might share a machine with other users. In that case, assuming each machine has a single user would lead to the mistaken conclusion that one person was interested in every subject researched and site visited by users of that machine. These difficulties are ameliorated somewhat by the increasing use of fixed IP addresses for DSL customers, but the vast majority of Internet users are still assigned dynamic IP addresses when they connect to the Internet. This portion of the chapter examines the means Web site administrators have at their disposal to track their visitors.

Web Usage Logs

The most basic way to track users that visit a Web site is to take advantage of the logs that server software packages maintain of every request for graphics and pages from that server. The structure and appearance of a Web page are set forth in HTML. A basic HTML document can include text, formatting and style notations, and images. As an example, Figure 7.1 shows a page from a Web site, while Figure 7.2 shows a portion of the HTML code used to create it. Note that the page includes an image (the Technology & Society logo) and textual bibliographic and rating information presented in tabular form. When a computer user requests this page, whether by clicking a link from another site or typing in the page's URL, the user's computer looks up the IP address of the computer hosting the page and transmits a request. The host computer examines the request, ensures the page asked for exists, reads the page into memory, and then sends the file plus any separate files mentioned in the HTML source code (such as titlegraphic.gif in the example) to the requesting computer.

As a means of ensuring the system is working properly, and to allow system administrators to track user movements throughout the site, Web servers maintain detailed logs of the files requested and the result of the request (i.e., whether it was successful or not, and if not, the type of failure). Most Web servers maintain the following four log files: transfer, error, referrer, and agent logs. There are also a number of combined logs formats, which consolidate the information in these four logs into one or two files.

Transfer Log

The transfer log is the workhorse of the visitor-tracking world in that it maintains a record of every file requested from a Web server. Figure 7.3 contains a sample log file listing accesses to the author's personal Web site. The log file contains several types of information:

- *Requesting Address.* The IP address of the computer requesting the file. In some cases this information is missing or is resolved to the human-readable name of the computer.

Figure 7.1
Sample Web Page—http://www.techsoc.com/commerce.shtml

Technology & Society

Book Reviews	Date	Title	Author(s)	Grade
Home				
What's New			Harvard	
Privacy & Individual Rights	12/18/99	*Harvard Business Review on*	Business	89%
Commerce, Security, & the Law		*Managing High-Tech Industries*	School Press	
Net Culture, Art, & Literature				
International Affairs & National Security	8/18/98	*The Death of Distance*	Cairncross	86%
Ethics, Rhetoric, & Metaphysics			Denning and	
Science Fiction	7/17/98	*Internet Besieged*	Denning	86%
Other Resources	7/10/98	*Virtual Private Networks*	Scott, Wolfe, and Erwin	83%
News				
Publishers			Davis and	
Other Book Review Sites	6/15/98	*Blur*	Meyer	89%
Letters				
Contact	6/7/98	*Corporate Espionage*	Winkler	90%
Copyright				
	5/22/98	*Computer Money*	Furche and Wrightson	79%

Source: Author's Web site.

- *User Codes.* The second and third fields in the transfer log are reserved for user authentication data, but they rarely contain anything other than a blank (represented by a hyphen).

- *Time.* This field contains a time/date stamp of when the request for the file occurred. The standard format of for this stamp is Day/Month/Year:Time +/– GMT (offset from Greenwich Mean Time). Investigators and software agents can use the gap between requests to derive the time a user spent looking at a specific page.

- *Action.* In Figure 7.3 the only action listed is GET, which instructs the Web server to retrieve and send the requested file. Another possible action is HEAD, which only retrieves information about the page, such as when it was last modified.

- *File Name.* This field contains the name of the file requested.

- *HTTP Version.* This field contains the version of the Hypertext Transfer Protocol used to make the request. As of January 2000, the current HTTP version is 1.1.

- *Transaction Code.* The next field contains a numerical code indicating the status of the transaction. The following is a list of the range of codes used to describe transactions.

```
100   Continue
101   Switching Protocols
200   OK
201   Created
202   Accepted
203   Non-Authoritative Information
204   No Content
205   Reset Content
206   Partial Content
300   Multiple Choices
301   Moved Permanently
```

Figure 7.2
Hypertext Markup Language Code Sample

```
<html><head><title>Commerce, Security, & the Law</title>

<meta name="keywords" content="technology, society, book
reviews,privacy, electronic commerce, security, internet,
national, techsoc, book,review"></head>

<BODY BGCOLOR="white", LINK="blue", TEXT="black",
VLINK="red">

<table border=0 cellpadding=5 cols=2 width=640>

<tr><td width=200></td>

<td width=440><center><img src="titlegraphic.gif" border=0
alt="Technology and Society"></center>

</td>

</tr>

<tr><td valign=top width=200><font face="tahoma" size=-
1><b>Book Reviews</b></font><br>

<font size=-2>
<a href="index.shtml">Home</a><br>
<a href="whatsnew.shtml">What's New</a><br>

<a href="privacy.shtml">Privacy & Individual Rights</a><br>

<a href="commerce.shtml">Commerce, Security, & the
Law</a><br>

<a href="culture.shtml">Net Culture, Art, &
Literature</a><br>

<a href="natsec.shtml">International Affairs & National
Security</a><br>

<a href="ethics.shtml">Ethics, Rhetoric, &
Metaphysics</a><br>

<a href="scifi.shtml">Science Fiction</a><p>


  302  Moved Temporarily
  303  See Other
  304  Not Modified
  305  Use Proxy
  400  Bad Request
```

Figure 7.3
Transfer Log File Example

```
216.26.10.30 - - [10/Feb/2000:16:03:12 -0500] "GET /postinfo.html HTTP/1.1" 200
2451
216.26.10.30 - - [10/Feb/2000:16:05:33 -0500] "GET /trnspsoc2.jpg HTTP/1.1" 200
8347
216.26.10.30 - - [10/Feb/2000:16:06:17 -0500] "GET /favicon.ico HTTP/1.1" 404
304
216.26.10.30 - - [10/Feb/2000:16:06:18 -0500] "GET /favicon.ico HTTP/1.1" 404
304
216.26.9.139 - - [10/Feb/2000:16:41:38 -0500] "GET /postinfo.html HTTP/1.1" 304
-
216.26.9.139 - - [10/Feb/2000:16:41:48 -0500] "GET /index.html HTTP/1.1" 200
1946
216.26.9.139 - - [10/Feb/2000:16:41:49 -0500] "GET /image/curttitle.gif
HTTP/1.1" 404 312
216.26.9.139 - - [10/Feb/2000:16:43:39 -0500] "GET /index.html HTTP/1.1" 200
1946
216.26.9.139 - - [10/Feb/2000:16:43:40 -0500] "GET /images/curttitle.gif
HTTP/1.1" 200 1320
216.26.9.139 - - [10/Feb/2000:16:50:28 -0500] "GET /resume.htm HTTP/1.1" 200
5986
216.26.9.139 - - [10/Feb/2000:16:58:54 -0500] "GET /index.html HTTP/1.1" 200
2223
216.26.9.139 - - [10/Feb/2000:16:58:55 -0500] "GET /images/curtsmall.jpg
HTTP/1.1" 200 7420
216.26.9.139 - - [10/Feb/2000:16:58:55 -0500] "GET /images/curttitle.gif
HTTP/1.1" 304 -
216.26.9.139 - - [10/Feb/2000:17:00:41 -0500] "GET /contact.htm HTTP/1.1" 200
5474
216.26.9.139 - - [10/Feb/2000:17:00:41 -0500] "GET /titlegraphic.gif HTTP/1.1"
404 309
216.26.9.139 - - [10/Feb/2000:17:00:42 -0500] "GET /curtsmall.jpg HTTP/1.1" 404
306
216.26.4.69 - - [11/Feb/2000:03:18:41 -0500] "GET /index.html HTTP/1.1" 304 -
216.26.4.69 - - [11/Feb/2000:03:18:41 -0500] "GET /images/curttitle.gif
HTTP/1.1" 304 -
216.26.4.69 - - [11/Feb/2000:03:18:41 -0500] "GET /images/curtsmall.jpg
HTTP/1.1" 304 -
216.26.4.69 - - [11/Feb/2000:03:41:35 -0500] "GET /index.html HTTP/1.1" 304 -
216.26.4.69 - - [11/Feb/2000:03:41:36 -0500] "GET /images/curttitle.gif
HTTP/1.1" 304 -
216.26.4.69 - - [11/Feb/2000:03:41:36 -0500] "GET /images/curtsmall.jpg
HTTP/1.1" 304 -
216.26.4.173 - - [14/Feb/2000:16:14:48 -0500] "GET /index.html HTTP/1.1" 304 -
216.26.4.173 - - [14/Feb/2000:16:14:48 -0500] "GET /images/curttitle.gif
HTTP/1.1" 304 -
216.26.4.173 - - [14/Feb/2000:16:14:49 -0500] "GET /images/curtsmall.jpg
HTTP/1.1" 304 -
216.26.8.67 - - [17/Feb/2000:17:02:59 -0500] "GET /index.html HTTP/1.1" 304 -
216.26.8.67 - - [17/Feb/2000:17:03:00 -0500] "GET /images/curttitle.gif
HTTP/1.1" 304 -
216.26.8.67 - - [17/Feb/2000:17:03:00 -0500] "GET /images/curtsmall.jpg
HTTP/1.1" 304 -
216.26.5.133 - - [21/Feb/2000:18:18:57 -0500] "GET /index.html HTTP/1.1" 304 -
216.26.5.133 - - [21/Feb/2000:18:18:57 -0500] "GET /images/curttitle.gif
HTTP/1.1" 304 -
216.26.5.133 - - [21/Feb/2000:18:18:58 -0500] "GET /images/curtsmall.jpg
HTTP/1.1" 304 -
```

```
401   Unauthorized
402   Payment Required
403   Permission Denied
404   Page Does Not Exist
405   Method Not Allowed
406   Not Acceptable
```

```
407  Proxy Authentication Required
408  Request Time-Out
409  Conflict
410  Gone
411  Length Required
412  Precondition Failed
413  Request Entity Too Large
414  Request-Uri Too Large
415  Unsupported Media Type
500  Process Failure/Broken Script
501  Not Implemented
502  Bad Gateway
503  Service Unavailable
504  Gateway Time-Out
505  HTTP Version Not Supported
```
Three of the most common codes are 200 (transfer OK), 304 (no change to the page since it was last requested by this user, which means the user still has the page on his or her computer), and 404 (page not found).

• *Bytes Transferred.* The final field of the transfer log indicates the number of bytes transferred in response to the request. This value corresponds to the size of the file requested; in the case of a 304 code (no change since last request), the value will be blank (represented by a hyphen).

Error Log

The second common log is the error log, which, as the name implies, keeps a record of any errors that occur. Figure 7.4 shows a sample error log of a site in the early stages of construction. This Web server software package uses the verbose version of the error codes already listed, so rather than returning a "404" error the log indicates a "file does not exist." The error log follows a similar format to the transfer log, but there are some important differences.

Figure 7.4
Error Log File Example

```
[Thu Feb 10 16:06:17 2000] [error] [client 216.26.10.30] File does not
exist:
/usr/local/plesk/apache/vhosts/curtisfrye.com/httpdocs/favicon.ico
[Thu Feb 10 16:06:18 2000] [error] [client 216.26.10.30] File does not
exist:
/usr/local/plesk/apache/vhosts/curtisfrye.com/httpdocs/favicon.ico
[Thu Feb 10 16:41:49 2000] [error] [client 216.26.9.139] File does not
exist:
/usr/local/plesk/apache/vhosts/curtisfrye.com/httpdocs/image/curttitle.
gif
[Thu Feb 10 17:00:41 2000] [error] [client 216.26.9.139] File does not
exist:
/usr/local/plesk/apache/vhosts/curtisfrye.com/httpdocs/titlegraphic.gif
[Thu Feb 10 17:00:42 2000] [error] [client 216.26.9.139] File does not
exist:
/usr/local/plesk/apache/vhosts/curtisfrye.com/httpdocs/curtsmall.jpg
```

- *Time Stamp.* Web servers that keep track of errors note the time and date of the error, but write the date using a different format than the transfer log.
- *Error Notation.* In the example the log merely notes there was an error; other packages provide the code for the error.
- *IP Address.* The IP address of the computer attempting to download the file in question. The requesting computer is referred to as a *client.*
- *Description.* A brief message describing the error, such as a note the file does not exist or that the connection was terminated.
- *File.* The file whose request generated the error, if applicable.

The error log is particularly useful for finding which pages on a site users are unable to reach and for what reason. Also, as Rick Stout points out in *Web Site Stats*, it is possible to use the error logs, in particular the "connection lost" errors, to determine which pages take too long to load. Most connections are lost because the user on the other end of the connection lost patience with the server and clicked the "stop" button on their browser to continue without bothering to download all of the graphics or other elements of an HTML page. Stout describes a method for finding those pages, reducing user frustration and ensuring the pages load fully.[4]

Referrer Log

The referrer log is a list of the pages that users were viewing when they made the jump to a page on the server where the log is kept. The referrer log also maintains a list of search terms used at popular search engines like Yahoo and Lycos. A line from a referrer log might read something like this:

http://lycospro.lycos.com/srchpro/?query=The+War+Of+The+Worlds-> warwrlds.shtml

In this case, the user searched for pages that contained all of the words in the query ("the," "war," "of," and "worlds"). The page it returned contained a review of a book with that title. The data from a referrer log can be derived from the transfer log, so many Web server administrators choose not to maintain a separate referrer log.

Agent Log

The final log maintained by some Web administrators is the agent log, which keeps track of the software used to view HTML pages requested from the server. In some cases the software is a browser, like Netscape Communicator or Microsoft's Internet Explorer, though in other cases the software is a *bot*, or automated program that crawls through Web sites cataloging their contents and returning the results to a search engine like Yahoo, AltaVista, or

Lycos. Figure 7.5 presents a number of lines from an agent log. Netscape's browsers are referred to using the code name for the original development project, "Mozilla." As with the referrer log, the contents of the agent log can be derived from the transfer log.

Combined Log Format

Rather than maintain the transfer, error, referrer, and agent logs separately, some Web servers allow administrators to maintain a single log that combines information from the four basic logs and presents it in a relatively easy-to-read format. Figure 7.6 shows the contents of a file in a combined log format. Note that each line contains the IP address of the client requesting the page, the two user authentication fields (as usual, represented by hyphens to indicate they were empty), a time/date stamp, the action requested, the name of the requested file, the HTTP version, the status code for the request, the number of bytes transferred, the referring URL (if any), and the name of the client software used to make the request.

Visit Tracking

Tracking a log full of simultaneous visitors is impossible for humans, but the log entries of a single user allow an analyst to take a quick look at the log and track that user's movements. In the case of the log file in Figure 7.6, the user connected to the page at http://www.teleport.com/~cfrye/techsoc/ at 4:03.36 PM Pacific time on February 27, 2000, after being referred there by a link at Vanderbilt University (that link is recorded as the refering page and is listed near the end of the log line). The visitor is using Microsoft's Internet Explorer Version 3.01, is running a PC with the Windows 95 operating system, and has an IP address of 216.26.20.195. Note that these last three values never vary during the visit.

The user immediately (twenty seconds later) moved to a new page, index.shtml, which is shown in Figure 7.7. After downloading four images

Figure 7.5
Sample Agent Log File

```
"logikabot"
"Mozilla/2.0 (compatible; MS FrontPage 4.0)"
"Mozilla/4.05 [en] (Win95; U)"
"Mozilla/4.05 [en] (Win95; U)"
"Mozilla/4.0 (compatible; MSIE 5.01; Windows 98; KATIESOFT 6.0)"
"Mozilla/3.0 (compatible; NetMind-Minder/4.0)"
"Mozilla/4.0 (compatible; MSIE 5.0; Windows 98; DigExt)"
"Mozilla/4.0 (compatible; MSIE 5.0; Windows 98; DigExt;
netLibrary.com)"
"Mozilla/4.0 (compatible; MSIE 5.0; Windows 98; oceanfree.net)"
"Mozilla/4.05 [en] (WinNT; I)"
```

Figure 7.6
Sample Combined Log File

```
216.26.20.195 - - [27/Feb/2000:16:03:36 -0800] "GET /~cfrye/techsoc/ HTTP/1.0" 200 174
"http://www.library.vanderbilt.edu/law/acqs/bookrev.html" "Mozilla/2.0 (compatible; MSIE
3.01; Windows 95)"
216.26.20.195 - - [27/Feb/2000:16:03:56 -0800] "GET /index.shtml HTTP/1.0" 200 2902
"http://www.teleport.com/~cfrye/techsoc/" "Mozilla/2.0 (compatible; MSIE 3.01; Windows
95)"
216.26.20.195 - - [27/Feb/2000:16:03:58 -0800] "GET /titlegraphic.gif HTTP/1.0" 200 6960
"http://www.techsoc.com/index.shtml" "Mozilla/2.0 (compatible; MSIE 3.01; Windows 95)"
216.26.20.195 - - [27/Feb/2000:16:03:58 -0800] "GET /wcspkr.gif HTTP/1.0" 200 1607
"http://www.techsoc.com/index.shtml" "Mozilla/2.0 (compatible; MSIE 3.01; Windows 95)"
216.26.20.195 - - [27/Feb/2000:16:04:02 -0800] "GET /MetroOfTomorrow.jpg HTTP/1.0" 200
11162 "http://www.techsoc.com/index.shtml" "Mozilla/2.0 (compatible; MSIE 3.01; Windows
95)"
216.26.20.195 - - [27/Feb/2000:16:04:02 -0800] "GET /nua.gif HTTP/1.0" 200 1969
"http://www.techsoc.com/index.shtml" "Mozilla/2.0 (compatible; MSIE 3.01; Windows 95)"
216.26.20.195 - - [27/Feb/2000:16:04:44 -0800] "GET /culture.shtml HTTP/1.0" 200 2257
"http://www.techsoc.com/index.shtml" "Mozilla/2.0 (compatible; MSIE 3.01; Windows 95)"
216.26.20.195 - - [27/Feb/2000:16:04:48 -0800] "GET /culttitl.gif HTTP/1.0" 200 2784
"http://www.techsoc.com/culture.shtml" "Mozilla/2.0 (compatible; MSIE 3.01; Windows 95)"
216.26.20.195 - - [27/Feb/2000:16:04:53 -0800] "GET /wrdnbrhd.shtml HTTP/1.0" 200 5314
"http://www.techsoc.com/culture.shtml" "Mozilla/2.0 (compatible; MSIE 3.01; Windows 95)"
216.26.20.195 - - [27/Feb/2000:16:04:58 -0800] "GET /wrdnbrhd.jpg HTTP/1.0" 200 25961
"http://www.techsoc.com/wrdnbrhd.shtml" "Mozilla/2.0 (compatible; MSIE 3.01; Windows 95)"
216.26.20.195 - - [27/Feb/2000:16:05:27 -0800] "GET /newcomm.shtml HTTP/1.0" 200 5064
"http://www.techsoc.com/culture.shtml" "Mozilla/2.0 (compatible; MSIE 3.01; Windows 95)"
216.26.20.195 - - [27/Feb/2000:16:05:26 -0800] "GET /newcomm.jpg HTTP/1.0" 200 48997
"http://www.techsoc.com/newcomm.shtml" "Mozilla/2.0 (compatible; MSIE 3.01; Windows 95)"
216.26.20.195 - - [27/Feb/2000:16:05:55 -0800] "GET /grwupdig.shtml HTTP/1.0" 200 5710
"http://www.techsoc.com/culture.shtml" "Mozilla/2.0 (compatible; MSIE 3.01; Windows 95)"
216.26.20.195 - - [27/Feb/2000:16:05:56 -0800] "GET /grwupdig.jpg HTTP/1.0" 200 30960
"http://www.techsoc.com/grwupdig.shtml" "Mozilla/2.0 (compatible; MSIE 3.01; Windows 95)"
216.26.20.195 - - [27/Feb/2000:16:10:08 -0800] "GET /index.shtml HTTP/1.0" 200 2902
"http://www.techsoc.com/culture.shtml" "Mozilla/2.0 (compatible; MSIE 3.01; Windows 95)"
216.26.20.195 - - [27/Feb/2000:16:10:15 -0800] "GET /ethics.shtml HTTP/1.0" 200 1967
"http://www.techsoc.com/index.shtml" "Mozilla/2.0 (compatible; MSIE 3.01; Windows 95)"
216.26.20.195 - - [27/Feb/2000:16:10:16 -0800] "GET /ethctitl.gif HTTP/1.0" 200 3023
"http://www.techsoc.com/ethics.shtml" "Mozilla/2.0 (compatible; MSIE 3.01; Windows 95)"
216.26.20.195 - - [27/Feb/2000:16:10:36 -0800] "GET /datasmog.shtml HTTP/1.0" 200 4034
"http://www.techsoc.com/ethics.shtml" "Mozilla/2.0 (compatible; MSIE 3.01; Windows 95)"
216.26.20.195 - - [27/Feb/2000:16:10:41 -0800] "GET /datasmog.jpg HTTP/1.0" 200 10925
"http://www.techsoc.com/datasmog.shtml" "Mozilla/2.0 (compatible; MSIE 3.01; Windows 95)"
216.26.20.195 - - [27/Feb/2000:16:16:53 -0800] "GET /softedge.shtml HTTP/1.0" 200 4470
"http://www.techsoc.com/ethics.shtml" "Mozilla/2.0 (compatible; MSIE 3.01; Windows 95)"
216.26.20.195 - - [27/Feb/2000:16:16:57 -0800] "GET /softedge.jpg HTTP/1.0" 200 20988
"http://www.techsoc.com/softedge.shtml" "Mozilla/2.0 (compatible; MSIE 3.01; Windows 95)"
216.26.20.195 - - [27/Feb/2000:16:17:56 -0800] "GET /index.shtml HTTP/1.0" 200 2902 "-"
"Mozilla/2.0 (compatible; MSIE 3.01; Windows 95)"
216.26.20.195 - - [27/Feb/2000:16:18:03 -0800] "GET /culture.shtml HTTP/1.0" 200 2257
"http://www.techsoc.com/index.shtml" "Mozilla/2.0 (compatible; MSIE 3.01; Windows 95)"
216.26.20.195 - - [27/Feb/2000:16:18:04 -0800] "GET /grwupdig.shtml HTTP/1.0" 200 5710
"http://www.techsoc.com/culture.shtml" "Mozilla/2.0 (compatible; MSIE 3.01; Windows 95)"
```

(titlegraphic.jpg, wcspkr.gif, MetroOfTomorrow.jpg, and nua.gif) and the text of the page, the user then requests the page labeled culture.shtml, which is a set of reviews about Net culture, art, and literature. From that list the user clicked on the link named wrdnbrhd.shtml, which leads to a review of Stephen Doheny-Farina's book *The Wired Neighborhood*. The user then visited the pages with reviews for *New Community Networks* and *Growing Up Digital* before moving back to the site's main page, index.shtml. Once there, the user clicked on the link for page ethics.shtml, which lists available reviews of books dealing with ethics, rhetoric, and metaphysics. After downloading the page text and the page's title .gif, the user visited the pages with reviews for

Figure 7.7
Home Page of Technology & Society Book Reviews

Technology & Society

Book Reviews
What's New
Privacy & Individual Rights
Commerce, Security, & the Law
Net Culture, Art, & Literature
International Affairs & National Security
Ethics, Rhetoric, & Metaphysics
Science Fiction

Other Resources
News
Publishers
Other Book Review Sites
Letters
Contact
Copyright

Feature Review

Hugh Ferriss's *The Metropolis of Tomorrow*, beyond being a beautiful collection of the artist's architectural drawings, invites comparisons to Tufte and inspires thoughts on the state of information space design.

Rating: 93%

Full review.

Source: <http://www.techsoc.com>.

David Shenk's *Data Smog* (datasmog.shtml) and Paul Levinson's *The Soft Edge* (softedge.shtml). After that the visitor returned to the main index page and returned to the Net culture, art, and literature page and then reopened the review of Don Tapscott's *Growing Up Digital*. The user's tracks leave off at that point, but that individual saw five different book reviews, visiting one of them twice. The time difference between the first and last log entry for that user is fourteen minutes and twenty-eight seconds, a healthy visit for an eclectic book review site.

Web Log Analysis Tools and Services

It is easy to imagine how much of a nightmare it would be for a human to scan through the log files of a busy Web site with multiple simultaneous users in an attempt to derive meaningful information. In response to that need, numerous companies and individuals offer Web log analysis software and services, ranging from free software packages that provide textual summaries of a log file's contents to sophisticated software suites that generate charts and graphs based on a site's logs. One such program group is WebTrends® Enterprise Suite™, produced by WebTrends Corporation in Portland, Oregon (http://www.webtrends.com). Figures 7.8 through 7.10 show three different reports

Figure 7.8
WebTrends® Enterprise Suite™ Activity Level by Day of the Week Summary Files

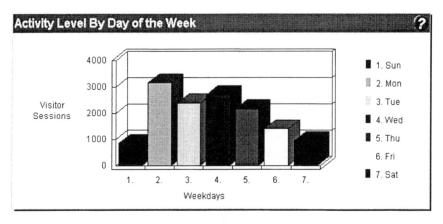

	Day	Hits	% of Total Hits	Visitor Sessions
1	Sun	15,915	8.62%	842
2	Mon	41,962	22.73%	3,155
3	Tue	30,927	16.75%	2,382
4	Wed	31,983	17.32%	2,691
5	Thu	25,646	13.89%	2,161
6	Fri	20,129	10.9%	1,402
7	Sat	17,996	9.75%	941
Total Weekdays		**150,647**	**81.62%**	**11,791**
Total Weekend		**33,911**	**18.37%**	**1,783**

Source: <http://www.webtrends.com/SampleReports/complete.htm>. Used by permission.

produced by WebTrends Enterprise Suite: reports describing site traffic by days of the week, by hours of the day, and by the North American states represented in the logs. Note that the reports indicate factors to keep in mind when interpreting the data, such as the warning that the report listing users' geographic distribution within North America reflects the state where the domain name of the computer connecting to the server is registered and may not be the actual state the user is logging in from.

Registration

One way to keep track of users on a system is to require users to register the first time they attempt to use a system and then to log in every time they come back. As noted in Chapter 2, the *New York Times* uses such a registration scheme for its visitors, requiring them to enter their ZIP code, age, and

Figure 7.9
WebTrends® Enterprise Suite™ Activity Level by Hour of the Day Summary Files

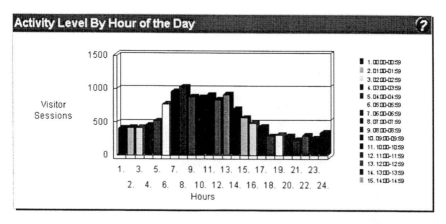

Hour	# of Hits	% of Total Hits	# of Visitor Sessions
00:00 - 00:59	5,597	3.03%	407
01:00 - 01:59	5,852	3.17%	417
02:00 - 02:59	5,967	3.23%	415
03:00 - 03:59	6,298	3.41%	451
04:00 - 04:59	7,556	4.09%	521
05:00 - 05:59	9,334	5.05%	768
06:00 - 06:59	11,566	6.26%	954
07:00 - 07:59	13,019	7.05%	1,029
08:00 - 08:59	11,498	6.23%	883
09:00 - 09:59	11,357	6.15%	872
10:00 - 10:59	11,677	6.32%	904

Source: <http://www.webtrends.com/SampleReports/complete.htm>. Used by permission.

gender during the registration process, and to pick a username and password for subsequent visits. While it is certainly possible for more than one user to access the *Times* site from the same computer, computer users are generally wary about giving out their passwords, so the likelihood of non–family members using the same account is reasonably low. Once a user has logged into a site, the hosting computer can note the time the user logged in and then assign that user's login name to every HTML page requested by the computer at that IP address.

Registration systems are a good way to get more information from a user than could normally be gained from tracking their movements within a site. Rather than guessing at the user's needs and interests, a site owner can ask (or require) users to fill out a registration form with items like the simple

Figure 7.10
WebTrends® Enterprise Suite™ Visitors by North American States and Provinces

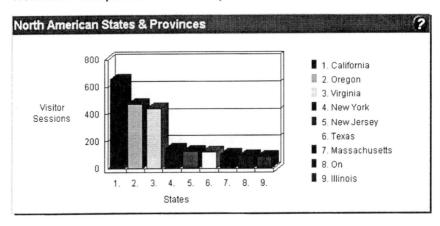

	State	Visitor Sessions
1	California	656
2	Oregon	475
3	Virginia	439
4	New York	142
5	New Jersey	126
6	Texas	118
7	Massachusetts	102
8	On	92
9	Illinois	89
10	Connecticut	86
11	Florida	64
12	Pennsylvania	63

Source: <http://www.webtrends.com/SampleReports/complete.htm>. Used by permission.

ZAG requested by the *New York Times* or a more detailed, multipage form like those traditionally used to qualify individuals for free subscriptions to industry newspapers and magazines. The danger of basing marketing decisions on this information is that users may lie, either unintentionally or with the intent to deceive and skew the site's demographics. With industry magazine registration forms it is usually possible to verify at least the size of the potential subscriber's company and the type of products they work with and are responsible for ordering.

Beyond tracking visitors, Stout mentions three uses for registration requirements. The first reason to require visitors to register with the site is to restrict access.[5] As with the industry magazines that only offer free subscriptions to qualified individuals in companies that could purchase advertisers' products, it may be in a site's interest to limit the number and type of users that can visit the site.[6] Professional organizations often establish members-only sections of their Web sites while providing press releases and other general information to the public at large. A second reason for requiring registration is to require users to pay for content not available to the main body of site visitors. Stout uses the example of the Web site run by ESPN, an American sports-oriented cable network. The site offers articles and statistics to the general public, but requires users to pay for access to in-depth articles and opinion pieces from the site's writers.[7] The final purpose for requiring registration is to allow radio stations and similar organizations to run contests. This type of registration requires visitors to provide accurate contact information so they can be informed in the event they win the contest.[8] In summary, Stout finds four benefits to allowing users to register with a site:

- To restrict access to private or confidential content.
- To enhance site revenues by selling premium content.
- To promote the site to encourage return visits.
- To enhance site revenues by selling mailing or telephone lists.[9]

COOKIES

So far this chapter has looked at tracking Web site visitors through log analysis and registration. The benefit of these methods is that they do not require a site's host to interact with the visitor's computer beyond the simple transferring of HTML pages and image files from the server to the client. While the requiring registration does allow a site administrator to track a user's movements across a site, it relies on the user being willing to register every time they visit the site. If registration is optional, there would be no way to know whether a registered user logged on to look at content available to the general public. Using Web logs to track user movements is even less effective: The best that can be done in that case is to hope that a user has a permanent IP address so that page views associated with that address can be associated with a single individual. Another method of tracking Web site visitors is much more effective and requires no action on the part of the user. In this method, the Web site server software writes a piece of text, called a *cookie*, on the user's hard drive. Cookies are the center of a heated privacy debate, with arguments ranging from assertions that cookies violate a user's property rights to the opposing view that cookies are beneficial to the user because their contents allow site administrators to personalize their offerings to best meet each user's tastes. This portion of the chapter defines cookies from a technical standpoint, illustrates their uses, describes what they are not capable of doing, and characterizes their role in the ongoing privacy debate.

What Cookies Are

As noted, cookies are text files written to a user's hard drive, usually in a file named "cookies.txt." (Any text file or other token written to a user's computer has been referred to as a "cookie" or "magic cookie" since the earliest days of the Unix operating system—the actual origin of the term has been lost.) The original cookie specification was developed by Netscape as a means of extending the capabilities of Web servers by allowing the server to write a file to the user's computer that stored information about that user. Whenever the user returned to the site, the server could query the user's cookie file to see if that user had been there before and, if so, to read the information from the cookie the server left and use it to aid in tracking the user's movements and customizing their experience. Figure 7.11 shows the contents of a cookie file as viewed through the Winmag.com Cookie Viewer, written by Karen Kenworthy. Actual cookie files are standard text files with every new cookie on a separate line. The Cookie Viewer makes the file more readable and allows the user to modify or delete the values in any or all of the cookies on their system.

Figure 7.11
Cookie File as Viewed with WinMag Cookie Viewer

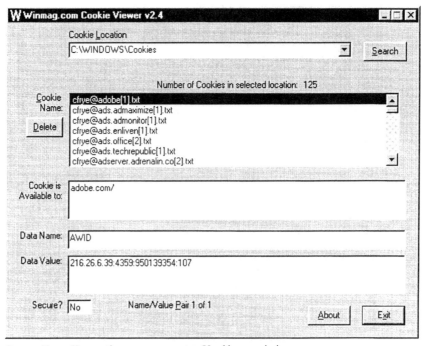

Source: Karen Kenworthy, program creator. Used by permission.

Cookie Specification

The cookie specification requires Web servers to create cookies using the following command:

Set-Cookie: NAME=VALUE; expires=DATE; path=PATH; domain=DOMAIN_ NAME; secure[10]

The only required element of the command, other than the Set-Cookie precursor, is the NAME field. In fact, the NAME label is a placeholder—the server can assign the cookie any name it likes, though the name cannot contain a comma, semicolon, or white space (such as a space, carriage return, or tab character). One example would be Set-Cookie: USER_ID=cfrye@techsoc.com. The NAME value could be anything—the only reason to make it readable by humans is to allow users to get an idea of the type of information stored in the cookie. The optional elements (expires, path, domain, and secure) allow the site administrator to better control how the cookie behaves.

- *Expires*. This property determines when the cookie should be erased automatically. If the expires property is left out, the cookie will never be erased.
- *Path*. This property indicates which directories on a server the cookie applies to. For instance, a sports information server could have a directory for baseball and another for basketball. If the site administrators decided to set separate cookies to track the user's activities in the two directories, they could set one cookie to work in /baseball and the other in /basketball.
- *Domain*. This property defines the domain (such as doubleclick.net) the cookie applies to. Servers may only read cookies set by computers in their same domain. That is, no Web server may read cookies set by a computer in another domain.
- *Secure*. If the word "secure" is included in the cookie, then the cookie may only be transmitted over an encrypted or otherwise secured link. If not, then the cookie's contents may be transmitted in the clear.

To avoid allowing cookies to take up too much space on a user's computer, the standard advises that programmers set the following limitations on the cookies file:

- 300 total cookies.
- 4 kilobytes per cookie, including the name and the text string.
- 20 cookies per server or domain.[11]

If a user's cookie file contains 300 cookies and a Web server attempts to set another cookie, the first cookie placed in the file is erased and the new one is written in its place. The same pattern (first in, first out) holds true if computers within a domain attempt to set more than twenty cookies on a single machine. With a limit of 4KB per cookie, the maximum size of the cookies file is 1.2MB. With the cost of hard-disk storage dropping rapidly, one megabyte of space is a negligible percentage of drives that can contain upwards of 10GB (gigabytes, or thousand megabytes) of data. Since most cookies consume far less than their allotted maximum space, the actual room required to store cookies is usually much less than a megabyte.

Cookie Contents

The contents of a cookie vary widely, reflecting the goals and practices of the organization that set them. Figure 7.12 shows the contents of a Netscape cookie file. Some of the cookies, notably those from DigitalThink (www. digital think.com) and DoubleClick (www.doubleclick.net), only store a user identification number, a user id, and password combination (as with www.listbot. com), while other cookies (like the one from www.imgis.com) store quite a bit more information on the user's computer. The primary reason to write lots of information to a cookie on a user's machine is to simplify the administrator's programming task: Rather than require the administrator to create and manage a database recording all of the transactions for every user, the administrator can write a program that stores information about the user's movements on that user's computer. Whenever that user returns to the site, the site can request the cookie, read the information about the user's activities, track the user's movements through the site during the current visit, and record them in the cookie. This information is usually coded so it takes up less space and is not legible by anyone outside the company (including the user).

Tracking Users Across Multiple Sites

Part of the cookie specification is that a computer can only read cookies set by a machine in the same domain. For example, a cookie set by a machine in the digitalthink.com domain could only be read by other machines with the extension digitalthink.com. It is possible to further limit the machines that can read a cookie by making the address more specific. For instance, assigning a cookie the domain learning.digitalthink.com would prevent any computer whose name did not end with the extension learning.digitalthink.com from reading the cookie, though a machine named custom.learning. digitalthink.com could read the cookie because its name ends with the proper sequence. Yet it is in advertisers' interests to monitor user movements across every site where their ads appear, so ad network administrators developed a simple work-around. Rather than store an advertiser's banner ads on the server where the ads are to appear, the ad service stores the graphics on their servers and requires the page displaying the ad to retrieve the graphics from their server. Figure 7.13 illustrates the process.

Figure 7.12
Netscape Cookie File

```
# Netscape HTTP Cookie File#
http://www.netscape.com/newsref/std/cookie_spec.html# This is a
generated file!  Do not edit

.deck.com    FALSE /cgi-bin/deck/createsite      FALSE 1163636146   count
      1
citiwallet.citibank.com FALSE /ssl-wallet FALSE 1103550427   HW      Y
.sitegauge.com    TRUE   /cgi-bin    FALSE 1823770797  safe_cookie
      4485663
www.1800flowers.com     FALSE /flowers    FALSE 981734873    800fname
      Curtis
.freedom.net      TRUE   /support    FALSE 1008483199  freedomTesting
      1
www.1800flowers.com     FALSE /flowers    FALSE 950285300    800fBanner
      vd2reg
info.greenwood.com      FALSE /shop FALSE 980499770    ISON  1
.netscape.com     TRUE   /     FALSE 1293839545   UIDC
      216.26.9.6:0929638770:237301
.bfast.com  TRUE   /     FALSE 1568659252   UID   2|449205513|20190916
.staples.com      TRUE   /     FALSE 2051222400   SITESERVER
      ID=1734f1e52f3a064429a947aa1c414c02
.listbot.com      TRUE   /     FALSE 2009658494   lb_subscriber
      subscriber_id%7C12480497%7Csubscriber_password%7CZqC%5BRhNWC
.go.com     TRUE   /     FALSE 961195394    SWID  45D914AE-7C5E-71A5-
2F8E-659646094786
.imgis.com  TRUE   /     FALSE 1087087130   JEB2
      4D88D878DDA658F4D81A07843004A719
.digitalthink.com TRUE   /     FALSE 993308482    user_id     cfrye
.avenuea.com      TRUE   /     FALSE 1245023559   AA002 929728560-
84347469/930938379
.doubleclick.net  TRUE   /     FALSE 1920498830   id    a0221600
.zdnet.com  TRUE   /     FALSE 1041310596   cgversion   4
.zdnet.com  TRUE   /     FALSE 1041310596   browser     D81A0715376E9BC2
.focalink.com     TRUE   /     FALSE 1293796396   SB_ID
      09300133980000461425181194270
.flycast.com      TRUE   /     FALSE 1293753600   atf   1_2473144696
www.soundforge.com      FALSE /     FALSE 962053889    UID   130022
www.sonicfoundry.com    FALSE /     FALSE 1008956833  MachineCode001
      3ZWJLQT
www.sonicfoundry.com    FALSE /     FALSE 1261417633  ContactID
```

In this scenario, a user connects to the Technology & Society Book Reviews site, triggering the download of information on that site's home page. The banner graphic at the top of the page is not stored on the machine hosting techsoc.com; rather, the HTML used to specify the image gives its address as residing on the machine named ads1.fakeadserver.com. The user's browser follows that link to ads1.fakeadserver.com and, by connecting to that machine, allows it to set a cookie on the user's computer. The cookie in question has the domain value of fakeadserver.com, so any computer in that domain (e.g., ads1.fakeadserver.com, ads2.fakeadserver.com, etc.) can read the cookie and use it to record information about that user. If the user visits another site

Figure 7.13
Process for Banner Ad and Cookie Placement

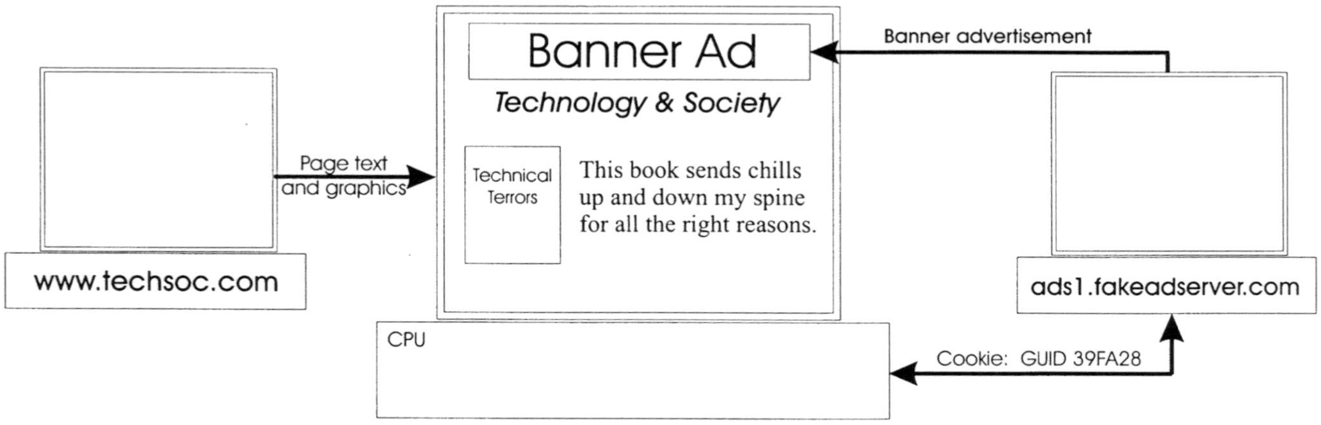

ads1.fakeadserver.com

Banner advertisement

Cookie: GUID 39FA28

Banner Ad

Technology & Society

Technical
Terrors

This book sends chills
up and down my spine
for all the right reasons.

CPU

Page text
and graphics

www.techsoc.com

that has its advertising banners served by a machine in the fakeadserver.com domain, the resulting connection to the machine hosting the advertisement will allow the company to read and update the contents of the cookie.

Also note how cookies alleviate the lack of user identification found in the standard transfer log. If a user signs on to a site and the server assigns that user's computer a cookie, Web log analysis software or services can correlate the cookie's contents to records in the logs, thus preserving information about the user and generating a more complete picture of that individual's activities at one or more sites. All of these benefits assume, however, that there is only one user per browser. As Zeff and Aronson note,

> At a college computer center where many students may be accessing a particular Web site through the same computer, the first time a student accesses the site from that computer, the computer will receive a cookie file. . . . Unfortunately, what the publisher thinks is one user is actually 100 different students using the same machine. The same problems (although to a lesser extent) are also caused by family computers that are used by more than one person.[12]

Personalization

A frequent use of cookies, in addition to user tracking, is to record user preferences and to use those preferences to modify a Web site so the visitor gets the most out of each visit. For example, a Web site might offer users a list of information categories (information technology news, stock quotes, sports scores, entertainment news, etc.) to be displayed on the site's main page when that user visits the site. The site operator can then store the visitor's stated preferences in the cookies, plus the collateral information inherent in their interests as expressed by the categories they chose and the type of information they seek out, in the cookie and arrange the site's appearance accordingly.

What Cookies Can't Do

As can be seen from the previous discussion, cookies by themselves have rather limited capabilities. Beyond writing a few lines of text (not executable instructions) to a well-defined place on a user's hard drive, they are not capable of affecting a user's computer. Cookies do wield considerable influence over how Web site operators can track and customize users' experiences on Web sites that use cookies, but there is nothing inherently nefarious about the technology beyond the minor intrusion of writing a relatively small chunk of text onto the user's hard drive. That many administrators of sites that set cookies choose to encode or encrypt the cookies' contents is an issue of choice, not design.

There has been considerable argument in the media, especially the online media, that allowing Web sites to set cookies on an individual's Web site poses an undue security and privacy threat. One popular example of how cookies were part of a privacy violation was a case where a programmer had used another technology (in this case a scripting language named JavaScript) to exploit flaws in a Web browser program and look on the user's hard drive to discover that user's e-mail address. The programmer then wrote the information to a cookie and used that mechanism to transfer the user's e-mail address back to his server.[13] The argument is that cookies are inherently privacy invading because they allow Web sites to track unwitting visitors who believe their actions are anonymous. One possible analogy is that of visiting a grocery store in another state and having the store clerk append the customer's vehicle license number to the store's copy of the receipt. The counterargument is that there is no way to duplicate the unique personal identifier of the vehicle license number in the online environment, but as will be noted later in this chapter it is indeed possible to correlate online information with offline sources to find a user's real name and contact information.

The Technologist Position

As with many debates over the proper application of technology, the discussion between technology implementers and technology commentators has revolved around the classic arguments of technology as a socially neutral force versus the competing view that every tool has important societal implications built in. As with most discussions of this type the absolutist positions on either side of the issue are untenable in the policy-making realm. To ignore technology's impact on society is irresponsible, though it is equally irresponsible to halt all progress and innovation until every ramification of a given technology is known. One view that shades to the side of technological neutrality, which this author terms the "technologist position," is that cookies can only contain information voluntarily submitted to a Web site, and because that information can only be read by computers in the same domain that issued the cookie, there is no harm to the individual. In *Web Site Stats*, Rick Stout states the case this way:

There's not really any motivation to turn cookies off—they're virtually completely benign. All they really do is allow the web server to associate hits from the user's browser with previous hits (and visits) from that browser.

Despite the facts, some people will still ask how to turn off cookies. The answer is that there is really no way to disable the acceptance of a cookie. . . . The two largest and most important browser developers are 100 percent behind supporting cookies, and they don't provide any way for users to turn them off. I expect other developers will follow suit and there will be fewer and fewer browsers that don't support cookies. I agree there should be no way to turn them off—there's no compelling reason for it. . . . Imagine getting mad at the phone company because a phone call could be traced.[14]

Jerry Kang paraphrases this sentiment from the consumer's perspective.

By contrast, in cyberspace, the exception becomes the norm: Every interaction is like the credit card purchase. In this alternate universe, you are invisibly stamped with a bar code as soon as you venture outside your home. There are entities called "road" providers, who provide the streets and ground you walk on, who track precisely where, when, and how fast you traverse the lands, in order to charge you for your wear on the infrastructure. As soon as you enter the cyber-mall's domain, the mall begins to track you through invisible scanners focused on your bar code. It automatically records which stores you visit, which windows you peer into, in which order, and for how long. The specific stores collect even more detailed data when you enter their domain. For example, the cyber-bookstore notes which magazines you flipped through, recording which pages you have seen, for how long, and notes the pattern, if any, of your browsing. It notes that you picked up briefly a health magazine featuring an article on St. John's Wort, read for seven minutes a news weekly detailing a politician's sex scandal, and flipped ever-so-quickly through a tabloid claiming that Elvis lives. Of course, whenever any item is actually purchased, the store as well as the credit, debit, or virtual cash company that provides payment through cyberspace take careful notes of what you bought.[15]

Both Netscape and Microsoft subsequently built in ways for users to manage cookies, whether by blocking them entirely or accepting them on an "ask first" basis. The issue of how cookies can be used to track user movements and correlate online information with offline records like phone listings will be explored in some depth later in this chapter.

GLOBAL UNIQUE IDENTIFIERS

While cookies often store information a user provides to a site, they can also be used to record information assigned to that user by the Web server software. A popular form of such information is the Global Unique Identifier (GUID), a random thirty-two-character string that is usually based on a site visitor's IP address and the address of the hosting site. In the same way that servers can combine cookies with banner advertising to track users movements, it is possible to link to a central site that maintains records of GUIDs (like http://www.guid.org) and associate the user's movements with the GUID. As with cookies, a GUID is assigned to a particular computer, not to a user. The worth of information associated with a GUID decreases quickly if more than one user uses a computer to surf the Web. There are other uses for GUIDs, such as assigning a user a GUID and requiring them to register a piece of software by providing information such as an e-mail address (to which the product activation code is sent, ensuring the address is correct), name, street address, and phone number. With that information on record and associated with a GUID, cooperating companies could create a detailed profile of the primary user of that machine.

Once a user's data has been captured, the data controller must be able to process the data to gain full advantage of it. The Web log processing software presented earlier offers a relatively simple way to perform such an analysis, but when a user is moving across sites and performing more actions than just changing Web pages (like viewing specific types of content), then the processing software must take that into account and make judgments about the user and his or her interests. One example of a software package that captures more than the standard log information is DoubleClick's AdServer Enterprise, which offers reports that answer questions like the following:

- How many clicks did each ad receive?
- What was the average reach and frequency?
- How many impressions did each ad and campaign receive?

AdServer Enterprise's powerful reporting package also does the following:

- Automatically generates reports into formats that follow specific agency spreadsheet guidelines, eliminating the need to cut and paste information.
- Using AdInsight, you can publish reports directly on the Internet for remote access and analysis of information by advertisers and ad agencies.
- Gives complete control over the types of reports each advertiser receives, as well as the schedule by which these reports get delivered.
- Extensive and detailed site reports enable you to quickly analyze advertising activity across your entire site. AdServer Enterprise's built-in site reports correlate usage patterns and user profiles to help answer a number of key questions, including
  - How does the ad media type affect user response?
  - Who is viewing an ad?
- Generate billing reports for entire ad campaigns.
- Using HTML or spreadsheet formats, you can easily customize reports for each advertiser or ad agency with logos or template headers.
- Use your favorite SQL reporting tools to develop entirely new reports.[16]

This type of analysis is called *data mining*: The data owner is looking for an interesting pattern in the data. In the case of DoubleClick's AdServer, that pattern could relate to a set of ads, a set of users, a time of day, or a given product line.

Two incidents where GUIDs brought privacy concerns to the fore involved a site-based customization program and a music managing and playing software program.

Comet Cursor

As mentioned earlier, one way to use cookies (and also GUIDs) is in site personalization; the more a site knows about a user, the better it can tailor its offerings for that user. But personalization does not always have to mean a unique presentation of a site's home page—the customization can be something as simple as an advertisement or a welcome message for the user. One relatively unobtrusive but visible way to change a user's experience of a Web site it is to change the appearance of the user's cursor, the on-screen indicator of where the user's mouse pointer is located. The standard shape for the cursor is an arrow, but one way to change that appearance is by installing custom software and a collection of images. In November 1999 a minor furor arose over the methods Comet Systems employed as part of a cursor customization program. The company created software that changes the cursor to a more interesting image than the arrow, including small-scale versions of logos of companies that pay Comet Systems for the privilege.

Comet Systems generates revenue by charging its clients a fee to include their logos in the software. Some clients pay a flat fee, while others pay on a "per impression" basis, meaning that every time a user clicks their mouse button, the advertiser whose logo is active is charged for one impression. As part of the Comet Cursor installation process, Comet Systems places a program to track the amount of time each cursor is visible on the user's computer. Web site hosts can modify their sites so users with My Comet Cursor installed will see a customized cursor rather than the standard arrow by adding a few simple lines of code to their site; that code allows them to change the user's cursor to a 32×32 pixel image of the advertiser's choosing while the user is visiting the site. If the user moves the cursor outside the Web browser window, the cursor changes back to the image the user chose.

The My Custom Cursor software sends the information it collects to Comet Systems via the Internet, allowing the company to calculate the total number of impressions for each advertiser and to bill accordingly. At no time during the installation process does Comet Systems ask for personally identifiable information, but the company does include a GUID with the software and associates the "face time" of a given cursor with that GUID. The software also notes when the cursor image on a computer changes and sends that information to the central server. Because the information is transmitted via a Web connection, there may also be a transfer or combined log entry that corresponds to the GUID, with that log containing the IP address of the machine the user has used to connect to the Internet. It is the possibility that the My Custom Cursor data, while innocuous by itself, could be combined with other information included in a user's Web transactions (like an IP address, the page the user is visiting when the transfer is made, the time of the transaction, etc.) to generate profiles of a user that raised alarm bells in the privacy and consumer-protection communities.

Another aspect of Comet Cursor's data collection activities that was particularly troubling for privacy advocates was that the company did not disclose to the users who downloaded their software (the company says there were 26 million in late February 2000) that information about their usage was being recorded. Wired News reported on November 30, 1999, that Richard

Smith, a software analyst credited with discovering and publishing information on numerous privacy-related concerns about popular programs, informed Comet Cursor that he had discovered that user data was being sent to the company's servers without disclosing that practice to users who installed the software. Within a week, the company had updated their Web site to disclose the practice.[17] The current policy reads as follows:

Our software contacts our servers to record logs of cursor impressions using a GUID (Globally Unique IDentifier). When you download the Comet Cursor software, it is issued a GUID from our servers. Using this GUID, we can keep track of how many people are using our software. The GUID is also used every time the software contacts our servers when we log cursors changing. . . . Collecting such statistics is an audit mechanism we use to bill our clients, since some of them pay us on a "per-cursor-impression" basis.

Second, our software checks in to see if a new version of the Comet Cursor software is available. If there is a bug fix or version upgrade available for the Comet Cursor, the software will retrieve the new code and replace the outdated code.[18]

One aspect of the Custom Cursor program that riled some observers is that some of the sites that implemented the program were targeted at children. Vice President Al Gore's Web site used the technology to make its kid's section more attractive but, after being informed that some user data was tracked by the company, chose to discontinue using the service.[19]

RealJukebox

Another company that chose to assign users GUIDs is RealNetworks, a company that creates software that allows site administrators to build and deliver audio and video files via the Web. Beyond its core production and editing package, RealNetworks distributes a number of programs that allow users to view online video and to listen to audio files. One of those programs is RealJukebox, a utility program that allows users to listen to audio CDs on their computers and to create music libraries by copying songs to their hard drives. RealNetworks also used the program to collect information about its users, beginning with the information requested when a user downloaded RealJukebox—the vendor required users to enter their e-mail address and demographic information as part of the registration process. The comingling of the e-mail address and the GUID made it possible to link a user's identity with their online behavior, a capability that brought strong objections from the privacy community. RealNetworks notes that they did not correlate any personally identifiable information with GUID-related data, but admits the possibility existed for them to do so. In the aftermath of the flare-up, RealNetworks released a patch (a program that modifies an existing software package) that set every user's GUID to all zeros and clarified their position on privacy.

The data RealNetworks was collecting was meant to provide statistics regarding aggregate use of RealJukebox, not individual use. Nonetheless the company will cease the collection of the type of data that led to the privacy concerns raised until such time as the company enhances how it provides for clear informed consent and reviews those enhancements with outside privacy experts.[20]

As of late October 1999 the RealNetworks privacy policy did not reflect the company's practice of assigning computers a GUID and tracking songs in users' libraries, the types of devices they used to listen to music, and whether they received automated music downloads from the Internet.[21] Jason Catlett, the founder of consumer-rights watchdog group Junkbusters, discovered that RealNetworks had changed their policy while he was writing a letter to TRUSTe, an online privacy-monitoring organization.[22]

Austin Hill, president of Zero-Knowledge Systems, a Montreal-based firm that specializes in Internet privacy technologies, points to online retailer Amazon as an example of a company that uses cookies and other identifying technologies responsibly. Amazon allows users to form "purchase circles." "Amazon is very clear about what they do, and they're using it to refer you books. As you browse around they're learning about what you're doing and where you're going. [The data] will be used in a profile, but it's done [with] openness and honesty," *Wired News* quoted Hill as saying.[23] The relevant part of Amazon's privacy page reads as follows:

For Purchase Circles, we group the items we send to particular ZIP and postal codes, and the items ordered from each domain name. We then aggregate this anonymous data and apply an algorithm that constructs bestseller lists of items that are more popular with each specific group than with the general population. None of the data is associated with any individual's name.[24]

DoubleClick

While both Comet Systems and RealNetworks have come under heavy fire from privacy advocates regarding their use of GUIDs, neither of those companies have faced the firestorm of protests raised against DoubleClick, a leading Web-based advertisement management and server firm. According to the company's Web site, DoubleClick serves over 1.5 billion advertisements per day, allowing the company to generate connections from users viewing the page where the ads are presented. Where possible, DoubleClick sets a cookie on the computer of the user viewing the ad. Figure 7.14 contains a shot of the cookie, as seen through Karen Kenworthy's Cookie Viewer program. Note that the cookie is available to any computer in the domain doubleclick.net and that it contains an identification number—in this case, dd3d90e9. This configuration indicates that DoubleClick uses a combination of a GUID and a cookie to mark each user's computer; when a machine from the domain doubleclick.net serves for a Web site, it downloads the computer's GUID

Figure 7.14
Double-Click Cookie as Viewed with WinMag Cookie Viewer

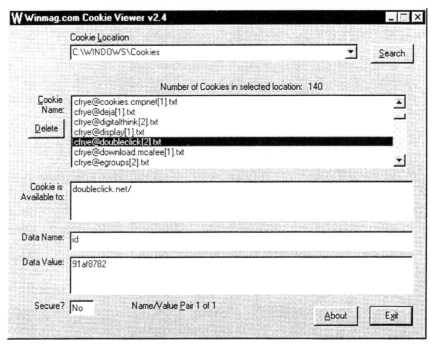

Source: Karen Kenworthy, program creator. Used by permission. Available <http://www.winmag.com/karen/ptcookie.htm>.

from the cookie and creates transaction records (most likely of the ad viewed, a time/date stamp, the number of times that ad has been viewed, and whether or not the user clicked the ad to visit the advertiser's site) with the GUID included. By compiling and analyzing a user's activities, DoubleClick can determine which ads a user is more likely to click and to use that information to justify higher rates for its advertisers and to benefit users by presenting them with information they are more likely to find interesting and useful.

Generating Profiles

The downside to collecting user transaction data is that over time DoubleClick and similar companies can develop extensive profiles of user behavior. It remains an open question as to whether individuals would willingly provide that sort of information if they were aware of the extent of the monitoring, so ad management firms tend to keep their activities out of the public eye. In the case of DoubleClick, changes to the company's privacy policy and corporate structure have set off alarm bells in the privacy community. One version of DoubleClick's privacy policy read as follows:

On June 14, 1999, DoubleClick and Abacus Direct Corporation announced their plan to merge in the third quarter of 1999.

Abacus currently maintains a database consisting of personally-identifiable information used primarily for off-line direct marketing. DoubleClick has no rights or plans to use Abacus' database information prior to the completion of the merger. Upon completion of the merger, should DoubleClick ever match the non-personally-identifiable information collected by DoubleClick with Abacus' database information, DoubleClick will revise this Privacy Statement to accurately reflect its modified data collection and data use policies and ensure that you have adequate notice of any changes and a choice to participate.[25]

DoubleClick subsequently revised its policy to notify users it planned to combine its online tracking data with personally identifiable information such as addresses and catalog order records compiled by Abacus. As Deirdre Mulligan of the Center for Democracy and Technology noted in her testimony to the Federal Trade Commission, the ability of an advertising network or other company to change the privacy policy originally presented to users put too much of a burden on consumers to monitor and exercise choice over their information. The ability to exercise choice, she notes, depends on the consumer's awareness of advertisers' practices. In many cases, consumers are not aware of the extent, or sometimes the existence, of tracking done by advertisers.[26] Consumers are becoming more aware of these practices, however, and the public outcry over DoubleClick's policy change caused the firm to refrain from combining personally identifiable information with users' Web use data.[27]

Industry groups have responded to the challenge from privacy advocates, creating new alliances with the goal of ensuring consumers are aware of what types of tracking are performed and what they can do to opt out of the practices:

In this instance, the ad server companies that are instrumental in tracking online activity and creating online profiles have also stepped up to the self-regulatory challenge. These companies have committed to providing notice to consumers of information collection at web sites and, where personal information is collected, providing consumers with the ability to opt-out of collection and use of their data. Ten of the companies have banded together to form the Network Advertising Initiative. This Initiative will include a web site where consumers can learn more about ad targeting and online profiling technology. The web site will also contain links to the individual companies web sites, where extensive privacy policies explain the methods used and types of information collected in ad delivery, from clickstream data, and from online registrations. Where personally identifiable information is collected or combined with non-personally identifiable information, these companies offer visitors an opportunity to opt-out. Some of the companies go even further and offer opt-out for non-personally identifiable information.[28]

What Is at Stake

Collecting and processing online information is the lynch pin of DoubleClick's current business model; the potential to correlate it with personally identifiable information from other sources to generate profiles of users, and sell the results to advertisers, would greatly enhance the value of their offerings to advertisers. As the company stated in a recent filing with the Securities and Exchange Commission,

> We collect and compile information in databases for the product offerings of all our businesses. Individuals have claimed, and may claim in the future, that our collection of this information is illegal. Although we believe that we have the right to use and compile the information in these databases, we cannot assure you that our ability to do so will remain lawful, that any trade secret, copyright or other intellectual property protection will be available for our databases, or that statutory protection that is or becomes available for databases will enhance our rights. In addition, others may claim rights to the information in our databases. Further, pursuant to our contracts with Web publishers using our solutions, we are obligated to keep certain information regarding each Web publisher confidential and, therefore, may be restricted from further using that information in our business.[29]

DoubleClick also recognized there was significant debate about the collection and correlation of online and offline information:

> Following our announcement of the Abacus merger, we have seen a heightened public discussion and speculation about the information collection practices that will be employed in the industry generally, and specifically by us. We have publicly committed that no personally identifiable offline information about a consumer will be associated with online information about that consumer for the delivery of personally-targeted Internet advertising without first providing the consumer with notice and an opportunity to opt out of the targeted advertising. In addition, some of our contracts with Web publishers prevent us from developing profiles of users of their Web sites. The current debate about data collection practices may cause additional Web publishers to seek similar contractual provisions in their agreements with us. Computer users may also use software designed to filter or prevent the delivery of advertising to their computers.[30]

The nature of the notice and the necessity of users to opt out of the service is at the heart of the current debate, though the changing legal environment could shift the consumer's burden to opt out of the service to an affirmative obligation on the part of DoubleClick and similar firms to get the informed consent of data subjects before being allowed to collect and process their information. In that vein, DoubleClick also noted that German privacy regulations prevent the company from using cookies to track visitors to German Web sites, though there is also a significant movement in the United States, both at the federal and state levels, to restrict how DoubleClick and similar companies do business.[31]

Investigations

Several consumer-protection groups and government bodies have taken action in an attempt to prevent DoubleClick from combining online and offline information. Many of the suits were brought in California, though two others were brought in New York. Each of the suits accuses DoubleClick of engaging in unfair and deceptive business practices, of violating electronic privacy statutes (detailed in Chapter 4), and of violating the common law privacy interests of Internet users. The company also noted it had received a letter from the Federal Trade Commission, dated February 8, 2000, that the FTC was making preliminary inquiries into whether DoubleClick had engaged in unfair and deceptive practices concerning Internet users.[32]

Just after DoubleClick filed its SEC document, Attorney General Jennifer Granholm initiated legal proceedings against the company.[33] The suit, which also named online sweepstakes arranger NetDeal.com and IAF.net, an e-mail search firm, alleges DoubleClick violated the Michigan's Consumer Protection Act by engaging in unfair and deceptive business practices. A C|Net news article notes that Granholm brought the suit on behalf of Michigan consumers as a response to DoubleClick's changing privacy policies and vagueness about how they would use the information gathered. The article also points out that DoubleClick has had four different privacy policies in the three years the company has been in business, though the reporter gave no details as to the differences among the policies beyond the recent modification informing consumers of the Abacus Direct acquisition and merger.[34]

Response

In addition to making plans to defend its practices in court, DoubleClick has taken several steps to inform consumers about what the company does and how consumers can opt out of its data collection. One aspect of that program is a site called PrivacyChoices (http://www.privacychoices.com) which will host an array of consumer privacy and opt-out resources. DoubleClick has committed to a $2-million ad campaign to promote the site.[35] Other organizations, such as the Center for Democracy and Technology (http://www.cdt.org), provide links on their sites that make it possible for consumers to opt out of DoubleClick's tracking program. And, as noted earlier in this chapter, DoubleClick did bow to pressure and held off from implementing its data-matching endeavor until the federal government provides privacy standards.

Not That Simple

The problems with sharing or not sharing user tracking data can run in both directions. In December 1999 Universal Image amended a suit originally brought in June to demand as much as $4 billion from Yahoo because the search engine firm had stopped transmitting data to Universal Image about subscribers to Broadcast.com, a company that broadcast sports, music, and business meetings over the Web.[36] Yahoo, which does not usually share consumer information with its business partners, stopped sharing the information after it acquired Broadcast.com. In an interview for the Bloomberg News/ C|Net article, Universal Image's attorney Larry Friedman noted the suit was about gaining compensation for Yahoo's refusal to transfer valuable user information. "They can direct-market to them, they can sell the names to advertisers. It's gold, it's currency."[37]

SELF-REGULATION

A recurring theme throughout the American debate over how to best ensure privacy interests are met is the idea of self-regulation, where advertisers and marketing firms police themselves to ensure compliance with applicable laws. As seen in Chapter 6, the U.S. Department of Commerce has negotiated with the European Union from the base position that self-regulatory means would be sufficient to meet the EU's concerns regarding the protection of personally identifiable information transferred from the EU or concerning EU citizens. There are two prominent online privacy monitoring organizations, one supported by the Council of Better Business Bureaus (CBBB) and the other by TRUSTe, an industry-supported group.

BBB*Online*

In March 1999 the Council of Better Business Bureaus launched BBB*Online*, a privacy seal organization used to put a CBBB "stamp of approval" on Web sites that protect user privacy. The organization requires Web sites to post privacy policies and to allow BBB*Online* or their designee to randomly investigate members to ensure the organization is following program guidelines. BBB*Online* also follows up on any complaints from users; organizations that violate their posted policies can have their seal revoked and their names put on a revocation list. The BBB*Online* allows potential participants to download an agreement that defines terms and sets out the program's expectations; the site also contains a draft privacy policy, but allows participants significant leeway in what they can and cannot do with personally identifiable information. The BBB*Online* policy page states the folowing:

The following sample privacy notice describes basic information practices for a single website directed to U.S. residents. Additional disclosures would be required for website operators that:

- limit the application of the privacy notice to U.S. residents,
- share individually identifiable information collected online with unaffiliated third parties or corporate affiliates not governed by the same privacy policy,

- direct part of their website to children or collect information from online visitors actually known to be children,
- enhance or merge individually identifiable information or prospect information collected online with data from third parties for the purposes of marketing products or services to the subject of that information,
- apply the privacy notice provisions to everyone except those operating solely in a business capacity,
- limit the scope of the BBB*OnLine* privacy seal by excluding in the application corporate subsidiaries, operating divisions, or websites devoted to other discrete product lines,
- condition access to any part of the website on the disclosure of individually identifiable information,
- allow other organizations to collect individually identifiable information or prospect information by interacting directly with online visitors at the applicant's website,
- collect passive information (including cookie information) that is linked to a name or similarly specific identifier,
- use prospect information for any purpose other than those for which the information was submitted, or
- limit access to maintained individually identifiable information or prospect information by limiting the frequency of requests or by requiring a processing fee; or limit access due to an inability to retrieve such information in the ordinary course of business.[38]

In addition to allowing these practices, given notice to the consumer in a site's privacy policy, the BBB*Online* program is specifically limited to monitoring how participants handle data acquired online: The program's participation agreement defines "individually identifiable information" to exclude information gathered about an individual offline.[39] It is worth noting that many of the practices the BBB*Online* program allows, given notice in a site's privacy policy, including the differentiation between information acquired online and offline, run contrary to the limitations required by the European Union's Data Directive.

TRUSTe

Another, perhaps better-known online "trust mark" program is that run by TRUSTe, formerly known as eTRUST. TRUSTe was founded in 1996 with the goal of creating a recognizable brand that, when displayed on a Web site, indicated to visitors that the site had a privacy policy and had signed up with a program to monitor their compliance with it. The original TRUSTe program allowed subscribing sites to display one of several logos, indicating whether the site shared data with third parties or not. The current program has only two logos: one for the main TRUSTe program and another for the group's children's privacy program. As with BBB*Online*, TRUSTe requires participants to publish a privacy policy disclosing their information practices and to allow TRUSTe to monitor subscriber compliance with those policies. The TRUSTe program does not prohibit participants from sharing or processing personally identifiable information, but it does require sites to inform visitors if they do so.

The TRUSTe licensing agreement defines personally identifiable information as anything that can be used to identify, locate, or contact an individual. If information that would normally not identify a specific individual (such as financial profiles, transaction records, and so forth) is combined with personally identifiable information, the lot of the information is considered personally identifiable information for the purposes of the contract.[40] The license agreement places the following requirement on subscribers:

Licensee shall not make Personally Identifiable Information and/or Third Party Personally Identifiable Information available to the general public in any form (including but not limited to on-line directories and customer lists) without the prior written or electronic consent of the individual identified, except that this paragraph shall not prevent or restrict Licensee from (i) distributing information that is already publicly available, including but not limited to information available in public telephone directories, classified ads, newspaper reports, publications, and the like.[41]

The nature of publicly available information is somewhat vague, even with the examples provided in the policy, giving rise to a number of questions. One situation where classifying information as "publicly available" is when a user's address and phone number are available in a telephone listing and the user provides that information to a TRUSTe-certified site.

Joel Reidenberg, a professor of law at Fordham University, argues that the level of trust engendered by a TRUSTe should be tempered because the organization has not followed through on its policies. Reidenberg writes,

These examples themselves demonstrate the structural defects in self-regulatory theory. TRUSTe, for example, is a program through which websites agree to dislcose their privacy policies and license the right to use a special logo designating the site as one that protects privacy. TRUSTe may audit licensees to verify compliance with the stated privacy policy. However, the program has a few major problems. Although about 450 companies are licensed to use the logo to date, this number is trivial compared to the number of website operators in the United States. In fact, one of the companies, GeoCities, holds the distinction of being the first company prosecuted by the Federal Trade Commission for information trafficking, and fifty percent of the TRUSTe sponsors do not bother to subscribe to the program and to license the logo.[42]

TRUSTe has also come under fairly sharp criticism for failing to investigate a number of privacy-related practices which went undisclosed by trustmark affiliates. The RealJukebox software case is one such incident; the other dealt with Microsoft's Windows 98 operating system software. In both instances the software placed a GUID on a user's computer, with neither company disclosing that practice on their company Web site. TRUSTe declined to investigate both practices because at that time the program was limited in scope to collecting and processing information via the Web site, but not through other Internet-based methods.[43]

CONCLUSIONS

The range of user tracking tools available to online merchants is staggering. From Web log file analysis services and programs to more advanced methods like cookies and GUIDs that allow advertisement managers and site administrators to track user movements, the tools for collecting and processing enormous amounts of data about users and correlating those data with individuals have never been stronger. There are two major trustmark programs available, but both programs are in their relative infancy and, as of January 2000, neither has revoked an affiliate's right to use their marks. Not surprisingly, users have taken measures that allow them to stave off such tracking and to protect their personally identifiable information. The next chapter looks at those tools and how they might impact online commerce.

NOTES

1. Heather Green, "A Little Net Privacy, Please," *Businessweek*, 16 March 1998. Available <http://www.businessweek.com/1998/11/b3569104.htm>.

2. Paul Albitz and Cricket Liu, *DNS and Bind*, 3d ed. (Sebastopol, Calif.: O'Reilly & Associates, 1998), 18.

3. One such source is <http://digitalid.verisign.com/ccodes.html>.

4. Rick Stout, *Web Site Stats: Tracking Hits and Analyzing Traffic* (New York: Osborne/McGraw-Hill, 1997), 35.

5. Ibid., 246.

6. Ibid., 247.

7. Ibid.

8. Ibid., 249.

9. Ibid., 249–250.

10. Netscape, *Persistent Client State HTTP Cookies*. Available <http://www.netscape.com/newsref/std/cookie_spec.html>.

11. Ibid.

12. Robbin Zeff and Brad Aronson, *Advertising on the Internet*, 2d ed. (New York: John Wiley & Sons, 1999), 110.

13. Stout, *Web Site Stats*, 84.

14. Ibid., 86.

15. Jerry Kang, "Information Privacy in Cyberspace Transactions," *Stanford Law Review* 50, no. 4 (1998): 1198–1199.

16. DoubleClick, *AdServer 3.5 Key Features*, 1999. Available <http://www.doubleclick.net:8080/publishers/software/adserver35enterprise/keyfeatures. htm>.

17. Chris Oakes, "Mouse Pointer Records Clicks," *Wired News*, 30 November 1999. Available <http://www.wired.com/news/print/0,1294,32788,00.html>.

18. Comet Systems, *Privacy Policy*. Available <http://www.cometcursor.com/help/privacy.shtml>.

19. Ibid.

20. RealNetworks, *RealNetworks Issues Patch to Address Privacy Concerns of Users* (press release), 1 November 1999. Available <http://www.realnetworks.com/company/pressroom/pr/99/updateadvisory.html>.

21. RealNetworks, *Privacy Policy*, 10 October 1999. Available <http://www.realnetworks.com/company/privacy/index.html>.

22. Courtney Macavinta, "RealNetworks Changes Privacy Policy Under Scrutiny," *C|NET News.com*, 1 November 1999. Available <http://news.cnet.com/category/0-1005-200-1426044.html>.

23. Chris Oakes, "The Electronic Tattoo To-Do," *Wired News*, 11 November 1999. Available <http://www.wired.com/news/technology/0,1282,32389-3,00.html>.

24. Amazon.com, *Privacy Policy*, 10 April 1999. Available <http://www.amazon.com/exec/obidos/subst/misc/policy/privacy.html>.

25. Jason Catlett, "Profiling: Comments to the Dept. of Commerce and Federal Trade Commission," *Online Profiling Project*, 18 October 1999. Available <http://www.ftc.gov/bcp/profiling/comments/catlett.htm>.

26. Deirdre Mulligan, "Testimony of the Center for Democracy and Technology Before the Federal Trade Commission," *Public Workshop on Online Profiling*, 30 November 1999, 3.

27. Chris Oakes, "A Turning Point for E-Privacy," *Wired News*, 4 March 2000. Available <http://www.wired.com/news/politics/0,1283,34734,00.html>.

28. Rita D. Cohen, "Comments from Magazine Publishers of America." *Online Profiling Project*, 30 November 1999. Available <http://www.ftc.gov/bcp/profiling/comments/cohen.htm>.

29. DoubleClick, Inc., *Amendment No. 1 to Form S-3 Registration Statement under the Securities Act of 1933* (SEC Document 0000950117-00-000281 as filed with the Securities and Exchange Commission on 14 February 2000), 12. Available <http://www.sec.gov/Archives/edgar/data/1049480/0000950117-00-000281-index.html>.

30. Ibid., 16.

31. Ibid., 15.

32. Ibid., 42.

33. Jennifer Cranholm, untitled press release, 17 February 2000. Available <http://167.240.254.37/AGWebSite/press_release/pr10164.htm>.

34. Patricia Jacobus, "Michigan Initiates DoubleClick Inquiry," *C|Net News.com*, 17 February 2000. Available <http://news.cnet.com/category/0-1005-200-1553030.html>.

35. Ibid.

36. Bloomberg News, "Yahoo Sued Over Business Partner's Claim to User Data," *C|Net News.com*, 23 December 1999. Available <http://news.cnet.com/category/0-1005-200-1505410.html>.

37. Ibid.

38. Council of Better Business Bureaus, *BBBOnline Sample Privacy Policy*, 1999. Available <http://www.bbbonline.org/businesses/privacy/sample.html>.

39. Council of Better Business Bureaus, *BBBOnline Privacy Program Participation Agreement*, 1999. Available <http://www.bbbonline.org/download/license.PDF>.

40. *TRUSTe License Agreement Rev. 5.01*, 19 August 1999. Available <http://www.truste.org/webpublishers/pub_agreement.html>.

41. Ibid.

42. Joel Reidenberg, "Restoring American Privacy," *Berkeley Technology Law Journal* 14, no. 2 (1999): 777.

43. Chris Oakes, "TRUSTe Declines Real Probe," *Wired News*, 9 November 1999. Available <http://www.wired.com/news/technology/0,1282,32388,00.html>.

8

Privacy-Enhancing Technologies

Chapter 7 described the technologies and methods online advertisers and site administrators can use to identify and track Web site visitors. Several groups, including the Electronic Privacy Information Center, the Center for Democracy and Technology, and the Electronic Frontier Foundation, have taken significant legal actions to halt what they perceive as overly invasive practices on the part of online advertisers. Because the Internet offers such groups the ability to propagate their message inexpensively to an audience that, as a general rule, has the knowledge and Internet experience to understand a fairly complex issue without a great deal of technical exposition, those messages have taken hold. Techniques for avoiding or confusing data trackers range from the very simple, such as friends exchanging supermarket buyer's club cards every time a reward level is reached or supplying false information on application forms, to using sophisticated cryptography formerly only available to government agencies. This chapter examines the tools available for users to maintain their privacy and to resist advertisers' attempts to collect information about them. Specifically, this chapter addresses the following:

- Cryptography.
- Digital certificates.
- Cookie management software.

- Anonymizing Web surfing proxies.
- Zero Knowledge's Freedom service.
- Infomediaries.

CRYPTOGRAPHY

From the very beginning of spoken human interaction, groups of individuals have undertaken to keep their communications secret from others. In some cases that drive for secrecy led to whispered conversations behind a curtain, but "security through obscurity" is no security at all: One must assume that any conversation that can be detected will be detected. To defeat eavesdropping, or at least to detect it, communicators developed *cryptography*, literally "secret writing." One type of encryption scheme is a *code*, where a word or other unique identifier (such as a flag wave or smoke signal) was substituted for another word. Another type of encryption scheme is the *cipher*, where individual letters or characters were substituted for others. One such example is the Caesar's cipher, used by postal agents in ancient Rome. That system saw each letter increased by three values in the alphabet; in English the effect would be to write the word "dog" as "grj." There are two serious problems with this simple cipher, the first of which is that it follows a regular pattern and, if a person who obtained the encrypted message, or *ciphertext*, knew or was able to guess the pattern then the original message, or *plaintext*, was readily available. Such guessing was made easier by the second weakness, that every letter in the original message was only represented in ciphertext by another letter. That is, using Caesar's cipher to encrypt a message meant that every "d" would be replaced by a "g."

A marginally more sophisticated method of encrypting data is to vary the number of spaces in the alphabet that each letter is incremented. One way to do that is to assign a *key*, which is a word that is used to increment the letters in the plaintext to generate the ciphertext (to *encrypt* the message). Figure 8.1 shows an example of how it works, using the plaintext message, "A message to be encrypted," and the key, "cab," which is repeated until the end of the text. Every letter that occurs above a "c" is incremented three places, every letter that occurs above an "a" is incremented one place, and every letter that occurs above a "b" is incremented two places. To derive the plaintext from the ciphertext, or *decrypt* the message, the key is once again lined up with the ciphertext and the value of the letter in the key is subtracted from the ciphertext to generate the plaintext. There are many more sophisticated ways of determining what letter to substitute for a letter in the plaintext—a comprehensive history of cryptography is Kahn's *The Codebreakers*, which covers the range of cryptographic schemes from ancient times through the present day.[1] Cryptography is essential to creating trustable communications on the Internet, especially for electronic commerce applications where sensitive personal data are being transmitted.

Figure 8.1
Encrypted Message Using the Key "cab"

```
amessagetobeencrypted
cabcabcabcabcabcabcab
dngvtcjfvrcghoeuzrwff
```

The next section of this chapter looks at two different types of methods to encrypt and decrypt messages: *symmetric* and *asymmetric* algorithms.

Symmetric Cryptography

Simply put, a symmetric encryption algorithm is an algorithm where the same key is used to encrypt and decrypt the message, meaning that both the sender and the recipient must know the key for the message to be sent successfully. The key could be communicated by phone, but in most cases the parties to the communication use a trusted courier to transfer the key from the sender to the recipient.[2] The necessity of transferring the key also puts the communicators in a bind: Either they need to use a key from a previous interchange, or *session*, or they need to wait until the key can be transmitted from the sender to the receiver. It is also the case the if an attacker is able to decrypt one message encrypted with a key, they will then be able to decrypt every message encrypted with that key. Simson Garfinkel and Gene Spafford offer the following list of factors influencing an algorithm's strength:

- The secrecy of the key.
- The difficulty of guessing the key or trying out all possible keys. . . .
- The difficulty of inverting the encryption algorithm without knowing the encryption key. . . .
- The existence (or lack) of *back doors*, or additional ways by which an encrypted file can be decrypted more easily without knowing the key.
- The ability to decrypt an entire encrypted message if you know the way that a portion of the message decrypts (called a *known plaintext attack*).
- The properties of the plaintext and knowledge of those properties by an attacker.[3]

There are a number of popular symmetric key encryption algorithms.

Data Encryption Standard

The Data Encryption Standard (DES), based on a IBM encryption algorithm named Lucifer, was adopted in 1977 as the U.S. government standard for encryption. In its original form, DES used a key that was 56 bits long, meaning that the number of potential keys (the *key space*) was just over 72 quadrillion keys. In the 1970s and 1980s the key space was large enough to prevent casual users from attempting every possible key and decrypting a message (a brute force attack), but many researchers assumed that cracking DES using special-purpose hardware would be relatively inexpensive. A Stanford computer-science professor estimated that building a machine that could crack a DES-encrypted message in a day would cost about $20 million, though over time that cost has fallen dramatically.[4] Michael J. Wiener estimated that in 1998 it would be possible to build a machine for $1 million that could crack a 56-bit DES key in an average of thirty-five minutes.[5] The book *Cracking DES* describes the design process and gives the design documentation for a custom DES cracker the Electronic Frontier Foundation, a San Francisco–based public interest advocacy group, designed and built for $200,000. That machine cracked a 56-bit DES key in fifty-six hours using somewhat outdated technology and largely donated time on the part of its software programmers and implementers.

DESX

The DESX algorithm is an improved version of DES that uses two additional rounds of data processing to make it impossible for parties to decrypt a message with a brute force attack. For a brute force attack to be successful, the software or hardware automating the attack must be able to recognize possible plaintexts so it can limit the amount of computational cycles it wastes on incorrect keys (usually the first eight or ten characters of a message are examined). Because the message has been modified so the correct plaintext is not recognizable as words in a known language, the software will never find the proper key. DESX is susceptible to other attacks, however.[6]

Triple-DES

Triple-DES entails encrypting a message three times with DES, each time using a new key. In theory this process doubles the security of the original DES algorithm and, like DESX, removes the possibility of finding a recognizable chunk of plaintext from the original message on the first or second pass.

Blowfish

According to Counterpane Internet Security's Web site,

Blowfish is a symmetric block cipher that can be used as a drop-in replacement for DES or IDEA. It takes a variable-length key, from 32 bits to 448 bits, making it ideal for both domestic and exportable use. Blowfish was designed in 1993 by Bruce Schneier as a fast, free alternative to existing encryption algorithms. Since then it has been analyzed considerably, and it is slowly gaining acceptance as a strong encryption algorithm. Blowfish is unpatented and license-free, and is available free for all uses.[7]

Blowfish's descendent Twofish is a candidate for the Advanced Encryption Standard, a competition run by the National Institute of Standards and Technology to pick a successor for DES.[8]

IDEA

This is the International Data Encryption Algorithm, the description of which was published in 1990 by Massey and Lai.[9] IDEA uses a 128-bit key but is not widely implemented because the algorithm is patented.

RC2, RC4, and RC5

These ciphers were developed by Ron Rivest, an originator of the RSA (Rivest, Shamir, Adelman) algorithm. The first two were originally held as trade secrets by RSA Data Security, though anonymous individuals posted RC2 and RC4 to newsgroups in 1996 and 1994, respectively. RC5 was published by Rivest in 1994.

Asymmetric Cryptography

The main problem with symmetric encryption algorithms is that regardless of an algorithm's security, there is no way to send messages spontaneously without reusing a key, a security nightmare. In 1975 Stanford researchers Whitfield Diffie and Martin Hellman published a paper describing the notion of *public key* cryptography, which solved the problem of key transfer associated with symmetric algorithms.[10] The details of the Diffie–Hellman scheme are well beyond the scope of this book, but the practical application of their conception was that a key could be broken into two pieces, with one half of the key published widely and the other half kept secret, and used to send and receive encrypted messages. That is, if a third party wanted to send an encrypted message to an individual whose published key was available from a database of keys (called a *key server*), the sender could encrypt the message with the recipient's public key and be sure the recipient would only be able to decrypt it using the matching half of the original key (called the *private key*). The process also works for multiple recipients: To encrypt a message to be read by more than one recipient, the sender encrypts the message with every recipient's public key. Other benefits of public key encryption are that messages may be signed electronically so they are indisputably from the controller of a private key, meaning the sender can prove he or she sent a particular message and the user cannot deny they sent it.

One problem with public key encryption methods is that they are computationally very expensive. They use much longer keys and are built on the premise that it is very difficult to factor numbers that are the multiplicative product of two large prime numbers. In this case, large means 100-digit prime numbers. Rather than slow down the communications process by using public key encryption for the entire session, most secure communications systems generate a symmetric key and then use public key encryption to send the key securely across the connection. Once the symmetric key is received and verified by sending it back to the device that initiated the communication, the devices may then use the much more efficient symmetric encryption method. Another problem concerns managing and verifying the authenticity of public keys. In other words, who verifies that an individual who has signed a message with a key is actually that individual? The answers lie in the formation of a public key infrastructure (PKI), an important component of which is *certification authorities*.

Public Key Infrastructure

The 1990s saw significant debate and technological development regarding the handling of public key encryption. From a technological standpoint, there were several difficulties in establishing a workable public key infrastructure, where users would be able to publish their public keys, revoke their keys when necessary, find the keys of other users, and prevent users from falsifying a key or key revocation. A workable PKI would need to consist of national databases that maintained lists of active and revoked keys. The difficulty in using public key systems is the huge number of active and revoked keys that accumulate in the system. For example, imagine a company with 50,000 employees that decided to create an internal PKI and administer it. The size of the key files, the need to issue and check key revocations, and the security measures that would need to be put in place could swamp even the most technologically savvy company's ability to handle their infrastructure. As noted in the discussion of the Clipper Chip in Chapter 5, the U.S. government attempted to create a PKI where the government maintained copies of individuals' and organizations' secret keys, both to prevent loss and to allow law-enforcement agencies to have access to a party's encrypted communications. Privacy concerns eventually caused the downfall of the scheme, but the lack of a central, trusted authority administering the public key infrastructure is a significant problem that must be overcome for public key cryptography to become truly widespread.

Certifying Authorities

At some point in any system there has to be someone or something you can trust. Organizations that establish themselves as those trustworthy bodies within a PKI are called certifying authorities (also known as certification authorities or CAs). One such authority is VeriSign (http://www.verisign.com), which recently acquired its largest competitor, the South African firm Thawte Consulting (http://www.thawte.com). A CA issues items called *digital cer-*

tificates, which are essentially additional secret keys that are bound to an individual's identity. The CA or its representative verifies information about the individual applying for the key (whether just that person's e-mail address or as extensive as their name, address, corporate affiliation, and Social Security Number), and includes that information in that user's digital certificate.[11] If a recipient of a digitally signed communication wants to verify the user's certificate is valid, the recipient can visit VeriSign's key server and check the signature versus the information VeriSign has stored in its database.

While having a certificate from a well-known certification authority is not absolute proof that the party on the other end of an Internet transaction is who they say they are, the presence of a certificate indicates that the CA or its representative checked the applicant's bona fides and was satisfied that they were who they claimed to be. If the information on a certificate can be correlated with public record data, such as corporation listing, then consumers can place their trust in the organization more completely.

Pretty Good Privacy

One of the earliest publicly available programs that allowed individuals to use public key encryption technologies was Phil Zimmerman's program Pretty Good Privacy (PGP). PGP was written in 1991 and released on the Internet in June of that year, sparking an investigation by the U.S. government into whether Zimmerman himself had violated American export laws by posting the program to the Internet and allowing non-Americans access to technology regulated under the International Trafficking in Arms Regulations (ITAR). The government eventually declined to prosecute Zimmerman, but only after the programmer had committed significant time and legal expense to his defense. PGP uses the RSA public key algorithm for key exchange and relies on the IDEA symmetric cipher for encrypted sessions once the connection has been established via the RSA public key exchange. The rights to distribute and package PGP are now owned by Network Associates (http://www.nai.com), though it is still available for free for noncommercial use over the Web from the Massachusetts Institute of Technology. The basic PGP tool runs as a stand-alone program, but the PGP engine has been included in a number of other security products from Network Associates, including tools that allow users to form *virtual private networks* (VPNs) by encrypting Internet communications between systems. PGP is an important tool from use and advocacy—the program gave users the ability to encrypt their communications and created a rallying point for the online privacy community that raised awareness among Internet users throughout the early and mid-1990s.

Secure Sockets Layer

On the World Wide Web, the leading practical application of these cryptographic techniques is through the Secure Sockets Layer (SSL) protocol. SSL allows Web surfers to make secure connections to sites and transfer their personal information, including credit card numbers, without concern that their information could be read easily. SSL, which was introduced in 1994 by Netscape and is currently on version 3.0, encrypts traffic sent between Internet-connected computers and can be used for World Wide Web, newsgroups, e-mail, file transfers, and so on without restriction. This flexibility does mean that SSL is not optimized for any single operation, so performing the requisite encryption and decryption means that the user will need to wait longer for their information to be transferred over the Internet.[12] Garfinkel and Spafford note that some users have reported slowdowns of up to 50 percent, but that users with fast computers and relatively slow Internet connections will see much less degradation, especially if they send high volumes of information among few sessions.[13]

How SSL Works

To establish an SSL connection over the World Wide Web, the computer that wishes to initiate the secure transaction links to a Web page with the prefix https://, which indicates an SSL-enabled page. The computers then go through a series of negotiations in which they attempt to establish the cryptographic algorithms that will be used to encrypt the session's contents. Figure 8.2 shows the mechanics of the operation. In the first step, the client computer (that is, the computer attempting to connect to the secure page) sends a request to initiate a secure connection. The server acknowledges the attempt, sends a copy of its digital certificate, and requests that the connecting computer send a copy of its digital certificate (many browsers have a built-in certificate that can be used for these transactions but do not identify the party holding the certificate). Once the server receives the client's digital certificate, it uses that certificate as a public key to encrypt and send a session key to encrypt the remainder of the traffic for this connection. The client receives the session key, decrypts it, re-encrypts it using the server's digital certificate, and transmits the result to the server. The server then decrypts the session key sent by the client computer—if the decrypted key matches the key the server sent originally, the machines have verifiably established a secure connection. The computers then mutually agree on a series of cryptographic algorithms they can use for the rest of the connection and, once the algorithms are agreed to, end the negotiation (or *handshake*) and begin transmitting encrypted data.[14]

Potential Problems with SSL

Early versions of SSL had a variety of security problems, including weaknesses in the random-number generators and in the protocol itself that allowed attackers either to guess the prime number factors used to generate a key or to bypass the encryption altogether. Those problems were subsequently

Figure 8.2
SSL Connection Handshake

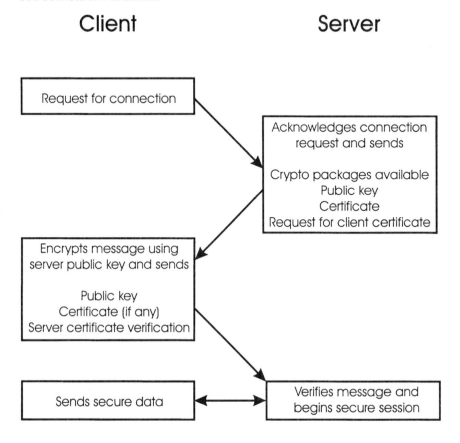

fixed, but there are still a number of potential problems users must be on the lookout for to avoid compromising personally identifiable information.

- *Site name mismatches.* In this case, the name of the organization or computer on a digital certificate does not match the name of the computer that sent the certificate. For instance, if the computer hosting www.techsoc.com had a digital certificate with the machine name hosting.techsoc.com, the user's browser would show a warning message indicating the names were different. For large companies that host commercial Web sites such a mismatch is not uncommon, but users must still exercise caution when the name of the machine and the name on the certificate do not match.

- *Pages with some secure and some insecure content.* In this case, the site's program-mers might collect a user's personally identifiable information, including credit card information and other details, on a secure page but then send the information to another computer over an insecure connection. By so doing, the server puts the user's information "in the clear" and allows anyone eavesdropping on the connection to read the information.

- *Weak cryptography.* Before January 2000 it was highly illegal for American citizens or businesses to export any cryptographically enabled products that used keys greater than 40 bits in length. Given the ability to build specialized hardware that can crack 56-bit DES keys in a matter of hours for less than the cost of a senior executive's salary, it should come as no surprise that the protection offered by keys of that length was completely inadequate for international business or, for the security conscious, personal privacy. In 1997 a French computer-science student used a network of computers at a university lab to crack a 40-bit DES key in three-and-a-half hours by writing a program that tried keys when the machine was not otherwise occupied.[15]

- *Certificate problems.* As mentioned earlier in this chapter, it becomes increasingly difficult to maintain a current list of which certificates have been issued and which have been revoked. It is also possible that an organization might have bought their own certificate-generation software and created a digital certificate for themselves. When a browser encounters a key from a certification authority it does not recognize it alerts the user and asks if the user is willing to accept the key. If so, the connection is established; if not, the connection is terminated or continues in insecure mode.

Conclusions Regarding Cryptography

The debate over the Clipper Chip and the changes in cryptography export controls at the beginning of 2000 signaled an admission on the part of the U.S. government that the spread of cryptographic tools had gone well beyond the control of a single country, especially one where individuals had proven that restrictions were practically unenforceable. Even had the potential for transferring cryptographic programs and source code (program listings) out of the country been shut down, the federal courts had found consistently in favor of the right of book publishers to export books containing cryptographic source code. Bruce Schneier's modern classic *Applied Cryptography* and the Electronic Frontier Foundation/O'Reilly & Associates publication *Cracking DES* showed the gap in the controls from a legal standpoint, while independent researchers, such as the Swiss inventors of IDEA, illustrated that advanced cryptographic capabilities existed in countries that did not place similar restrictions on the technology.

Even though cryptographic tools have not been widely adopted by Internet users (beyond the relatively weak built-in systems in the Netscape and Microsoft browsers), cryptography is an important part of the online privacy debate. As will be seen later in this chapter, it is more than possible for users to use cryptographic and other technological means to block organizations' abilities to track their movements on the Web. If there are questions about user motivation to use cryptography, remember the Vanderbilt study in Chapter 1, which found that up to 40 percent of users have provided false information to a Web site to gain access. That type of misinformation is damaging, but it also demonstrates that if users are given an easy way to limit the amount of information they provide to third parties, they will do so.

OTHER TECHNOLOGIES

While cryptography forms an important foundation of personal security both on the Internet and in home computers, it is not by itself a guarantee that a user's movements and personally identifiable information are safeguarded completely. One element of user tracking that can mitigate the effectiveness of cryptography is *traffic analysis*, where a third party tracks a user's movements through Web logs or by tracing individual data packets as they traverse the Internet. There are a number of other ways of defeating cryptographic controls, including placing a listening device (which can be either software or hardware) on a user's computer or network connection or by using physical persuasion (euphemistically referred to as *rubber hose cryptanalysis*) to extract the desired information. Absent such radical methods, however, users can do quite a bit to safeguard their privacy. This section looks at a number of these technologies and methods.

Cookie Management Software

As noted in Chapter 7, it is possible for Web site operators to keep careful watch on users by placing cookies (small text files with identifying information) on visitors' computers. Karen Kenworthy's Cookie Viewer, also mentioned in Chapter 7, is but one of many programs and methods available to users who want to manage their cookies. The means described here range in a rough order from the easiest to the hardest to implement, though they are all valid.

Within Web Browsers

Despite Rick Stout's contention that there would never and should not be any way for users to turn cookies off, Netscape and Microsoft both allow users to disable cookies or to have the browser get permission from the user on a per-cookie basis. The means for setting one's cookies preferences has become increasingly hard to find—in version 5.0 of both browsers, the settings are buried under several layers of menus. Also, Jason Catlett of Junkbusters takes issue with "the language used by Microsoft's Internet Explorer (a Web browser) when a user asks to be notified of cookies. The notice states that the site would like to "personalize" the visitor's experience by placing a file on their PC. No consumer would even vaguely anticipate what is happening with ad networks based on this notice."[16]

Modifying or Deleting Cookies.txt

There are other options available to users if they know where cookies are stored on their machine and they are aware of how file permissions on a personal computer work. If a user wants to allow Web sites to set cookies on his or her machine but does not want to make those cookies available for later use (if, for instance, a Web site required its users to accept cookies), the user could erase their cookies.txt file at regular intervals and be able to visit Web sites that required cookies but without the sites being able to assign the user's browser software a permanent GUID or to maintain records of that user's movements by storing information about the user in a cookie. The user would lose the benefits of the cookie, but would give up little personal information along the way, assuming the user logged onto the Internet through an Internet Service Provider that assigned its users random IP addresses. If the user were connected to the Internet through a permanent connection, such as a Digital Subscriber Line or as part of a corporate network, then the Web site's logs would show the user's fixed IP address, which could subsequently be attached to the user's identity. If the user is more sophisticated, the same effect can be accomplished by setting the properties of the cookies.txt file to "Read Only," or "Write Protect." Doing so, which is usually an option available through the user's operating system, allows the browser to read the contents of cookies.txt and write potential changes to a buffer, but when the browser attempts to save the changes to the cookies.txt file, the operating system prevents the new information from being added.

Cookie Management Software

There are a wide variety of cookie management and blocking software programs available. Karen Kenworthy's Cookie Viewer is one such program—it allows users to view the contents of their cookie file one cookie at a time and to edit or delete individual cookies. In addition to offering users the ability to block or manage cookies, there are other software packages that allow users to prevent Web sites from loading time-consuming additions like music and animated images to the user's computer. The following are software packages that allow users to block cookies and/or banner advertisements:

- interMute (http://www.intermute.com). Put out by Ad Subtract, this software package allows users to determine whether they want to view advertisements, animated images, cookies, pop-up windows, referrers, background music, Java, JavaScript, and so on. interMute allows the user to choose on a domain-by-domain basis what types of content he or she is willing to download. As of January 2000 interMute (a play on "Wintermute," the name of an artificial intelligence system in William Gibson's novel *Neuromancer*) retails for $19.95.
- Web Washer (http://www.webwasher.com). Developed by Siemens, Web Washer is an ad and active content blocker that uses signatures of banner ads (the standard

graphic sizes mentioned in Chapter 2, for instance, or HTML patterns) and other active objects (such as animated images) to prevent them from being downloaded. The Web Washer site claims that the software has over 2 million users and that the software, by preventing ads and other relatively high-bandwidth content from being sent over the network, reduces page download time by up to 45 percent. As with interMute, Web Washer allows the user to customize the program's behavior and maintains logs of the program's activities. Web Washer also retails for $19.95.

- At Guard (http://www.atguard.com). This ad blocking and cookie management software was developed by WRQ, Inc., but the company decided that it did not have the resources to make the product a commercial success and licensed the core technology to Symantec, which indicated it would use the technology in their Norton Internet Security 2000 product.

- Internet Watcher 2000 (http://www.internetwatcher.com). Internet Watcher was developed by the German firm Bernard D&G. Their software, which can also be used to block pornography and inappropriate Web sites, is available in four languages and retails for $49.95. Unlike other applications, a single copy of Internet Watcher can manage downloads for more than one user.

- InterQuick (http://interquick.deerfield.com). InterQuick is a Web accelerator that blocks advertisements and, like Internet Watcher, can limit the type of Web sites users are able to access. InterQuick also serves as a *proxy* server, meaning that it can be programmed to download designated pages while the user is not at the computer (usually during off-peak hours) and to make those pages available offline. A single user license for InterQuick costs $39.95.

- Anonymizer Window Washer (http://www.anonymizer.com/3.0/anonwash). In addition to the usual cookie management tools, Anonymizer Window Washer deletes any record of where users have gone on the Internet from more programs than just Web browsers. For example, Microsoft Office programs like Word and Excel also maintain an internal record of recently visited Web sites. Anonymizer Window Washer deletes those records, removes any record of what files were placed in the Recycle Bin, and "bleaches" deleted files by overwriting the disk space where the file was stored with random characters, making it much harder to undelete the files. The full version of Anonymizer Window Washer retails for $29.95.

- A variety of freeware (no cost) and shareware (payment on the honor system) programs are available for managing cookies. Some of those programs are Cookie Crusher, Cookie Jar, Cookie Monster, Cookie Pal, No Cookie, ZDNet Cookie Master 2, and Cookie Cutter PC. Many of these programs, plus others, may be found through <http://www.cookiecentral.com>.

Proxy Services

One of the functions of the software program InterQuick is to operate as a proxy, or a software program that downloads Web pages the user specifies and, rather than take the time to download the page from its server, stores the page on the user's computer and writes it to the screen when the user types in its URL. Proxies of that nature can be programmed to go back to popular sites at regular intervals (a few hours, every day, or once a week, for example) to get a more recent version of the page. Another type of proxy serves as a go-between moderating the connection between the user's computer and the destination site. The best-known proxy server is the Anonymizer (http://www.anonymizer.com). The Anonymizer allows users to surf the Web without giving away their machine's IP address or receiving cookies for the fee of $5 a month. It is possible to use the service for free, though there is a slight delay (perhaps fifteen seconds) built into the system. Another proxy is the Internet Junkbuster Proxy, which is available as a server to be installed on an ISP's computers or on a user's personal computer. The proxy operates much like InterQuick, but has the advantage of being totally free.

Zero Knowledge Systems' Freedom

A software package that melds the secure transaction capabilities of cryptography with the intermediary services provided by anonymizing proxies is Freedom, from Zero Knowledge Systems (ZKS) of Montreal. The goal of ZKS's Freedom product is to create an easy-to-use system that allows users to create one or more pseudonyms (referred to as *nyms*) that cannot be linked with their computer or any personally identifiable information. Every pseudonym has its own digital signature and encryption key, so Freedom purchasers can create as many nyms as they like (at a cost of $10 apiece—five nyms are included in the initial purchase price of $50). Much like the SSL protocol, Freedom encrypts all traffic between the destination computer and the user's machine, making it impossible to eavesdrop on the transmissions. As an extra measure of security, all data sent from a Freedom subscriber's machine to the Internet is rerouted through a series of at least three other machines, called the Freedom Network. The user's computer, which downloads and updates the public keys of the machines on the Freedom Network, randomly determines a path for the message, and encrypts the message using the public keys of every machine in the message's path. The nature of this encryption scheme is such that each node on the network is only able to determine the node a packet came from and the node it is to forward the data on to—there is no unencrypted information in a message that can be traced to the originator of the transmission after it passes the first node. In addition, Freedom introduces a random delay at each stopover on the network, making traffic analysis much more difficult if not impossible. This delay, plus the time needed for encryption and decryption, does add significant delay to the system, though users with fast computers and quick Internet connections are able to handle the load.

One potential hole in the Freedom security scheme is cookies, especially those that use GUIDs to track user movements, so an integral part of the Freedom software is its ability to separate cookies into separate cookie jars for each nym. If a user decides to leave the cookies on the machine, the only thing the cookie can identify is that nym; because all Web traffic is routed through a series of machines, the originating IP address is lost. Indeed, if a

Freedom user is careful not to include any personally identifiable information in their e-mail messages, such as automatically included signature blocks, then not even the Zero Knowledge Systems staff is able to link a nym with a user's true name. Zero Knowledge reserves the right to remove any users from their system if it can be proven that someone using a particular nym violated the system's terms of service agreement, but the nature of the system used to purchase and establish nyms removes all traces of a connection between the nym and its owner.

Platform for Privacy Preferences

In the middle ground between the insecure world of cookies and GUIDs and the absolute secrecy of Zero Knowledge System's Freedom Network is the Platform for Privacy Preferences (P3P) standard under development by the World Wide Web Consortium.[17] According to the project FAQ list, the goal of P3P is to create a technology that allows users and Web site owners to negotiate what personally identifiable information a user is willing to disclose in exchange for specific types of access to a Web site.[18] For instance, if a Web site is willing to allow a user open access to the site in exchange for placing a cookie on the user's computer and the user is willing to accept cookies from that type of site, then the Web server software and the user's browser will be able to determine that compatibility automatically and not require the user and site to enter into negotiations. If the user's preferences and the site's requirements are not compatible, a P3P-compatible browser would inform the user of the problem and allow the parties to the transaction to negotiate an agreement. The technological question to be answered, of course, concerns automating the negotiation for the server (which could be dealing with literally thousands of simultaneous users) while maintaining a useful dialog with the user.

Two engineers from Citigroup (speaking for themselves) argued in a 1998 critique of the system that creating such a burden for Web site operators would destroy their ability to collect personal information:

P3P allows a user to dictate under what sort of conditions she is willing to give out personal information. If Citibank does not agree to whatever conditions the user puts forth, the user may opt not to transact with the bank at all . . . thus putting the onus on the bank to tighten the privacy protection until users are willing to transact i.e., to the lowest common denominator.

There is a concern that P3P would let ordinary users see, in full gory detail, how their personal information might be misused by less trusted or responsible Web site operators. Such knowledge may cause users to resist giving out information altogether. Some individual business groups have done focus studies on users, and . . . concluded that most users would prefer to give out only the information needed for the transaction and that they do not like the idea of someone monitoring their browsing behavior.[19]

The objection seems to be that users would not be able to differentiate between trustworthy and untrustworthy sites and that informing users of the risks of sending personally identifiable information over the Internet would result in substantial harm to business. This sentiment is certainly in line with Rick Stout's argument in favor of cookies, but the notion that relatively unsophisticated users need to be protected from an ugly truth for their own good is probably not the best way for Web site operators to establish and maintain trusting relationships with their visitors.

In other quarters, the P3P proposal has been roundly praised. In 1998 the *Harvard Law Review* noted as follows:

The multitude of potential substitutes for any particular type of Internet content, coupled with the intense competition among content providers for Internet traffic, ensures a high level of site responsiveness to user preferences. . . . A P3P regime will result in the optimal level of privacy protection because it permits individuals to value privacy according to their personal preferences. Individual users will configure their privacy preferences to protect privacy according to the value that they attach to it. In the resulting privacy market, those who value their personal information less will part with it more easily than those who value it more. . . . When aggregated, these individual preferences will exert pressure on site operators to conform their privacy practices to user preferences.[20]

After years as a draft standard, working implementations of P3P appeared in June 2000. For updates on P3P and a list of compliant sites, visit the P3P home page at <http://www.w3.org/P3P>.

INFOMEDIARIES

From the "privacy as a human right" perspective, a problem with the P3P proposal is that it puts the onus on the user to negotiate the amount of personally identifiable information they are willing to give up for a given transaction. If the organization holds information the user cannot do without, then that user can be forced to give up whatever personally identifiable information the Web site operator desires to gain access to the site's contents. A compromise between the user-based privacy negotiations inherent to the P3P system and the total openness of the status quo is the infomediary, an organization that accumulates user profiles and allows users to surf the Web without allowing the destination sites to acquire any personally identifiable information, or potentially personally identifiable information, about the infomediary's members. Instead, the business model for the infomediary is to collect information about its users' habits and to tell its advertisers, "We have positively identified fifteen hundred users between the ages of forty-nine and fifty-nine [living] in households with an annual income of over $120,000 who will probably purchase a luxury automobile in the next six months. Advertising your automobiles to this group will cost you three times the normal rate, but the quality of the prospects should more than make up for the outlay."

The infomediary model is similar to the model followed by Zero Knowledge Systems for its Freedom Network, though the level of security that prevents ZKS from discovering the identity of Freedom participants will almost certainly be missing from the standard infomediary. (However, in February 2000 ZKS gained the services of a scientist who holds several patents for anonymous electronic cash methodologies, so it is certainly possible that ZKS will choose to develop a completely anonymous, Internet-based payment system as an extension to Freedom.) Figure 8.3 shows how an infomediary might choose to configure its contact-management and information-gathering net-

Figure 8.3
Infomediary Network Configuration

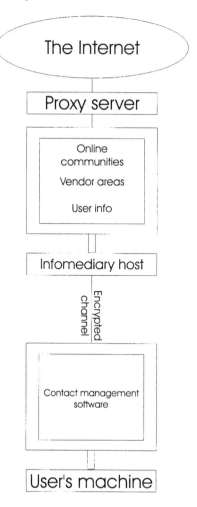

work. At one end of the process is the user, who interacts with the infomediary through an information management agent. The current method is to create information-management tools that are compatible with Web browsers, a trend that is likely to continue. At the other end of the process are vendors who provide information to the infomediary about their products, services, and pricing. In the middle of it all is a series of data repositories and blinding agents that allow users to examine the information provided by vendors or gathered by the infomediary, manage the type and amount of information they are willing to give up for a given level of access, and request more information or make purchases.

This ability to aggregate consumer information is the real strength of infomediaries. The infomediary business model was first put forth by Hagel and Singer in 1998 in their book *Net Worth*, which recognized the growing tide of sentiment that consumers wanted more control over how their personally identifiable information is used and offered businesses a way to take advantage of that sentiment while benefiting consumers.[21] Hartman, Sinfonis, and Kador elaborated the infomediary model in their 2000 book *Net Ready: Strategies for Success in the E-conomy* by noting that infomediaries have the following essential functions:

- Aggregation of needs.
- Aggregation of services.
- Bid/ask engines.
- Consultative adviser.
- Hidden demand.
- Matchmaking.
- Negotiation.
- Notification service.
- Smart needs adviser.
- Upsell.[22]

Aggregation of Needs

This function of an infomediary provides "one stop shopping" for a number of user needs, such as an online financial institution bringing together loan, mortgage, and credit card information on a single site.

Aggregation of Services

The flip side of the aggregation of needs function, an infomediary's ability to bring the services available from its vendors into a single, searchable location, potentially with additional commentary (such as from other consumers who have used a vendor's services or independent review organizations like *Consumer Reports*), makes consumers' searches for services and goods much more efficient. It also allows vendors the opportunity to offer entirely new services consumers, like the online car-buying service provided by AutoByTel.com (http://www.autobytel.com).

Bid/Ask Engines

This function is embodied by sites like Priceline.com (http://www.priceline. com), which allows users to bid on airplane tickets in an effort to find a price they are willing to pay. If no vendor will sell the user a ticket for the specified price, the user can change their bid. Because airline ticket fares are in a constant state of flux due to demand, sales, and competitive pressures, consumers gain less than the usual advantage from being "natives" (described in Chapter 5).

Consultative Adviser

Infomediaries can also serve as consultants by gathering information about the products and services available to their members, whether on their sites or elsewhere. In this case, the infomediary is less a broker between the consumer and the vendor and more an accumulator of information and independent authority on the available products and services.

Hidden Demand

Perhaps one of the best ways an infomediary can benefit vendors is to field questions from consumers about products or services they want but have been unable to find. By bringing out this "hidden demand," vendors that cooperate with infomediaries will have the benefit of definite leads on new products and services users want, not just sales information or direct contacts that might not be correlated due to communication problems within the company. Under the popular model of tracking user activities through lists of terms users put into search engines, this information is indirect (at best) and easily misunderstood.

Matchmaking

This function, one of the basic elements of a successful infomediary, sees the infomediary bringing buyers and sellers together based on stated interests and available products. It is not necessary for the infomediary to have detailed information about the consumer for these one-off transactions, as the request should provide sufficient information for the infomediary to identify likely solution providers.

Negotiation

Like the bid/ask engine, consumers can negotiate with vendors to affect the makeup of a purchase, price, and included services. In some cases the negotiation could be automated using autonomous agent technology like that described in the section on shopping robots.

Notification Service

Many Web sites have services that allow users to request the site send them an e-mail message whenever an item of interest appears on a site, a vendor issues a new product, or a Web page changes. An example of the latter service is provided by NetMind (http://www.netmind.com), which allows users to register a list of pages and receive messages whenever any of those pages are updated.

Smart Needs Adviser

In this case, the infomediary anticipates a user's requirements and offers them alternatives to the product or service they have chosen. The alternatives could be based on price (a better fare on another airline), service (a better warranty scheme if the product is purchased from another vendor), or benefits (purchasing from another merchant offers frequent-flier miles).

Upsell

Finally, an infomediary can offer consumers additional items, such as warranties or product bundles that increase the overall price but offer the individual products or services at a discount. One Web site that follows this strategy is TechSmith (http://www.techsmith.com), makers of the SnagIt screen-shot utility and related products. The company sells its products individually for prices ranging from $39.95 to $89.95, but offers substantial discounts if the user purchases more than one product at a time.

Makeup of an Infomediary

To perform the services its users and vendors require, an infomediary must develop and implement technologies that allow users to search for products, services, and information without inadvertently revealing their personally identifiable information. Hagel and Singer note that an infomediary needs several items to fulfill its role:

- A privacy toolkit.
- A profiling toolkit.
- A filtering, agent, targeting, and data analysis toolkit.

Privacy Toolkit

The first element an infomediary needs to have in place is the privacy toolkit that protects user privacy. In many cases the cryptographic tools mentioned earlier in this chapter, such as the technologies used as part of the Freedom network, will suffice. The user will require an anonymous e-mail address the vendor cannot link with the user's real name or online travels, the use of a proxy server while visiting the infomediary's site, and a credit or debit card associated with the user's account that is, once again, not traceable to the user unless they choose to reveal their information to a vendor.[23] Users will need to reveal their names and addresses for order fulfillment and shipping of physical products, but if the product can be downloaded over the Internet the transaction may not even require users to give up that information if they do not wish to do so.

Profiling Toolkit

Raw log information can be useful but is often too plentiful to review by hand, so infomediaries will need to develop or license technologies to profile user activities. One way to do so is through the interest-matching technologies found on Reel.com (http://www.reel.com), though another approach would be to develop proprietary methods to correlate user activities and interests with the type of ads they are most likely to click.

Filtering, Agent, Targeting, and Data Analysis Toolkit

These tools allow the infomediary to automate the processes of ensuring unwanted messages do not reach consumers, automating the process of negotiating prices and information exchanges, determining which users would be most interested in a given advertisement, and representing user click-through and conversion rates to find advertisements that work well and those that should be retooled or replaced.

Critical Information Mass

Like any other business, infomediaries must find consumers who are willing to share their personal information and allow themselves to be tracked as they use the Internet. A substantial obstacle to gaining those profiles is creating an atmosphere of trust. Hagel and Singer indicate the issue of trust is quite complex:

No matter how sincere the infomediary is regarding privacy, no matter how many processes it puts in place to protect privacy, and no matter what it says about being loyal to clients ahead of vendors, the proof of the infomediary's trustworthiness will be in its track record. This track record will accumulate over time, client by client.

The more clients an infomediary has and the longer it has served those clients, the more each client is likely to trust the infomediary to do the right thing. . . .

Powerful network effects, resulting from the interplay between trust and value delivered to the client, characterize this challenge. The increasing value a consumer receives from an infomediary that understands not just that particular individual, but also others with similar tastes and habits, reinforces trust. The more interaction an infomediary has with consumers, the more insight it gains into their needs, and the more proactive and precise it can be in delivering agent and filter services. The information profiles of consumers that it can subsequently offer to vendors in turn become more compelling and thus generate larger revenues. As consumers see the value of the infomediary's understanding, their trust grows deeper.[24]

Existing Infomediaries

A number of companies have started operating as infomediaries of the type described by Hagel and Singer, but a larger number of companies that refer to themselves as infomediaries are actually taking on the role of virtual community sponsor. Those virtual communities, where the organizer takes on the role of information broker and matchmaker, do not offer their users any privacy protections and are therefore not infomediaries in the sense used here and by Hagel and Singer. The infomediaries that do offer privacy protections have developed their technologies without waiting for the P3P standard to be finalized and, while they are not interoperable, do offer many of the same benefits.

digitalme

Run by Novell, digitalme (http://www.digitalme.com) is a service that allows users to create *meCards*, which represent the information users choose to give out in certain situations. For instance, for recreational sites where a user would only want to give out a specific e-mail address and no other information a user could create a meCard with a nickname and the e-mail address. digitalme also allows users to fill in forms automatically based on information that is part of a meCard and, if any of the information in that meCard is changed, the Novell server automatically updates the information in the address books of other digitalme users who had copied or linked to the meCard. Novell encrypts transmissions of personally identifiable information between the digitalme servers and user computers with 128-bit SSL encryption, the highest encryption available for Netscape and Internet Explorer, though the browser must be capable of handling that key length. All personal information is stored in Novell Directory Services (NDS), a highly scalable and secure directory. NDS uses cryptographically secure authentication protocols, such as digital signatures, to protect digitalme account information and to detect intruders. The digitalme servers are located in a physically secure facility with controlled and limited access.

Lumeria

Lumeria (http://www.lumeria.com) is a Berkeley, California, infomediary that is developing its SuperProfile technology that will allow users to manage their personally identifiable information and trade it to vendors in exchange for received value. Lumeria's technical philosophy is based on the Fair Information Practices embodied in the OECD's guidelines and the EU Data Directive and, at least on paper, implements many of the functions called for in Hagel and Singer. The Lumeria Web site claims,

The SuperProfile system allows individuals to appoint agents (such as Lumeria or other third parties including banks) who will actively seek the best deals for the individual. The agent can provide software that highlights deficiencies of any transaction or warns the individual about a scrupulous deal. Moreover, the SuperProfile system allows the individual to sell or trade some data about themselves (e.g. their habits or preferences) while protecting their identity. If the individual suspects the veracity of the company, they can provide extremely limited or anonymous data to the company until a relationship has been established and the merchant is trusted.[25]

As of January 2000, the only way to sign up for the SuperProfile service is to put one's name on a mailing list and wait for notification that the system is ready.

PrivacyBank

Like digitalme, PrivacyBank (http://www.privacybank.com) allows users to fill out forms automatically. In this case, users may do so by using the company's Drag 'N Fill technology to move information from the user's PrivacyBank account to online forms. PrivacyBank has trademarked their FormL technology, which allows the PrivacyBank software to learn from an online form and to add information to that user's profile to be automatically added to subsequent forms. A central part of PrivacyBank's control is that they allow users to give Web sites permission, on a case-by-case basis, to use their information for helping purchases, site customization, research, contact purposes, or disclosure to third parties.

PrivaSeek

PrivaSeek (http://www.privaseek.com) is another infomediary that provides users with automatic form fill-in capabilities and the power to determine what information to provide to sites on a per-site basis. The original version of the company's software was very difficult to use, but the new version is much simpler and easier to handle.

AllAdvantage

AllAdvantage (http://www.alladvantage.com) is an infomediary of a different and interesting type. Rather than providing users with profile management software, AllAdvantage adds a banner advertisement bar to the user's computer screen and pays users for every hour the window (called the ViewBar) is active. Users can also earn money by referring others to the program.

INTERVIEW WITH RAY EVERETT-CHURCH

The following is a telephone interview of Ray Everett-Church of AllAdvantage.com with the author on 28 February 2000:

How do you develop user profiles and target ads to them?

The best way to explain how we do targeting is to explain how AllAdvantage works generally. AllAdvantage is an infomediary, which means we work as an agent for our members to assist them with obtaining value for the use of their personally identifiable information. We have a piece of proprietary software called the ViewBar, which is the conduit through which we serve ads. It is the application that actually talks to people's Web browser and sends back data about their travels across the Web. People sign up, download ViewBar, and are in control of the profiling process. They can turn the ViewBar on or off depending on when they want us to track them. When turned off or minimized, the ViewBar is not on the screen and the user is not compensated. When the ViewBar is on the screen we pay fifty cents an hour, to a maximum of twenty-five hours per month, but there is no cap on amounts to be earned through referrals. If you refer someone, we pay you ten cents an hour for time they are surfing. You can refer any number of people and get a cut. As a result of our referral program we had one fellow who received a check for six grand in January [2000]. It's kind of a true multi-level arrangement where you don't have to buy anything—it's all positive cash flow for you.

As a result of the way the ViewBar works, we can track pretty much all of your Web surfing while you're online, including Web sites viewed, search terms (used at Yahoo, etc.), and to some extent can trigger off content on those pages. In other words, if the ViewBar recognizes that certain topics are mentioned on a page, we have the capability to track and target based on that content. Right now we focus on targeting URLs because they are the easiest and most useful information to capture.

With the current version of the ViewBar we have the ability to implement full profiling based on traffic. Our goal is to do "key site targeting," which means if a user goes to United Airlines we could serve an ad for TWA purely by looking at what site you're at. The current practice is mostly keyword targeting, where a search engine sells a keyword to a certain vendor (for example, "golf balls" on Yahoo gets Titleist). The next generation of that technology is key site targeting. We hope to go to "key person targeting" where, based upon a profile, we can realize it's getting close to spring break and start serving ads for great hotel deals in Daytona Beach. We couldn't do that as accurately or as usefully if we were waiting for someone to enter keywords.

What size company is AllAdvantage? Specifically, do you have the necessary staff to ensure user privacy?

It has actually taken some time to find the right folks, but we are right now in the process of bringing staff on board. I have made a couple of offers and, in fact, have a new legislative director coming on board to help on the other aspects of my role here, which is to project our privacy practices to the rest of the industry, legislators, and regulators. We've also just gotten an acceptance from a person who will be our director of privacy programs; that individual will essentially be my number two and he'll help expand my coverage to other parts of the company and have people looking over the business plan, production, and development plans, all with a mind to privacy issues.

Our company as a whole is just about to crest the 500-employee mark. We have twenty offices around the world, most of which are sales and media strategy offices. They are located in places like London, Sydney, New York, Seattle, Paris, and Chicago. Creating so many local offices is actually a recognition that we can do targeting based on ZIP code. In fact, we can target ads to consumers geographically, because Joe's Pizza would never buy an ad on Yahoo but could on the ViewBar and would reach people who are just down the street. As I tell people on Capitol Hill, we can target down to the precinct level.

What personal information do you request from your subscribers?

We require users to give us their name, mailing address, age, and gender. We don't correlate with third-party sources because most targeting is based on real-time surfing data and other stuff isn't as useful to us. We may try correlating to ZIP codes to make guesses as to probable income levels and profiles based on ZIP codes but that's the extent of it. Most third-party information vendors would require us to give up personal information about our subscribers, which we will never do. Consumer information is never released to a third party.

Advertisers come to us all the time and ask us "what's your demographic?" and we answer, "what are you looking for?" We have all ages, all locations; if an advertiser is looking for a particular demographic (such as GM wanting to send an ad to people looking for model of car in last fourteen days), we can show an ad to those people without ever giving the consumer's information to the advertiser.

What is the size of your user base?

Right now we have about 6 million members, of which 2 million are active ViewBar users (have used the ViewBar in the last thirty days). We have millions of individuals that want it in areas we haven't rolled it out yet. We're signing up folks at the rate of about 30,000 a day. In the first ten days we were in business we signed up half a million people.

We only pay people for twenty-five hours of surfing per month, but we've found that the ViewBar actually stays on a lot longer than that. One reason is that the ViewBar has a search engine built in and allows you to search Ask Jeeves, About.com, Excite, Go, Goto, LookSmart, and DirectHit. Hopefully we'll add more soon. For folks it winds up being a fairly handy thing.

There is some exciting potential. Because the ViewBar is always talking to the server, it loads ads in the background. That is, it waits to see when you're not busy, then it downloads the ads in the background so you don't get additional slowdown of service. What's really neat is because you can do downloading in the background you never need to upgrade. The ViewBar can download a little bit more, then a little bit more until it's done. We call it seamless auto-upgrading. We have also cut a deal with the McAfee antivirus software people . . . our users can rent the virus software for fifty cents per month, and the ViewBar can query the McAfee site and, if it finds a new virus signature file, it can download it automatically.

Have you noticed an improved click-through rate for AllAdvantage surfers? Have advertisers received more orders, or is there only "the illusion of action"?

Our media strategy and sales folks believe that it's fairly similar to standard industry numbers, though they tend not to talk about click-through because it doesn't necessarily correlate to conversion. What I understand is that we've heard from a number of advertisers that conversion rates have been very strong. My initial sense is that they've been pretty pleased with the conversion rates.

What level of emphasis do senior managers at AllAdvantage place on user privacy?

When I came aboard here it was a big change from private legal practice in D.C. to here, but from our earliest conversations it was clear they had privacy front and center in their planning and in their own personal visions of the future of the company. In discussions with the founders from the first it was clear they understood the issues and were trying to come up with a way for consumers to get a piece of the huge value created by trade in personally identifiable information. We essentially put consumers in a position of control over the collection of that information and how much they want to share and make sure they get value for that information without losing control. As a result we built a system that is based on the notion that people should have control over how that information is collected; we give them total control, they can turn the ViewBar on and off at will.

What happens to an individual's personally identifiable information if they drop out of the program?

If someone leaves the service, when they walk away we delete their data. For us it's all about giving them the right ad at the right time, to give incentives to share information with us but also to give control. It's functional, but we want people to share their data with us and need to give incentives beyond money . . . that incentive is trust. We promise to them while we store their data and use it on their behalf that we won't share it with third parties and will delete it when they walk away.

How does a new company establish that trust? I didn't see a TRUSTe or BBBOnline mark on the AllAdvantage site.

We have specifically decided not to sign up with any trustmark organization because we find that because of the way these trustmark organizations work, we feel it creates a false sense of security in consumers. Essentially the way these organizations work is that they certify you have a privacy policy and that you adhere to it, but they make no qualitative judgments about the policies. In fact, some companies have privacy policies that aren't . . . it's extremely clear they have no interest in consumer privacy or in protecting consumer privacy, and by slapping a trustmark on it, you wind up simply with a rather cynical guarantee that this company promises they will do the rotten things they say they will. It creates a false set of expectations and we would rather be held to the word of our privacy policy rather than have consumers think they somehow get some protection they're not just by seeing a logo.

We are right now engaged in beginning a process with Ernst & Young to complete a full-scale review of all our internal practices. In the interim, part of my role as chief privacy officer is to ensure throughout the process that we adhere to our privacy policy and by engaging a third-party auditor our hope is to back up our pledge with a trusted third-party statement that we're actually doing this and in the meantime project to our membership that there is someone here in the company whose job it is to make sure our promises are kept in this regard. I report directly to the CEO and we promote our policy through an ad that promotes my role in the company.

What kind of security infrastructure is in place to protect user information?

We had an outside audit and investigation of our systems and network by the folks at the International Computer Security Association (icsa.net), do a certification program called TrueSecure, and, within the next couple of weeks, we will probably be fully certified by them for meeting industry standards for computer and network security.

Is there any possibility of offering credit cards linked to an infomediary-granted i.d. where the credit report for that i.d. is not linked to the user's real name?

We've been looking at some deals related to credit cards and debit cards, but nothing has been finalized. We don't anticipate getting into the credit reporting business and we certainly aren't a bank.

How does your business model hold up under stricter privacy regulations, perhaps ones similar to those in the Canadian bill C-6 or the EU's Data Directive?

We have already launched in the EU and are fully EU compliant. We knew we would be global comp[etition] and did so early in the game. We have gone about trying to determine the highest standards throughout the world for all of our policies and have set those standards as our baseline. When it comes to consumer data protection we have looked to the EU as they are far and away the strictest. Many countries are still in the process of implementing the directive, but the trick has been in some of these cases to have local counsel test the wind to see where the policies are going to land and encompass their laws. We will need to continue to revise our policies and have had to make little tweaks based on local implementations.

Most of these tweaks relate to registration requirements. We had to register with various data authorities and have had various requirements. In one case we had to revise our policy in the United Kingdom to state that, because the databases are housed in the United States, we had to more clearly state that we were passing member data out of the EU and therefore needed to get consent, with a clear explanation of the process. Things like that come up as we talk to each country's data authority and we need to revisit issues. The premise of the company is to offer greater protection than any other company in this space.

The reverse is interesting as well. Again, we take the highest standards and set as our baseline. In the United States, the Children's Online Privacy Protection Act is much more strict than the law the EU has in place in that it requires parental consent for anyone under thirteen—and must be verifiable adult consent. All members under thirteen, regardless of country, must send in written parental consent forms. That exceeds the EU's requirement, but meets U.S. law. It's pretty onerous, but it's important to us to show it's being done. In fact, the regulations don't take effect until April [2000], but we began the process in January. To prevent circumvention we require parental contact information on the form and do random check-ups.

What are your company's activities in D.C.?

We are very active in Washington, less so but still engaged with various state legislatures. There is lots of concern with privacy and Internet privacy issues in Washington, D.C., and state legislatures. We are concerned with how privacy issues are perceived in the legislative and regulatory environment and are making sure the infomediary is important to the privacy debate. Previously the focus was on tensions between consumers and marketers. Infomediaries add a third party to that debate as an agent and forum for solving the disputes between the two sides. An infomediary comes in and says "we'll help you do business on your terms and we'll get you the people you want but do it in a way that is responsive to consumer concerns." The infomediary creates a lubricant where there previously was friction. Folks in Washington have been very receptive to our ideas. They are starting to understand what an infomediary is. Once they see a business model is built around solving these problems, maybe they'll start to think there's hope to get by without precipitous or intrusive regulation.

I'm not sure how any of the new privacy bills are going to fare. I know there is significant concern amongst both congressmen and senators about regulating the Internet. McCain and Bliley have said they aren't eager to see legislation without a strong consensus behind it, especially in privacy, because they do not want to strangle the baby in the crib and the Internet e-commerce marketplace is just getting rolling. But certainly there are desires to keep the market growing, but that growth has to be tempered with concern for consumers responses to things like privacy. If consumers don't have faith in the medium, they will kill the medium faster than any ill-advised legislation.

Do you anticipate AllAdvantage expanding beyond its current model to include some of the functions described in Net Worth?

We are quite actively considering an array of services and features to benefit our members, many of which are very well outlined in *Net Worth*. We see ourselves as growing into the kind of infomediary that Hagel and Singer describe. Lots of folks call themselves infomediaries that don't necessarily deliver the kind of direct value to members that is encompassed by the infomediary model that Hagel and Singer outline.

Note that AllAdvantage.com's strategy neatly solves the problem of establishing a critical mass of customer profiles. By providing a substantial incentive for users to surf and to bring in others who do the same, AllAdvantage has quickly generated a substantial profile base that can be differentiated by demonstrable behavior, not potentially falsifiable interest surveys.

NOTES

1. David Kahn, *The Codebreakers* (New York: Scribner, 1996).

2. Curtis Frye and Richard Peck, *The State of Web Commerce* (Sebastopol, Calif.: O'Reilly & Associates, 1997), 11. Online summary available <http://www.ora.com/research/netcraft/index.html>.

3. Simson Garfinkel and Gene Spafford, *Web Security & Commerce* (Sebastopol, Calif.: O'Reilly & Associates, 1997), 195.

4. Electronic Frontier Foundation, *Cracking DES* (Sebastopol, Calif.: O'Reilly & Associates, 1998), ix.

5. Ibid., 11–14.

6. RSA Security, *What is DESX?* 1998. Available <http://www.rsasecurity.com/rsalabs/faq/3-2-7.html>.

7. Counterpane Internet Security Inc., *The Blowfish Encryption Algorithm*, 1999. Available <http://www.counterpane.com/blowfish.html>.

8. National Institute of Standards and Technology, *Advanced Encryption Standard (AES) Development Effort*, 1998. Available <http://www.nist.gov/aes>.

9. X. Lai, J. L. Massey, and S. Murphy, "Markov Ciphers and Differential Cryptanalysis," in *Advances in Cryptology—EUROCRYPT '91*, ed. D. W. Davies, pp. 17–38 (New York: Springer-Verlag).

10. Whitfield Diffie and Martin E. Hellman, "New Directions in Cryptography," *IEEE Transactions in Information Theory* IT-22 (November 1976): 644–654.

11. Gail L. Grant, *Understanding Digital Signatures* (New York: McGraw-Hill, 1998), 38.

12. Lincoln Stein, *Web Security: A Step-by-Step Reference Guide* (Boston: Addison-Wesley, 1998), 38.

13. Garfinkel and Spafford, *Web Security & Commerce*, 241.

14. Frye and Peck, *The State of Web Commerce*, 16–17.

15. Stein, *Web Security*, 37.

16. Jason Catlett, "Profiling: Comments to the Dept. of Commerce and Federal Trade Commission," *Online Profiling Project*, 18 October 1999. Available <http://www.ftc.gov/bcp/profiling/comments/catlett.htm>.

17. The Platform for Privacy Preferences Web site may be found at <http://www.w3.org/P3P>.

18. Joseph M. Reagle, Jr. and Rigo Wenning, *P3P and Privacy on the Web FAQ*, 18 April 2000. Available <http://www.w3.org/P3P/P3FAQ.html>.

19. Kenneth Lee and Gabriel Speyer, *White Paper: Platform for Privacy Preferences Project (P3P) & Citibank*, 12 October 1998. Available <http://www.we.org/P3P/Lee_Speyer.html>.

20. Harvard Law Review, "The Law of Cyberspace," *Harvard Law Review* 112 (1999): 1574–1704.

21. John Hagel, III and Marc Singer, *Net Worth: Shaping Markets When Customers Make the Rules* (Boston: Harvard Business School Press, 1999), 29.

22. Amir Hartman and John Sifonis, with John Kador, *Net Ready: Strategies for Success in the E-conomy* (New York: McGraw-Hill, 2000), 119–120.

23. Hagel and Singer, *Net Worth*, 29.

24. Ibid., 121.

25. Lumeria, *An Infomediary Approach to the Privacy Problem*, 1999. Available <http://www.superprofile.com/paper1/privacypartner6.html>.

9

Policy Scenarios

American politics often has the feel of Japanese *kabuki*—the audience knows where the story will end up before the characters do. That also seems to be the case in the privacy arena for the United States over the next several years. Several laws have been proposed to limit how personally identifiable information can be used in the online environment, but the Clinton administration's strong preference is for self-regulation, except in cases of unfair and deceptive trade practices that could be investigated by the Federal Trade Commission, and Ray Everett-Church has commented that there is significant resistance in the American federal legislature to any law that could stifle Internet commerce (see Chapter 8). So, at the federal level it seems unlikely that policy will change any time in the next few years regardless of the outcome of the political process, though action at the state level and industry's application of privacy technologies may very well have a sufficient impact on the policy-making apparatus to make those changes foregone conclusions or, at the extreme, irrelevant. This chapter examines the range of possible regulatory scenarios under which electronic commerce could take place, with a special emphasis on privacy policy. The analysis is time based, looking at the most probable scenarios for the short term (to 2003), the medium term (to 2007), and the long term (to 2010). The final part of this chapter offers businesses a flexible approach to working within any of these scenarios.

SHORT-TERM PROSPECTS

As already noted, it is highly unlikely that there will be any major shake-up in American privacy policy over the next two or three years. The biggest change one might expect on the domestic front is an increase in Federal Trade Commission activities aimed at Web site operators who change their privacy policies in ways that decrease the amount of protection offered to their user base. The FTC has undertaken a number of such investigations in the recent past, and the success of those actions can be used as strong arguments against any laws that might stifle electronic commerce.

Prospects at the Federal Level

If any laws are passed at the federal level, they will most likely be relatively weak or an extension of existing opt-out protections to electronic commerce. An opt-in regime is especially unlikely in the near term, though Senator Robert Torrecelli (Democrat–New Jersey) filed just such a bill, S.2063. The speaker noted in a January 23, 2000, speech that he had introduced

S. 2063, the Secure Online Communication Enforcement Act of 2000. This legislation is not a final product, I stress to privacy advocates and to the Internet industries and online companies. It is not a final product. It is establishing, I hope, a national dialog first to educate ourselves about the privacy problem in cyberspace. It is a beginning document to which I invite comment and amendment. Its purpose is simply to begin collecting ideas of how to enhance privacy. But it is built on the concept of opting in versus opting out; that is, that the consumer, the citizen, must make a choice about whether they want this information shared. So the consumer, the individual, holds the power.

If I believe a company can better market to me—and, indeed, I believe a company can better market to me if they know my taste in music, my taste in reading, my taste in clothing or automobiles—I can decide that I want that information shared, given to other companies, and come back to me with good information. However, if I don't want something shared—perhaps I have gone online with a health care company and I prefer my health information not be shared—I do not opt in, I do not give anybody the right to give that information.

A second vital part of this bill: I strongly believe government oversight and regulation of the Internet should be kept to a minimum. That is one reason I have opposed steadfastly a sales tax on Internet purchases. This is one area of American life where the government should keep its presence to an absolute minimum in taxation and regulation. For that reason, this legislation is self-enforcing. No government bureaucracy will be calling if there is a violation. If, indeed, a company violates a citizen's privacy, the right of action is with the citizen, not the government. There is a legal right of action when sharing my personal information which I have said will not be shared. If I did not give anyone that right, then I as a citizen will hold them liable for doing so.

Those twin pillars are: As a citizen, I decide whether to share my private service; second pillar, as a citizen, I and not the government have the right of action to enforce it.[1]

There are several aspects of the law per se and the senator's goals that make it highly unlikely the Secure Online Communication Enforcement Act (SOCEA) will become law. The first consideration is the senator's own statement that the bill is a work in progress and is only offered to catalyze debate on the issue of online privacy. Given the sponsor's offering of the bill as a worst-case scenario and the overhaul of online services that the bill would require, it is highly unlikely that the bill would pass as is, even without the lobbying efforts of the direct-marketing industry. The second shortcoming is that the law creates a property right with regard to online personal information, a proposal that would have serious repercussions for marketers of all stripes. For example, if an Internet user subscribed to a magazine and could somehow prove the information they provided was stored on, processed on, or transferred via a remote communications system or Web site, then the SOCEA might apply. Finally, such a property right could spur significant litigation, much as has been seen in the DoubleClick case, though under the SOCEA there would be significant room to expand individuals' claims to the offline world.

On an international front Senator Torrecelli's proposal, while a significant departure from the American approach to privacy rights to date, would still not meet the requirements set forth by the European Union's Data Directive with regard to establishing adequate protection for personally identifiable information. The first limitation is that, like the self-regulatory schemes administered by TRUSTe and BBB*Online*, the SOCEA as written only applies to online information. Unless the bill's intent or interpretation were changed to comprehend offline information handling, its restrictions would not be in line with the directive's requirements. The second limitation, which the bill again has in common with the online trustmark programs, is the lack of a national enforcement agent. Senator Torrecelli emphasizes that the right granted in his bill is a private right, offering private individuals a cause of action if the law's strictures are violated, but the reliance on citizens policing organizations that deal in personally identifiable information is specifically rejected by the directive. As Viktor Mayer-Schönberger's chapter "Generational Development of Data Protection in Europe" in Agre and Rotenberg's *Technology and Privacy: The New Landscape* points out, the second generation of data protection laws in Europe, generally passed in the early to mid-1980s, also required an individual's consent before their information could be processed.[2] Whether citizens will have the knowledge and wherewithal to investigate and challenge companies' uses of their personally identifiable information is open to serious question. President Clinton did say that the chances were even that Congress would enact legislation this year to protect online medical and financial privacy, but those regulations would likely be no more than an extension of existing health privacy restrictions and the provisions of the Gramm–Leach–Bliley Act.[3]

Other proposals, such as calls for an Office of Electronic Commerce and Privacy Policy (OECPP) within the Department of Commerce or for an independent privacy commission, seem much less likely over the next few years.[4] President Clinton did create a new privacy post in the Office of Management and Budget (manned as of January 2000 by Peter Swire, professor of law at Ohio State University and lead author of *None of Your Business*), but Reidenberg notes that the office "is placed within the layers of the OMB bureaucracy and does not fulfill all the needed roles. Instead, the post has a coordinating role and does not have policy decision-making authority nor does the position have authority for the international negotiations with Europe."[5]

Prospects at the State Level

The picture is quite different at the state level. With several states considering or actually initiating consumer-protection actions against DoubleClick, it is evident that the reluctance to take action against companies that change their practices significantly does not exist in state governments. While the outcome of these suits and the private class action lawsuits is uncertain, especially after any appeals reach the federal courts, it is likely that state governments will pass legislation extending the privacy rights of their citizens. New York is one state where such a policy could take hold, though the advertising and marketing lobby is quite strong there. The most likely outcome in the short term is a version of the opt-out clause in the Gramm–Leach–Bliley Act of 1999, which could force online advertisers to contact individuals on whom they have collected personally identifiable information and offer them the chance to opt out of their programs.

Other Areas

On a technological level, the next few years should see the first implementations of the Platform for Privacy Preferences standard, though if current trends hold then the default setting for browsers with the standard enabled will be to allow all information to be collected by site operators. The Article 29 Working Party, commissioned under the EU Data Directive, has found fault with P3P in that "a technical platform for privacy protection will not in itself be sufficient to protect privacy on the Web. It must be applied within the context of a framework of enforceable data protection rules, which provide a minimum and non-negotiable level of privacy protection for all individuals."[6] That infomediaries like digitalme, PrivaSeek, and AllAdvantage have implemented privacy negotiation standards ahead of P3P takes quite a bit of the luster off of the standard.

In Canada, the passage of the Personal Information Protection and Electronic Documents Act (Bill C-6) seems very likely in the near term, though it is unclear whether Canada's minister of industry, the Honorable John Manley, will attempt to block the bill because of the one-year implementation delay the Senate granted the health industry. Regardless, the bill or a close relative will most certainly pass in the near future and offer greatly enhanced privacy protections to Canadians.

The prospect for negotiations between the United States and the European Union are quite intriguing in the short term. Ambassador David Aaron is set to leave the U.S. Department of Commerce at the end of March 2000, so there was great incentive to have reached a preliminary accord by then. The downside of their efforts is that even if the two sides are able to reach a tentative agreement, the pact must then be ratified by eleven of the fifteen EU nations and the U.S. Senate for it to take effect. If the U.S. negotiating position does not change from the Safe Harbor proposal and Frequently Asked Questions list submitted in November 1999, then an agreement, even one in principle, seems quite unlikely. Such an accord would face a long uphill battle to ratification as well.

MID-TERM PROSPECTS

Over the mid-term, meaning the years 2004 to 2007, the most likely policy environment in the United States is one of increasing tension between privacy laws at the state and federal levels. At the far end of the spectrum of approaches is the possibility that states could grant individuals strong property rights over their personally identifiable information, above and beyond the right established by Senator Torrecelli's proposed Secure Online Communications Enforcement Act. Rule and Hunter advocate such a right, which is actually a bit more strict than the EU Data Directive:

The essential principle would be simplicity itself: No information could legally be sold or traded from any personal data file, for any commercial purpose, without express permission from the person concerned. Subject to this stricture would be the release of personal data from credit card companies, medical care providers, periodical subscription lists, mail order houses and other retail establishments, and any other source. All these forms of release . . . would be illegal without evidence of permission from the data subject.[7]

A far more likely scenario would be a continuation of the self-regulatory practices advocated by online advertisers and the Clinton administration, again with the threat of action by the Federal Trade Commission if companies engaged in unfair or deceptive practices. It is also just as likely that these self-regulatory measures would continue to be challenged at the state level and to be proven to be inadequate to protect consumer privacy. The existing trustmark programs, such as those run by TRUSTe and BBB*Online*, are simply guarantees that the company has and follows a privacy policy, making no distinction between policies that provide adequate protection for personally identifiable information and those that do not. The policies in place are also limited to the online environment and, as noted by Joel Reidenberg, are not particularly well enforced.[8]

It is also during this time frame that the EU and the United States will need to reopen negotiations if the March 2000 agreement on the Safe Harbor Principles is not ratified by the European Commission and the Senate. By this time the privacy landscape in the United States will have changed significantly. It is most likely that more than a few states will have passed significant privacy legislation, perhaps even granting the type of property right to personally identifiable information advocated by Rule and Hunter. It is also likely, particularly in 2006–2007, that one or more infomediaries will have created an online environment and user base that allow them to wield considerable influence over the practicalities of commerce both online and offline. As always, the legislature will be struggling to catch up with current business practices, but the precedent of the Telephone Consumer Privacy Act (discussed in Chapter 4) offers some insights into how the drama might unfold. The TCPA was passed to fill a gap in similar laws passed by the states, with Congress acknowledging that "over half the States now have statutes restricting various uses of the telephone for marketing, but telemarketers can evade their prohibitions through interstate operations; therefore, Federal law is needed to control residential telemarketing practices."[9]

In the mid-term, the most likely business configuration for organizations wishing to do business with entities in the EU will be to combine a contractual approach with cooperation with existing infomediaries, either as data guardians who can lend their trustworthiness to the transaction or as advisers who can show the contracting party best practices with regard to information security. While the EU and the United States will certainly continue negotiating, the importance of an agreement between governments will decrease in importance for industries that need to do business with the EU. Instead, the mid-term will see companies adopting, at least with regard to data transferred from the EU or regarding EU citizens, information protection practices consistent with the EU Data Directive.

LONG-TERM PROSPECTS

The more years one looks out into the privacy debate, the hazier the picture becomes. Domestically, the years 2007 to 2010 are likely to see an ever-rising tide of state laws regarding information privacy as the concept of infomediaries and the impact of privacy laws in other states become apparent to the citizens of states without such laws, as educated by privacy rights organizations. The federal legislature will still probably not have passed an opt-in law regarding consumers' personally identifiable information, but it is very likely that the majority of citizens who can afford a computer (a sociological distinction that is important but beyond the scope of this discussion) and want to protect their privacy will have done so through infomediaries. On the international front, it is likely that the EU and the United States will still be negotiating over privacy protections, but that the negotiations will be concluded with a Safe Harbor agreement that acknowledges the role of infomediaries in the online economy and offers sufficient protection for offline information to warrant wrapping up an agreement. It is unlikely, however, that the United States will agree to such a part until its hand is forced by the technological and commercial realities of the day. A look at how the Clinton administration handled cryptographic export controls (resisting change for years and, only after its position was proved to be completely untenable, giving in incompletely) is sufficient to set the pattern for the U.S. government in such matters.

A PLAN FOR THE PRIVACY-ENHANCED ECONOMY

The central truth that must be comprehended when examining the future of commerce is that the balance of power with regard to information process and control has swung to the side of the consumer. That most consumers do not take full advantage of that control at present, whether due to inability to do so, ignorance, or choice, should not blind managers to the fact that privacy-enhancing technologies and services give consumers effective control over the collection of their personally identifiable information. The legal protections put in place by the European Union and Canada, which may be mirrored by some U.S. states, also provide an impetus for studying industry best practices in preparation for new ways to do business. Underneath the legal requirements and profit-and-loss statements, however, lies the customer, so often treated as a commodity. Earning customer trust is imperative to succeeding in the new economy.

Organizational Structure

The specific structure an organization adopts to monitor changes to privacy laws and internal adherence to privacy procedures will depend on the size and scope of the organization, but a good place to start looking is the chief information officer (CIO). In many cases the CIO will have technical and policy responsibilities to ensure information security, which encompasses data flow within the company and to outside recipients, so it is a natural extension to add privacy protections to that individual's portfolio. Because adherence to privacy policies will probably increase the workload substantially, it is important to create a privacy committee that sets the direction of and builds consensus for the organization's policies. That committee should be led, if possible, by the chief executive officer (CEO), though administration of the meetings and many of the other oversight functions will likely rest with the CIO. There is also the option to establish an independent privacy committee within an organization. In response to the heavy criticism leveled against it for announcing plans to merge online and offline information, DoubleClick hired two individuals to build its privacy policies. New York City Consumer Affairs Commissioner Jules Polonetsky was brought on as chief privacy officer, while Bob Abrams, a former New York attorney general, will chair the company's new privacy advisory board.[10]

Information on the World Wide Web

For the short term, where privacy protection remains optional but beneficial for many businesses, Garfinkel and Spafford offer a simple list of steps to take to protect user information on a Web site:

- Do not require users to register to use your site.
- Allow users to register with their e-mail addresses if they wish to receive bulletins.
- Do not share a user's e-mail address with another company without that user's explicit permission for each company with which you wish to share the e-mail address.
- Whenever you send an e-mail message to users, explain to them how you obtained their e-mail addresses and how they can get off your mailing list.
- Do not make your log files publicly available.
- Delete your log files when they are no longer needed.
- If your log files must be kept online for extended periods of time, remove personally identifiable information from them.
- Encrypt your log files if possible.
- Do not give out personal information regarding your users.
- Discipline or fire employees who violate your privacy policy.
- Tell people about your policy on your home page, and allow your company to be audited by outsiders if there are questions regarding your policies.[11]

Routine Consumer Interactions

The next choice to make is how to interact with customers in a way that allows companies to continue to collect information about them without turning them away. Bear in mind that there are a wide range of businesses that may not benefit immediately by outsourcing their information functions to infomediaries. As Hagel and Rayport note,

Businesses that deal directly with consumers, such as retailers, hotels, and airlines, will be able to continue collecting information about their customers in the near term just as they do today. However, as more consumers purchase goods and seek information over networks, or as they begin to use smart cards or other forms of electronic cash (which preserve their anonymity), it may become harder for those businesses to obtain information without the assistance of infomediaries. . . . To forestall or limit their dependence on infomediaries, such businesses could begin to think now about how they will obtain information about their best customers and forge strong relationships with them to earn their trust and loyalty. They also should start to consider how they will develop the capabilities to provide customized services that address their customers' future needs and desires.[12]

Former Harvard Business School professor John J. Sviokla argues that businesses can take advantage of some of the technologies developed for use with infomediaries to form solid relationships with consumers that will benefit both parties:

Allowing customers to own their personal behavior does not mean losing them to competitors. It will create a new and deeper relationship. Companies that open up to customers—and have the effective, efficient business processes to execute the orders—will get more of them. The only thing lost will be the illusion of control.[13]

International Business

The potential for European Union member nations to prohibit the transfer of personally identifiable information from within their borders is a significant issue for many American businesses. A substantial part of the privacy committee's duties within any company should be to monitor the state of negotiations between the EU and the United States closely, with an eye to anticipating privacy-related issues before they arise and establishing controls that can be documented internally and verified by outside authorities. Except in cases where state law requires consent for data processing, it appears that contracts that establish adequate protection between American organizations and their EU counterparts will be the preferred method of doing business for the near future. In the mid- to long-term scenarios, businesses must be prepared to move to a consent-based model.

CONCLUSIONS

Now more than ever, consumers understand what can be done with the personal information they reveal explicitly and implicitly when using the Internet; they also know what can be done with computers to collect and process their personally identifiable information from online and offline sources. The outcry over *Lotus Marketplace: Households* in the early 1990s and the more recent furor over DoubleClick's practices have brought the issue squarely into the public eye. While there are no serious legislative proposals to implement a federal privacy protection system similar to that in place in the European Union, there is the real possibility that either the American states will pass equivalent laws or that the EU member nations will choose to enforce their laws more rigorously. Organizations must, at a minimum, study the issue and map out a plan to adapt to differing restrictions, but the path that offers the best results at present seems to the strategy mapped out by AllAdvantage.com. Rather than fight to the bitter end to resist privacy restrictions, companies should take their customers' expectations, plus their power to enforce those expectations, into account and build personally identifiable information protection practices into their everyday operations.

NOTES

1. Robert G. Torrecelli, *Senator Torrecelli Speaks on Your Privacy Online*, 23 January 2000, pp. 5–7. Available <http://www.senate.gov/~torricelli/speeches/speech_online_privacy.htm>.

2. Viktor Mayer-Schönberger, "Generational Development of Data Protection in Europe," in *Technology and Privacy: The New Landscape*, ed. Philip E. Agre and Marc Rotenberg (Cambridge, Mass.: MIT Press, 1999), 227.

3. David Streitfeld, "Clinton Sees Chances as Good for Online Privacy Bill This Year," *Washington Post*, 4 March 2000, A5.

4. Peter P. Swire and Robert E. Litan, *None of Your Business: World Data Flows, Electronic Commerce, and the European Privacy Directive* (Washington, D.C.: Brookings Institution Press, 1998), 185; Joel Reidenberg, "Restoring Americans' Privacy in Electronic Commerce," *Berkeley Technology Law Journal* 14, no. 2 (1999): 792.

5. Reidenberg, "Restoring Americans' Privacy," 791.

6. Article 29 Working Party, *Working Document: Platform for Privacy Preferences (P3P) and the Open Profiling Standard (OPS)* (Opinion 1/98), 16 June 1998. Available <http://www.europa.eu.int/comm/dg15/en/media/dataprot/wpdocs/wp11en.htm>.

7. James Rule and Lawrence Hunter, "Property Rights in Personal Data," in *Visions of Privacy: Policy Choices for the Digital Age*, ed. Colin J. Bennett and Rebecca Grant (Toronto: University of Toronto Press, 1999), 170.

8. Reidenberg, "Restoring Americans' Privacy," 777.

9. Public Law 102-243.

10. Ben Hammer, "DoubleClick Hires Private Eyes," *The Industry Standard*, 8 March 2000. Available <http://www.thestandard.com/article/display/1,1151,12751,00.html>.

11. Simson Garfinkel and Gene Spafford, *Web Security & Commerce* (Sebastopol, Calif.: O'Reilly & Associates, 1997), 96.

12. John Hagel and Jeffrey Rayport, "The Coming Battle for Customer Information," in *Creating Value in the Network Economy*, ed. Don Tapscott (Boston: Harvard Business School Press, 1999), 170.

13. John J. Sviokla, "The Customer Information Backlash," *CIO Magazine*, 15 January 2000. Available <http://www.cio.com/archive/011500_new.html>.

EU Data Protection Directive

CODEC 92
Common Position (EC) No /95
Adopted by the Council on 20 February 1995
With a View to Adopting Directive 94/ /EC of the European
Parliament and of the Council on the Protection of Individuals
With Regard to the Processing of Personal Data and on the
Free Movement of Such Data
Directive 95/ /EC of the European Parliament
and of the Council
On the protection of individuals with regard to the processing
of personal data and on the free movement of such data

THE EUROPEAN PARLIAMENT AND THE COUNCIL OF THE EU-
ROPEAN UNION,

Having regard to the Treaty establishing the European Community, and in
particular Article 100a thereof,

Having regard to the proposal from the Commission 1,

Having regard to the opinion of the Economic and Social Committee 2,

Acting in accordance with the procedure referred to in Article 189b of the
Treaty 3,

1. Whereas the objectives of the Community, as laid down in the Treaty, as amended by the Treaty on European Union, include creating an ever closer union among the peoples of Europe, fostering closer relations between the States belonging to the Community, ensuring economic and social progress by common action to eliminate the barriers which divide Europe, encouraging the constant improvement of the living conditions of its peoples, preserving and strengthening peace and liberty and promoting democracy on the basis of the fundamental rights recognized in the constitution and laws of the Member States and in the European Convention for the Protection of Human Rights and Fundamental Freedoms;

2. Whereas data-processing systems are designed to serve man; whereas they must, whatever the nationality or residence of natural persons, respect their fundamental rights and freedoms, notably the right to privacy, and contribute to economic and social progress, trade expansion and the well-being of individuals;

3. Whereas the establishment and functioning of an internal market in which, in accordance with Article 7a of the Treaty, the free movement of goods, persons, services and capital is ensured require not only that personal data should be able to flow freely from one Member State to another, but also that the fundamental rights of individuals should be safeguarded;

4. Whereas increasingly frequent recourse is being had in the Community to the processing of personal data in the various spheres of economic and social activity; whereas the progress made in information technology is making the processing and exchange of such data considerably easier;

5. Whereas the economic and social integration resulting from the establishment and functioning of the internal market within the meaning of Article 7a of the Treaty will necessarily lead to a substantial increase in cross-border flows of personal data between all those involved in a private or public capacity in economic and social activity in the Member States; whereas the exchange of personal data between undertakings in different Member States is set to increase; whereas the national authorities in the various Member States are being called upon by virtue of Community law to collaborate and exchange personal data so as to be able to perform their duties or carry out tasks on behalf of an authority in another Member State within the context of the area without internal frontiers as constituted by the internal market;

6. Whereas, furthermore, the increase in scientific and technical cooperation and the coordinated introduction of new telecommunications networks in the Community necessitate and facilitate cross-border flows of personal data;

7. Whereas the difference in levels of protection of the rights and freedoms of individuals, notably the right to privacy, with regard to the processing of personal data afforded in the Member States may prevent the transmission of such data from the territory of one Member State to that of another Member State; whereas this difference may therefore constitute an obstacle to the pursuit of a number of economic activities at Community level, distort competition and impede authorities in the discharge of their responsibilities under Community law; whereas this difference in levels of protection is due to the existence of a wide variety of national laws, regulations and administrative provisions;

8. Whereas, in order to remove the obstacles to flows of personal data, the level of protection of the rights and freedoms of individuals with regard to the process-

ing of such data must be equivalent in all Member States; whereas this objective is vital to the internal market but cannot be achieved by the Member States alone, especially in view of the scale of the divergences which currently exist between the relevant laws in the Member States and the need to coordinate the laws of the Member States so as to ensure that the cross-border flow of personal data is regulated in a consistent manner that is in keeping with the objective of the internal market as provided for in Article 7a of the Treaty; whereas Community action to approximate those laws is therefore needed;

9. Whereas, given the equivalent protection resulting from the approximation of national laws, the Member States will no longer be able to inhibit the free movement between them of personal data on grounds relating to protection of the rights and freedoms of individuals, and in particular the right to privacy; whereas Member States will be left a margin for manoeuvre, which may, in the context of implementation of the Directive, also be exercised by the business and social partners; whereas Member States will therefore be able to specify in their national law the general conditions governing the lawfulness of data processing; whereas in doing so the Member States shall strive to improve the protection currently provided by their legislation; whereas, within the limits of this margin for manoeuvre and in accordance with Community law, disparities could arise in the implementation of the Directive, and this could have an effect on the movement of data within a Member State as well as within the Community;

10. Whereas the object of the national laws on the processing of personal data is to protect fundamental rights and freedoms, notably the right to privacy, which is recognized both in Article 8 of the European Convention for the Protection of Human Rights and Fundamental Freedoms and in the general principles of Community law; whereas, for that reason, the approximation of those laws must not result in any lessening of the protection they afford but must, on the contrary, seek to ensure a high level of protection in the Community;

11. Whereas the principles of the protection of the rights and freedoms of individuals, notably the right to privacy, which are contained in this Directive, give substance to and amplify those contained in the Council of Europe Convention of 28 January 1981 for the Protection of Individuals with regard to Automatic Processing of Personal Data;

12. Whereas the protection principles must apply to all processing of personal data by any person whose activities are governed by Community law; whereas there should be excluded the processing of data carried out by a natural person in the exercise of activities which are exclusively personal or domestic, such as correspondence and the holding of records of addresses;

13. Whereas the activities referred to in Titles V and VI of the Treaty on European Union regarding public safety, defence, State security or the activities of the State in the area of criminal laws fall outside the scope of Community law, without prejudice to the obligations incumbent upon Member States under Article 56 (2), Article 57 or Article 100a of the Treaty establishing the European Community; whereas the processing of personal data that is necessary to safeguard the economic well-being of the State does not fall within the scope of this Directive where such processing relates to State security matters;

14. Whereas, given the importance of the developments under way, in the framework of the information society, of the techniques used to capture, transmit, manipulate, record, store or communicate sound and image data relating to natural persons, this Directive should be applicable to processing involving such data;

15. Whereas the processing of such data is covered by this Directive only if it is automated or if the data processed are contained or are intended to be contained in a filing system structured according to specific criteria relating to individuals, so as to permit easy access to the personal data in question;

16. Whereas the processing of sound and image data, such as in cases of video surveillance, does not come within the scope of this Directive if it is carried out for the purposes of public security, defence, national security or in the course of State activities relating to the area of criminal law or of other activities which do not come within the scope of Community law;

17. Whereas, as far as the processing of sound and image data carried out for purposes of journalism or the purposes of literary or artistic expression is concerned, in particular in the audiovisual field, the principles of the Directive are to apply in a restricted manner according to the provisions laid down in Article 9;

18. Whereas, in order to ensure that individuals are not deprived of the protection to which they are entitled under this Directive, any processing of personal data in the Community must be carried out in accordance with the law of one of the Member States; whereas, in this connection, processing carried out under the responsibility of a controller who is established in a Member State should be governed by the law of that State;

19. Whereas establishment on the territory of a Member State implies the effective and real exercise of activity through stable arrangements; whereas the legal form of such an establishment, whether simply branch or a subsidiary with a legal personality, is not the determining factor in this respect; whereas, when a single controller is established on the territory of several Member States, particularly by means of subsidiaries, he must ensure, in order to avoid any circumvention of national rules, that each of the establishments fulfils the obligations imposed by the national law applicable to its activities;

20. Whereas the fact that the processing of data is carried out by a person established in a third country must not stand in the way of the protection of individuals provided for in this Directive; whereas in these cases, the processing should be governed by the law of the Member State in which the means used are located, and there should be guarantees to ensure that the rights and obligations provided for in this Directive are respected in practice;

21. Whereas this Directive is without prejudice to the rules of territoriality applicable in criminal matters;

22. Whereas Member States shall more precisely define in the laws they enact or when bringing into force the measures taken under this Directive the general circumstances in which processing is lawful; whereas in particular Article 5, in conjunction with Articles 7 and 8, allows Member States, independently of general rules, to provide for special processing conditions for specific sectors and for the various categories of data covered by Article 8;

23. Whereas Member States are empowered to ensure the implementation of the protection of individuals both by means of a general law on the protection of individuals as regards the processing of personal data and by sectorial laws such as those relating, for example, to statistical institutes;

24. Whereas the legislation concerning the protection of legal persons with regard to the processing data which concerns them is not affected by this Directive;

25. Whereas the principles of protection must be reflected, on the one hand, in the obligations imposed on persons, public authorities, enterprises, agencies or other bodies responsible for processing, in particular regarding data quality, technical security, notification to the supervisory authority, and the circumstances under which processing can be carried out, and, on the other hand, in the right conferred on individuals, the data on whom are the subject of processing, to be informed that processing is taking place, to consult the data, to request corrections and even to object to processing in certain circumstances;

26. Whereas the principles of protection must apply to any information concerning an identified or identifiable person; whereas, to determine whether a person is identifiable, account should be taken of all the means likely reasonably to be used either by the controller or by any other person to identify the said person; whereas the principles of protection shall not apply to data rendered anonymous in such a way that the data subject is no longer identifiable; whereas codes of conduct within the meaning of Article 27 may be a useful instrument for providing guidance as to the ways in which data may be rendered anonymous and retained in a form in which identification of the data subject is no longer possible;

27. Whereas the protection of individuals must apply as much to automatic processing of data as to manual processing; whereas the scope of this protection must not in effect depend on the techniques used, otherwise this would create a serious risk of circumvention; whereas, nonetheless, as regards manual processing, this Directive covers only filing systems, not unstructured files; whereas, in particular, the content of a filing system must be structured according to specific criteria relating to individuals allowing easy access to the personal data; whereas, in line with the definition in Article 2 (c), the different criteria for determining the constituents of a structured set of personal data, and the different criteria governing access to such a set, may be laid down by each Member State; whereas files or sets of files as well as their cover pages, which are not structured according to specific criteria, shall under no circumstances fall within the scope of this Directive;

28. Whereas any processing of personal data must be lawful and fair to the individuals concerned; whereas, in particular, the data must be adequate, relevant and not excessive in relation to the purposes for which they are processed; whereas such purposes must be explicit and legitimate and must be determined at the time of collection of the data; whereas the purposes of processing further to collection shall not be incompatible with the purposes as they were originally specified;

29. Whereas the further processing of personal data for historical, statistical or scientific purposes is not generally to be considered incompatible with the purposes for which the data have previously been collected provided that Member States furnish suitable safeguards; whereas these safeguards must in particular rule out the use of the data in support of measures or decisions regarding any particular individual;

30. Whereas, in order to be lawful, the processing of personal data must in addition be carried out with the consent of the data subject or be necessary for the conclusion or performance of a contract binding on the data subject, or as a legal requirement, or for the performance of a task carried out in the public interest or in the exercise of official authority, or in the legitimate interests of a natural or legal person, provided that the interests or the rights and freedoms of the data subject are not overriding; whereas, in particular, in order to maintain a balance between the interests involved while guaranteeing effective competition, Member States may determine the circumstances in which personal data may be used or disclosed to a third party in the context of the legitimate ordinary business activities of companies and other bodies; whereas Member States may similarly specify the conditions under which personal data may be disclosed to a third party for the purposes of marketing whether carried out commercially or by a charitable organization or by any other association or foundation, of a political nature for example, subject to the provisions allowing a data subject to object to the processing of data regarding him, at no cost and without having to state his reasons;

31. Whereas the processing of personal data must equally be regarded as lawful where it is carried out in order to protect an interest which is essential for the data subject's life;

32. Whereas it is for national legislation to determine whether the controller performing a task carried out in the public interest or in the exercise of official authority should be a public administration or another natural or legal person governed by public law, or by private law such as a professional association;

33. Whereas data which are capable by their nature of infringing fundamental freedoms or privacy should not be processed unless the data subject gives his explicit consent; whereas, however, derogations from this prohibition must be explicitly provided for in respect of specific needs, in particular where the processing of these data is carried out for certain health-related purposes by persons subject to a legal obligation of professional secrecy or in the course of legitimate activities by certain associations or foundations the purpose of which is to permit the exercise of fundamental freedoms;

34. Whereas Member States must also be authorized, when justified by grounds of important public interest, to derogate from the prohibition on processing sensitive categories of data where important reasons of public interest so justify in areas such as public health and social protection—especially in order to ensure the quality and cost-effectiveness of the procedures used for settling claims for benefits and services in the health insurance system—scientific research and government statistics; whereas it is incumbent on them, however, to provide specific and suitable safeguards so as to protect the fundamental rights and the privacy of individuals;

35. Whereas, moreover, the processing of personal data by official authorities for achieving aims, laid down in constitutional law or international public law, of officially recognized religious associations is carried out on important grounds of public interest;

36. Whereas where, in the course of electoral activities, the operation of the democratic system requires in certain Member States that political parties compile data on people's political opinion, the processing of such data may be permitted

for reasons of important public interest, provided that appropriate safeguards are established;

37. Whereas the processing of personal data for purposes of journalism or for purposes of literary of artistic expression, in particular in the audiovisual field, should qualify for exemption from the requirements of certain provisions of this Directive in so far as this is necessary to reconcile the fundamental rights of individuals with freedom of information and notably the right to receive and impart information, as guaranteed in particular in Article 10 of the European Convention for the Protection of Human Rights and Fundamental Freedoms; whereas Member States should therefore lay down exemptions and derogations necessary for the purpose of balance between fundamental rights as regards general measures on the legitimacy of data processing, measures on the transfer of data to third countries and the power of the supervisory authority; whereas this should not, however, lead Member States to lay down exemptions from the measures to ensure security of processing; whereas at least the supervisory authority responsible for this sector should also be provided with certain ex-post powers, e.g. to publish a regular report or to refer matters to the judicial authorities;

38. Whereas, if the processing of data is to be fair, the data subject must be in a position to learn of the existence of a processing operation and, where data are collected from him, must be given accurate and full information, bearing in mind the circumstances of the collection;

39. Whereas certain processing operations involve data which the controller has not collected directly from the data subject; whereas, furthermore, data can be legitimately disclosed to a third party, even if the disclosure was not anticipated at the time the data were collected from the data subject; whereas, in all these cases, the data subject should be informed when the data are recorded or at the latest when the data are first disclosed to a third party;

40. Whereas, however, it is not necessary to impose this obligation if the data subject already has the information; whereas, moreover, there will be no such obligation if the recording or disclosure are expressly provided for by law or if the provision of information to the data subject proves impossible or would involve disproportionate efforts, which could be the case where processing is for historical, statistical or scientific purposes; whereas, in this regard, the number of data subjects, the age of the data, and any compensatory measures adopted may be taken into consideration;

41. Whereas any person must be able to exercise the right of access to data relating to him which are being processed, in order to verify in particular the accuracy of the data and the lawfulness of the processing; whereas, for the same reasons, every data subject must also have the right to know the logic involved in the automatic processing of data concerning him, at least in the case of the automated decisions referred to in Article 15 (1); whereas this right must not adversely affect trade secrets or intellectual property and in particular the copyright protecting the software; whereas these considerations must not, however, result in the data subject being refused all information;

42. Whereas Member States may, in the interest of the data subject or so as to protect the rights and freedoms of others, restrict rights of access and information; whereas they may, for example, specify that access to medical data may be obtained only through a health professional;

43. Whereas restrictions on the rights of access and information and on certain obligations of the controller may similarly be imposed by Member States in so far as they are necessary to safeguard, for example, national security, defence, public safety, or important economic or financial interests of a Member State or the Union, as well as criminal investigations and prosecutions and action in respect of breaches of ethics in the regulated professions; whereas the list of exceptions and limitations should include the tasks of monitoring, inspection or regulation necessary in the three last-mentioned areas concerning public security, economic or financial interests and crime prevention; whereas the listing of tasks in these three areas does not affect the legitimacy of exceptions or restrictions for reasons of State security or defence;

44. Whereas Member States may also be led, by virtue of the provisions of Community law, to derogate from the provisions of this Directive concerning the right of access, the obligation to inform individuals, and the quality of data, in order to secure certain of the purposes referred to above;

45. Whereas, in cases where data might lawfully be processed on grounds of public interest, official authority or the legitimate interests of a natural or legal person, any data subject should nevertheless be entitled, on legitimate and compelling grounds relating to his particular situation, to object to the processing of any data relating to himself; whereas Member States may nevertheless lay down national provisions to the contrary;

46. Whereas the protection of the rights and freedoms of data subjects with regard to the processing of personal data requires that appropriate technical and organizational measures be taken, both at the time of the design of the processing system and at the time of the processing itself, particularly in order to maintain security and thereby to prevent any unauthorized processing; whereas it is incumbent on the Member States to ensure that controllers comply with these measures; whereas these measures must ensure an appropriate level of security, taking into account the state of the art and the costs of their implementation in relation to the risks inherent in the processing and the nature of the data to be protected;

47. Whereas where a message containing personal data is transmitted by means of a telecommunications or electronic mail service, the sole purpose of which is the transmission of such messages, the controller in respect of the personal data contained in the message will normally be considered to be the person from whom the message originates, rather than the person offering the transmission services; whereas, nevertheless, those offering such services will normally be considered controllers in respect of the processing of the additional personal data necessary for the operation of the service;

48. Whereas the procedures for notifying the supervisory authority are designed to ensure disclosure of the purposes and main features of any processing operation for the purpose of verification that the operation is in accordance with the national measures taken under this Directive;

49. Whereas, in order to avoid unsuitable administrative formalities, exemptions from the obligation to notify and simplification of the notification required may be provided for by Member States in cases where processing is unlikely adversely to affect the rights and freedoms of data subjects, provided that it is in accordance with a measure taken by a Member State specifying its limits; whereas

exemption or simplification may similarly be provided for by Member States where a person appointed by the controller ensures that the processing carried out is not likely adversely to affect the rights and freedoms of data subjects; whereas such a data protection official, whether or not an employee of the controller, must be in a position to exercise his functions in complete independence;

50. Whereas exemption or simplification could be provided for in cases of processing operations whose sole purpose is the keeping of a register intended, according to national law, to provide information to the public and open to consultation by the public or by any person demonstrating a legitimate interest;

51. Whereas, nevertheless, simplification or exemption from the obligation to notify shall not release the controller from any of the other obligations resulting from this Directive;

52. Whereas, in this context, ex post facto verification by the competent authorities must in general be considered a sufficient measure;

53. Whereas, however, certain processing operations are likely to pose specific risks to the rights and freedoms of data subjects by virtue of their nature, their scope or their purposes, such as that of excluding individuals from a right, benefit or a contract, or by virtue of the specific use of new technologies; whereas it is for Member States, if they so wish, to specify such risks in their legislation;

54. Whereas with regard to all the processing undertaken in society, the amount posing such specific risks should be very limited; whereas Member States must provide that the supervisory authority, or the data protection official in cooperation with the authority, check such processing prior to it being carried out; whereas following this prior check, the supervisory authority may, according to its national law, give an opinion or an authorization regarding the processing; whereas such checking may equally take place in the course of the preparation either of a measure of the national parliament or of a measure based on such a legislative measure, which defines the nature of the processing and lays down appropriate safeguards;

55. Whereas, if the controller fails to respect the rights of data subjects, national legislation must provide for a judicial remedy; whereas any damage which a person may suffer as a result of unlawful processing must be compensated for by the controller, who may be exempted from liability if he proves that he is not responsible for the damage, in particular in cases where he establishes fault on the part of the data subject or in case of force majeure; whereas sanctions must be imposed on any person, whether governed by private of public law, who fails to comply with the national measures taken under this Directive;

56. Whereas cross-border flows of personal data are necessary to the expansion of international trade; whereas the protection of individuals, guaranteed in the Community by this Directive does not stand in the way of transfers of personal data to third countries which ensure an adequate level of protection; whereas the adequacy of the level of protection afforded by a third country must be assessed in the light of all the circumstances surrounding the transfer operation or set of transfer operations;

57. Whereas, on the other hand, the transfer of personal data to a third country which does not ensure an adequate level of protection must be prohibited;

58. Whereas provisions should be made for exemptions from this prohibition in certain circumstances where the data subject has given his consent, where the trans-

fer is necessary in relation to a contract or a legal claim, where protection of an important public interest so requires, for example in cases of international transfers of data between tax or customs administrations or between services competent for social security matters, or where the transfer is made from a register established by law and intended for consultation by the public or persons having a legitimate interest; whereas in this case such a transfer should not involve the entirety of the data or entire categories of the data contained in the register and, when the register is intended for consultation by persons having a legitimate interest, the transfer should be made only at the request of those persons or if they are to be the recipients;

59. Whereas particular measures may be taken to compensate for the lack of protection in a third country in cases where the controller offers appropriate safeguards; whereas, moreover, provision must be made for procedures for negotiations between the Community and such third countries;

60. Whereas, in any event, transfers to third countries may be effected only in full compliance with the provisions adopted by the Member States pursuant to this Directive, and in particular Article 8 thereof;

61. Whereas Member States and the Commission, in their respective spheres of competence, must encourage the trade associations and other representative organizations concerned to draw up codes of conduct so as to facilitate the application of this Directive, taking account of the specific characteristics of the processing carried out in certain sectors, and respecting the national provisions adopted for its implementation;

62. Whereas the establishment in Member States of supervisory authorities, exercising their functions with complete independence, is an essential component of the protection of individuals with regard to the processing of personal data;

63. Whereas such authorities must have the necessary means to perform their duties, including powers of investigation and intervention, particularly in cases of complaints from individuals, and powers to engage in legal proceedings; whereas such authorities must help to ensure transparency of processing in the Member States within whose jurisdiction they fall;

64. Whereas the authorities in the different Member States will need to assist one another in performing their duties so as to ensure that the rules of protection are properly respected throughout the European Union;

65. Whereas, at Community level, a Working Party on the Protection of Individuals with regard to the Processing of Personal Data must be set up and be completely independent in the performance of its functions; whereas, having regard to its specific nature, it must advise the Commission and, in particular, contribute to the uniform application of the national rules adopted pursuant to this Directive;

66. Whereas, with regard to the transfer of data to third countries, the application of this Directive calls for the conferment of powers of implementation on the Commission and the establishment of a procedure as laid down in Council Decision 87/373/EEC 4;

67. Whereas an agreement on a modus vivendi between the European Parliament, the Council and the Commission concerning the implementing measures for acts adopted in accordance with the procedure laid down in Article 189b of the EC Treaty was reached on 20 December 1994;

68. Whereas the principles set out in this Directive regarding the protection of the rights and freedoms of individuals, notably their right to privacy, with regard to the processing of personal data may be supplemented or clarified, in particular as far as certain sectors are concerned, by specific rules based on those principles;

69. Whereas Member States should be allowed a period of not more than three years from the entry into force of the national measures transposing this Directive in which to apply such new national rules progressively to all processing operations already under way; whereas, in order to facilitate their cost-effective implementation, a further period expiring 12 years after the date on which this Directive is adopted will be allowed to Member States to ensure the conformity of existing manual filing systems with certain of the Directive's provisions; whereas, where data contained in such filing systems are manually processed during this extended transition period, those systems must be brought into conformity with these provisions at the time of such processing;

70. Whereas it is not necessary for the data subject to give his consent again so as to allow the controller to continue to process, after the national provisions taken pursuant to this Directive enter into force, any sensitive data necessary for the performance of a contract concluded on the basis of free and informed consent before the entry into force of these provisions;

71. Whereas this Directive does not stand in the way of a Member State's regulating marketing activities aimed at consumers residing in territory insofar as such regulation does not concern the protection of individuals with regard to the processing of personal data;

72. Whereas this Directive allows the principle of public access to official documents to be taken into account when implementing the principles set out in this Directive,

CHAPTER 1
GENERAL PROVISIONS

Article 1
Object of the Directive

1. In accordance with this Directive, Member States shall protect the fundamental rights and freedoms of natural persons, and in particular their right to privacy, with respect to the processing of personal data.

2. Member States shall neither restrict nor prohibit the free flow of personal data between Member States for reasons connected with the protection afforded under paragraph 1.

Article 2 Definitions

For the purposes of this Directive:

(a) "personal data" shall mean any information relating to an identified or identifiable natural person ("data subject"); an identifiable person is one who can be identified, directly or indirectly, in particular by reference to an identification number or to one or more factors specific to his physical, physiological, mental, economic, cultural or social identity;

(b) "processing of personal data" ("processing") shall mean any operation or set of operations which is performed upon personal data, whether or not by automatic means, such as collection, recording, organization, storage, adaptation or alteration, retrieval, consultation, use, disclosure by transmission, dissemination or otherwise making available, alignment or combination, blocking, erasure or destruction;

(c) "personal data filing system" ("filing system") shall mean any structured set of personal data which are accessible according to specific criteria, whether centralized, decentralized or dispersed on a functional or geographical basis;

(d) "controller" shall mean the natural or legal person, public authority, agency or any other body which alone or jointly with others determines the purposes and means of the processing of personal data. Where the purposes and means of processing are determined by national or Community laws or regulations, the controller or the specific criteria for his nomination may be designated by a national or Community law.

(e) "processor" shall mean the natural or legal person, public authority, agency or any other body which processes personal data on behalf of the controller;

(f) "third party" shall mean the natural or legal person, public authority, agency or any other body other than the data subject, the controller, the processor and the persons who, under the direct authority of the controller or the processor, are authorized to process the data;

(g) "recipient" shall mean the natural or legal person, public authority, agency or any other body to whom data are disclosed, whether a third party or not; however, authorities which may receive data in the framework of a particular inquiry shall not be regarded as recipients;

(h) "the data subject's consent" shall mean any freely given specific and informed indication of his wishes by which the data subject signifies his agreement to personal data relating to him being processed.

Article 3 Scope

1. This Directive shall apply to the processing of personal data wholly or partly by automatic means, and to the processing otherwise than by automatic means of personal data which form part of a filing system or are intended to form part of a filing system.

2. This Directive shall not apply to the processing of personal data:

— in the course of an activity which falls outside the scope of community law, such as those provided for by Titles V and VI of the Treaty on European Union and in any case to processing operations concerning public security, defence, State security (including the economic well-being of the State when the processing operation is bound up with questions of State security) and the activities of the State in areas of criminal law;

— by a natural person in the course of a purely personal or household activity.

Article 4 National Law Applicable

1. Each Member State shall apply the national provisions it adopts pursuant to this Directive to the processing of personal data where:

    (a) the processing is carried out in the context of the activities of an establishment of the controller on the territory of the Member State; when the same controller is established on the territory of several Member States, he must take the necessary measures to ensure that each of these establishments complies with the obligations laid down by the national law applicable;

    (b) the controller is not established on the Member State's territory, but in a place where its national law applies by virtue of international public law;

    (c) the controller is not established on Community territory and, for purposes of processing personal data makes use of equipment, automated or otherwise, situated on the territory of said Member State, unless such equipment is used only for purposes of transit through the territory of the Community.

2. In the circumstances referred to in paragraph 1(c), the controller must designate a representative established in the territory of that Member State, without prejudice to legal actions which could be initiated against the controller himself.

CHAPTER II
GENERAL RULES ON THE LAWFULNESS OF
THE PROCESSING OF PERSONAL DATA

Article 5

Member States shall, within the limits of the provisions of this Chapter, determine more precisely the conditions under which the processing of personal data is lawful.

SECTION 1
PRINCIPLES RELATING TO DATA QUALITY

Article 6

1. Member States shall provide that personal data must be:

    (a) processed fairly and lawfully;

    (b) collected for specified, explicit and legitimate purposes and not further processed in a way incompatible with those purposes. Further processing of data for historical, statistical or scientific purposes shall not be considered as incompatible provided that Member States provide appropriate safeguards;

    (c) adequate, relevant and not excessive in relation to the purposes for which they are collected and/or for which they are further processed;

    (d) accurate and, where necessary, kept up to date; every reasonable step must be taken to ensure that data which are inaccurate or incomplete, having regard to the purposes for which they were collected or for which they are further processed, are erased or rectified;

(e) kept in a form which permits identification of data subjects for no longer that is necessary for the purposes for which the data were collected or for which they are further processed. Member States shall lay down appropriate safeguards for personal data stored for longer periods for historical, statistical or scientific use.

2. It shall be for the controller to ensure that paragraph 1 is complied with.

SECTION II
PRINCIPLES RELATING TO THE REASONS FOR MAKING DATA PROCESSING LEGITIMATE

Article 7

Member States shall provide that personal data may be processed only if:

(a) the data subject has given his consent unambiguously;

or

(b) processing is necessary for the performance of a contract to which the data subject is party or in order to take steps at the request of the data subject entering into a contract;

or

(c) processing is necessary for compliance with a legal obligation to which the controller is subject;

or

(d) processing is necessary in order to protect the vital interests of the data subject;

or

(e) processing is necessary for the performance of a task carried out in the public interest or in the exercise of official authority vested in the controller or in a third party to whom the data are disclosed;

or

(f) processing is necessary for the purposes of the legitimate interests pursued by the controller or by the third party or parties to whom the data are disclosed, except where such interests are overridden by the interests or fundamental rights and freedoms of the data subject which require protection under Article 1(1).

SECTION III
SPECIAL CATEGORIES OF PROCESSING

Article 8
The Processing of Special Categories of Data

1. Member States shall prohibit the processing of personal data revealing racial or ethnic origin, political opinions, religious or philosophical beliefs, trade-union membership, and the processing of data concerning health or sex life.

2. Paragraph 1 shall not apply where:

(a) the data subject has given his explicit consent to the processing of those data, except where the laws of the Member State provide that the prohibition referred to in paragraph 1 may not be waived by the data subject giving his consent; or

(b) processing is necessary for the purposes of carrying out the obligations and specific rights of the controller in the field of employment law insofar as it is authorized by national law providing for adequate safeguards; or

(c) processing is necessary to protect the vital interests of the data subject or of another person where the data subject is physically or legally incapable of giving his consent; or

(d) processing is carried out in the course of its legitimate activities with appropriate guarantees by a foundation, association or any other non-profit-seeking body with a political, philosophical, religious or trade-union aim and on condition that the processing relates solely to the members of the body or to persons who have regular contact with it in connection with its purposes and that the data are not disclosed to a third party without the consent of the data subjects; or

(e) the processing relates to data which are manifestly made public by the data subject or is necessary for the establishment, exercise or defense of legal claims.

3. Paragraph 1 shall not apply where processing of the data is required for the purposes of preventive medicine, medical diagnosis, the provision of care or treatment or the management of health-care services, and where those data are processed by a health professional subject under national law or rules established by national competent bodies to the obligation of professional secrecy or by another person also subject to an equivalent obligation of secrecy.

4. Subject to the provision of suitable safeguards, Member States may lay down for reasons of important public interest, exemptions in addition to those laid down in paragraph 2 either by national law or by decision of the supervisory authority.

5. Processing of data relating to offences, criminal convictions or security measures may be carried out only under the control of official authority, or if suitable specific safeguards are provided under national law, subject to derogations which may be granted by the Member State under national provisions providing suitable specific safeguards. However, a complete register of criminal convictions may be kept only under the control of official authority.

Member States may provide that data relating to administrative sanctions or civil trials shall also be processed under the control of official authority.

6. Derogations from paragraph 1 provided for in paragraphs 4 and 5 shall be notified to the Commission.

7. Member States shall determine the conditions under which a national identification number or any other identifier of general application may be processed.

Article 9
Processing of Personal Data and Freedom of Expression

Member States shall provide for exemptions or derogations from the provisions of this Chapter, Chapter IV and Chapter VI for the processing of personal data carried out solely for journalistic purposes or the purpose of artistic or literary expression only if they are necessary to reconcile the right to privacy with the rules governing freedom of expression.

SECTION IV
INFORMATION TO BE GIVEN TO THE DATA SUBJECT

Article 10
Information in Cases of Collection of Data from the Data Subject

Member States shall provide that the controller or his representative must provide a data subject from whom data relating to himself are collected with at least the following information, except where he already knows:

(a) the identity of the controller and of his representative, if any,

(b) the purposes of the processing for which the data are intended,

(c) any further information such as

— the recipients or categories of recipients of the data;

— whether replies to the questions are obligatory or voluntary, as well as the possible consequences of the failure to reply;

— the existence of the right of access to and the right to rectify the data concerning him insofar as they are necessary, having regard to the specific circumstances in which the data are collected, to guarantee fair processing in respect of the data subject.

Article 11
Information Where the Data Have Not
Been Obtained from the Data Subject

1. Where the data have not been obtained from the data subject, Member States shall provide that the controller or his representative must at the time of undertaking the recording of personal data or if a disclosure to a third party is envisaged, no later than the time when the data are first disclosed provide the data subject with at least the following information, except where he already knows:

   (a) the identity of the controller and of his representative, if any,

   (b) the purposes of the processing,

   (c) any further information such as

      — the categories of data concerned

      — the recipients or categories of recipients;

      — the existence of the right of access to and the right to rectify the data concerning him insofar as they are necessary, having regard to the specific circumstances in which the data are processed, to guarantee fair processing in respect of the data subject.

2. Paragraph 1 shall not apply where, in particular for processing for statistical purposes or for the purposes of historical or scientific research, the provision of

information proves impossible or involves a disproportionate effort or if recording or disclosure is expressly laid down by law. In these cases Member States shall provide appropriate safeguards.

SECTION V
THE DATA SUBJECT'S RIGHT OF ACCESS TO DATA

Article 12
Right of Access

Member States shall guarantee for every data subject the right to obtain from the controller:

1. without constraint at reasonable intervals and without excessive delay or expense:

   —confirmation as to whether or not data relating to him are processed and information at least as to the purposes of the processing, the categories of data concerned, and the recipients or categories of recipients to whom the data are disclosed;

   —communication to him in an intelligible form of the data undergoing processing and of any available information as to their source;

   —knowledge of the logic involved in any automatic processing of data concerning him at least in the case of the automated decisions referred to in Article 15(1);

2. as appropriate the rectification, erasure or blocking of data, the processing of which does not comply with the provisions of this Directive, in particular because of the incomplete or inaccurate nature of the data;

3. notification to third parties to whom the data have been disclosed of any rectification, erasure or blocking carried out in compliance with paragraph 2, unless this proves impossible or involves a disproportionate effort.

SECTION VI
EXEMPTIONS AND RESTRICTIONS

Article 13
Exemptions and Restrictions

1. Member States may adopt legislative measures to restrict the scope of the obligations and rights provided for in Articles 6(1), 10, 11(1), 12 and 21 when such a restriction constitutes a necessary measure to safeguard:

   (a) national security;

   (b) defence;

   (c) public security;

   (d) the prevention, investigation, detection and prosecution of criminal offences, or of breaches of ethics for regulated professions;

(e) an important economic or financial interest of a Member State or of the European Union, including monetary, budgetary and taxation matters;

(f) a monitoring, inspection or regulatory function connected, even occasionally, with the exercise of official authority in cases referred to in (c), (d) and (e);

(g) the protection of the data subject or of the rights and freedoms of others.

2. Subject to adequate legal guarantees, in particular that the data are not used for taking measures or decisions regarding any particular individual data subject, Member States may restrict, by a legislative measure, the rights provided for in Article 12 when data are processed solely for purposes of scientific research or are kept in personal form for a period which does not exceed the period necessary for the sole purpose of creating statistics.

SECTION VII
THE DATA SUBJECT'S RIGHT TO OBJECT

Article 14
The Data Subject's Right to Object

Member States shall grant the data subject the right:

(a) at least in the cases referred to in Article 7(e) and (f), to object at any time on compelling legitimate grounds relating to his particular situation to the processing of data relating to him, save where otherwise provided by national legislation. Where there is a justified objection, the processing instigated by the controller may no longer involve those data;

(b) to object, on request and free of charge, to the processing of personal data relating to him which the controller anticipates being processed for the purposes of direct marketing;

or

to be informed before personal data are disclosed for the first time to third parties or used on their behalf for the purposes of direct marketing, and to be expressly offered the right to object free of charge to such disclosures or uses.

Member States shall take the necessary measures to ensure that data subjects are aware of the existence of the right referred to in the first subparagraph of (b).

Article 15
Automated Individual Decisions

1. Member States shall grant the right to every person not to be subject to a decision which produces legal effects concerning him or significantly affects him and which is based solely on automated processing of data intended to evaluate certain personal aspects relating to him, such as his performance at work, creditworthiness, reliability, conduct, etc.

2. Subject to the other Articles of this Directive, Member States shall provide that a person may be subjected to a decision of the kind referred to in paragraph 1 if that decision:

(a) is taken in the course of entering into or performance of a contract, provided the request by the data subject has been satisfied, or that there are suitable measures to safeguard his legitimate interests, such as arrangements allowing him to defend his point of view; or

(b) is authorized by a law which also lays down measures to safeguard the data subject's legitimate interests.

SECTION VIII
CONFIDENTIALITY AND SECURITY OF PROCESSING

Article 16
Confidentiality of Processing

Any person acting under the authority of the controller or of the processor, including the processor himself, who has access to personal data must not process them except on instructions from the controller, unless he is required to do so by law.

Article 17
Security of Processing

1. Member States shall provide that the controller must implement appropriate technical and organizational measures to protect personal data against accidental or unlawful destruction or accidental loss and against unauthorized alteration, disclosure or access, in particular where the processing involves the transmission of data over a network, and against all other unlawful forms of processing.

    Having regard to the state of the art and the costs of their implementation, such measures shall ensure a level of security appropriate to the risks represented by the processing and the nature of the data to be protected.

2. The Member States shall provide that the controller must, where processing is carried out on his behalf, choose a processor who provides sufficient guarantees in respect of the technical security measures and organizational measures governing the processing to be carried out and must ensure compliance with those measures.

3. The carrying out of processing by way of a processor must be governed by a contract or legal act binding the processor to the controller and stipulating in particular that:

    —the processor shall act only on instructions from the controller;

    —the obligations set out in paragraph 1, as defined by the law of the Member State in which the processor is established, shall also be incumbent on the processor.

4. For the purposes of keeping proof, the parts of the contract or legal act relating to data protection and the requirements relating to the measures referred to in paragraph 1 shall be in writing or in another equivalent form.

SECTION IX
NOTIFICATION

Article 18
Obligation to Notify the Supervisory Authority

1. Member States shall provide that the controller or his representative, if any, must notify the supervisory authority referred to in Article 28 before carrying out any wholly or partly automatic processing operation or set of such operations intended to serve a single purpose or several related purposes.

2. Member States may provide for the simplification of or exemption from notification only in the following cases and under the following conditions:

   —where, for categories of processing operations which are unlikely, taking account of the data to be processed, to affect adversely the rights and freedoms of data subjects, they specify the purposes of the processing, the data or categories of data undergoing processing, the category or categories of data subject, the recipients or categories of recipient to whom the data are to be disclosed and the length of time the data are to be stored and/or

   —where the controller appoints, in compliance with the national law which governs him, a data protection official, responsible in particular

   = for ensuring in an independent manner the internal application of the national provisions taken pursuant to this Directive

   = for keeping the register of processing operations carried out by the controller, containing the items of information referred to in Article 21(2), thereby ensuring that the rights and freedoms of the data subjects are unlikely to be adversely affected by the processing operations.

3. Member States may provide that paragraph 1 does not apply to processing whose sole purpose is the keeping of a register, which according to laws or regulations is intended to provide information to the public and which is open to consultation either by the public in general or by any person demonstrating a legitimate interest.

4. Member States may provide for an exemption from the obligation to notify or a simplification of the notification in the case or processing operations referred to in Article 8(2)(d).

5. Member States may stipulate that certain or all non-automatic processing operations involving personal data shall be notified, or provide for these processing operations to be subject to a simplified notification.

Article 19 Contents of Notification

1. Member States shall specify the information to be given in the notification. It shall include at least:

   (a) the name and address of the controller and of his representative, if any;

   (b) the purpose or purposes of the processing;

(c) a description of the category or categories of data subject and of the data or categories of data relating to them;

(d) the recipients or categories of recipient to whom the data might be disclosed;

(e) proposed transfers of data to third countries;

(f) a general description allowing a preliminary assessment to be made of the appropriateness of the measures taken pursuant to Article 17 to ensure security of processing.

2. Member States shall specify the procedures under which any change affecting the information referred to in paragraph 1 must be notified to the supervisory authority.

Article 20
Prior Checking

1. Member States shall determine the processing operations likely to present specific risks for the rights and freedoms of data subjects and shall check that these processing operations are examined prior to the start thereof.

2. Such prior checks shall be carried out by the supervisory authority following receipt of a notification from the controller or by the data protection official, who in cases of doubt must consult the supervisory authority.

3. Member States may also carry out such checks in the context of preparation of a measure decided on by the national parliament or based on such a decision, defining the nature of the processing operation and laying down appropriate safeguards.

Article 21
Publicizing of Processing Operations

1. Member States shall take measures to ensure that processing operations are publicized.

2. Member States shall provide that a register of processing operations notified in accordance with Article 18 shall be kept by the supervisory authority. The register shall contain at least the information listed in Article 19(1)(a) to (e). The register may be inspected by any person.

3. Member States shall provide, in relation to processing operations not subject to notification, that controllers or another body appointed by the Member States make available at least the information referred to in Article 19(1)(a) to (e) in an appropriate fashion to any person on request. Member States may provide that this provision does not apply to processing whose sole purpose is the keeping of a register, which according to laws or regulations is intended to provide information to the public and which is open to consultation either by the public in general or by any person who can provide proof of a legitimate interest.

CHAPTER III
JUDICIAL REMEDIES, LIABILITY AND PENALTIES

Article 22
Remedies

Without prejudice to any administrative remedy for which provision may be made, inter alia before the supervisory authority referred to in Article 28, prior to referral to the judicial authority, Member States shall provide for the right of every person to a judicial remedy for any breach of the rights guaranteed him by the national law applicable to the processing in question.

Article 23
Liability

1. Member States shall provide that any person who has suffered damage as a result of an unlawful processing operation or of any act incompatible with the national provisions adopted pursuant to this Directive is entitled to receive compensation from the controller for the damage suffered.

2. The controller may be exempted from this liability, in whole or in part, if he proves that he is not responsible for the event giving rise to the damage.

Article 24 Sanctions

The Member States shall adopt suitable measures to ensure the full implementation of the provisions of this Directive and shall in particular lay down the sanctions to be imposed in case of infringement of the provisions adopted pursuant to this Directive.

CHAPTER IV
TRANSFER OF PERSONAL DATA TO THIRD COUNTRIES

Article 25
Principles

1. Member States shall provide that the transfer to a third country of personal data which are undergoing processing or are intended for processing after transfer may take place only if, without prejudice to compliance with the national provisions adopted pursuant to the other provisions of this Directive, the third country in question ensures an adequate level of protection.

2. The adequacy of the level of protection afforded by a third country shall be assessed in the light of all the circumstances surrounding a data transfer operation or set of data transfer operations; particular consideration shall be given to the nature of the data, the purpose and duration of the proposed processing operation or operations, the country of origin and country of final destination, the

rules of law, both general and sectoral, in force in the third country in question and the professional rules and security measures which are complied with in those countries.

3. Member States and the Commission shall inform each other of cases where they consider that a third country does not ensure an adequate level of protection within the meaning of paragraph 2.

4. Where the Commission finds, under the procedure provided for in Article 31(2), that a third country does not ensure an adequate level of protection within the meaning of paragraph 2 of this Article Member States shall take the measures necessary to prevent the transfer of data of the same type to the third country in question.

5. At the appropriate time, the Commission shall enter into negotiations with a view to remedying the situation resulting from the funding made pursuant to paragraph 4.

6. The Commission may find, in accordance with the procedure referred to in Article 31(2), that a third country ensures an adequate level of protection within the meaning of paragraph 2 of this Article, by reason of its domestic law or of the international commitments it has entered into, particularly upon conclusion of the negotiations referred to in paragraph 5, for the protection of the private lives and basic freedoms and rights of individuals. Member States shall take the measures necessary to comply with the Commission's decision.

Article 26
Derogations

1. By way of derogation from Article 25 and save where otherwise provided by domestic law governing particular cases, Member States shall provide that a transfer or a set of transfers of personal data to a third country which does not ensure an adequate level of protection within the meaning of Article 25(2) may take place on condition that:

1) the data subject has given his consent unambiguously to the proposed transfer, or

2) the transfer is necessary for the performance of a contract between the data subject and the controller or the implementation of precontractual measures taken in response to the data subject's request, or

3) the transfer is necessary for the conclusion or for the performance of a contract concluded in the interest of the data subject between the controller and a third party, or

4) the transfer is necessary or legally required on important public interest grounds, or for the establishment, exercise or defence of legal claims, or

5) the transfer is necessary in order to protect the vital interests of the data subject, or

6) the transfer is made from a register which according to laws or regulations is intended to provide information to the public and which is open to consultation either by the public in general or by any person who can demonstrate legitimate interest, to the extent that the conditions laid down in law for consultation are fulfilled in the particular case.

2. Without prejudice to paragraph 1, a Member State may authorize a transfer or a set of transfers of personal data to a third country which does not ensure an adequate level of protection within the meaning of Article 25(2), where the controller adduces sufficient guarantees with respect to the protection of the privacy and fundamental rights and freedoms of individuals and as regards the exercise of the corresponding rights; such guarantees may in particular result from appropriate contractual clauses.

3. The Member State shall inform the Commission and the other Member States of the authorizations granted pursuant to paragraph 2.

   If a Member State or the Commission objects on justified grounds involving the protection of the privacy and fundamental rights and freedoms of individuals, the Commission shall take appropriate measures in accordance with the procedure laid down in Article 31(2).

   Member States shall take the necessary measures to comply with the Commission's decision.

4. Where the Commission decides, in accordance with the procedure referred to in Article 31(2), that certain standard contractual clauses offer sufficient guarantees required by paragraph 2, Member States shall take the necessary measures to comply with the Commission's decision.

CHAPTER V
CODES OF CONDUCT

Article 27

1. The Member States and the Commission shall encourage the drawing up of codes of conduct intended to contribute to the proper implementation of the national provisions adopted by the Member States pursuant to this Directive, taking account of the specific features of the various sectors.

2. Member States shall make provision for trade associations and other bodies representing other categories of controllers which have drawn up draft national codes or which have the intention of amending or extending existing national codes to be able to submit them to the opinion of the national authority.

   Member States shall make provision for this authority to ascertain, among other things, whether the drafts submitted to it are in accordance with the national provisions adopted pursuant to this Directive. If it sees fit, the authority shall seek the views of data subjects or their representatives.

3. Draft Community codes, and amendments or extensions to existing Community codes, may be submitted to the Working Party referred to in Article 29. This Working Party shall determine, among other things, whether the drafts submitted to it are in accordance with the national provisions adopted pursuant to this Directive. If it sees fit, the authority shall seek the views of data subjects or their representatives. The Commission may ensure appropriate publicity for the codes which have been approved by the Working Party.

CHAPTER VI
SUPERVISORY AUTHORITY AND WORKING PARTY ON THE PROTECTION OF INDIVIDUALS WITH REGARD TO THE PROCESSING OF PERSONAL DATA

Article 28
Supervisory Authority

1. Each Member State shall provide that one or more public authorities are responsible for monitoring the application within its territory of the provisions adopted by the Member States pursuant to this Directive.

   These authorities shall act with complete independence in exercising the functions entrusted to them.

2. Each Member State shall provide that the supervisory authorities are consulted when drawing up administrative measures or regulations relating to the protection of individuals' rights and freedoms with regard to the processing of personal data.

3. Each authority shall in particular be endowed with:

   — investigative powers, such as powers of access to data forming the subject-matter of processing operations and powers to collect all the information necessary for the performance of its supervisory duties;

   — effective powers of intervention, such as, for example, that of delivering opinions in accordance with Article 20, before processing operations are carried out and ensuring appropriate publication of such opinions, or that of ordering the blocking, erasure or destruction of data, or of imposing a temporary or definitive ban on processing, or that of warning or admonishing the controller or that of referring the matter to national parliaments or other political institutions;

   — the power to engage in legal proceedings where the national provisions adopted pursuant to this Directive have been violated or to bring these violations to the attention of the judicial authorities.

   Decisions by the supervisory authority which give rise to complaints may be appealed against through the courts.

4. Each supervisory authority shall hear claims lodged by any person, or by an association representing that person, concerning the protection of his rights and freedoms in regard to the processing of personal data. The person concerned shall be informed of the outcome of the claim.

   Each supervisory authority shall, in particular, hear claims for checks on the lawfulness of data processing lodged by any person when the national provisions adopted pursuant to Article 13 of this Directive apply. The person shall at any rate be informed that a check has taken place.

5. Each supervisory authority shall draw up a report on its activities at regular intervals. The report shall be made public.

6. Each supervisory authority is competent, whatever the national law applicable to the processing in question, for exercising, on the territory of its own Member

State, the powers attributed to it in accordance with paragraph 3. Each authority may be requested to exercise its powers by an authority of another Member State.

The supervisory authorities shall cooperate with one another to the extent necessary for the performance of their duties, in particular by exchanging all useful information.

7. Member States shall provide that the members and staff of the supervisory authority, even after their employment has ended, are to be subject to a duty of professional secrecy with regard to confidential information to which they have access.

Article 29
Working Party on the Protection of Individuals with Regard to the Processing of Personal Data

1. A Working Party on the Protection of Individuals with regard to the Processing of Personal Data, hereinafter referred to as "the Working Party", is hereby set up.

   It shall have advisory status and act independently.

2. The Working Party shall be composed of a representative of the supervisory authority or authorities designated by each Member State and of a representative of the authority or authorities established for Community institutions and bodies, and of a representative of the Commission.

   Each member of the Working Party shall be designated by the institution, authority or authorities which he represents. Where a Member State designates more than one supervisory authority, they shall nominate a joint representative. The same shall apply for the authorities established for Community institutions and bodies.

3. The Working Party shall take decisions by a simple majority of the representatives of the supervisory authorities.

4. The Working Party shall elect its chairman. The chairman's term of office shall be two years. His appointment shall be renewable.

5. The Working Party's secretariat shall be provided by the Commission.

6. The Working Party shall adopt its own rules of procedure.

7. The Working Party shall consider items placed on its agenda by its chairman, either on his own initiative or at the request of a representative of the supervisory authorities or at the Commission's request.

Article 30

1. The Working Party shall:

   (a) examine any question covering the application of the national measures adopted under this Directive in order to contribute to the uniform application of such measures;

   (b) give the Commission an opinion on the level of protection in the Community and in third countries;

   (c) advise the Commission on any proposed amendment of this Directive, on any additional or specific measures to safeguard the rights and freedoms of natural persons with regard to the processing of personal data and on any other proposed Community measures affecting such rights and freedoms;

(d) give an opinion on codes of conduct drawn up at Community level.

2. If the Working Party finds that divergences likely to affect the equivalence of protection for persons with regard to the processing of personal data in the Community are arising between the laws or practices of Member States, it shall inform the Commission accordingly.

3. The Working Party may, on its own initiative, make recommendations on all matters relating to the protection of persons with regard to the processing of personal data in the Community.

4. The Working Party's opinions and recommendations shall be forwarded to the Commission and to the committee referred to in Article 31.

5. The Commission shall inform the Working Party of the action it has taken in response to its opinions and recommendations. It shall do so in a report which shall also be forwarded to the European Parliament and the Council. The report shall be made public.

6. The Working Party shall draw up an annual report on the situation regarding the protection of natural persons with regard to the processing of personal data in the Community and in third countries, which it shall transmit to the Commission, the European Parliament and the Council. The report shall be made public.

CHAPTER VII
COMMUNITY IMPLEMENTING MEASURES

Article 31
The Committee

1. The Commission shall be assisted by a committee composed of the representatives of the Member States and chaired by the representative of the Commission.

2. The representative of the Commission shall submit to the committee a draft of the measures to be taken. The committee shall deliver its opinion on the draft within a time limit which the chairman may lay down according to the urgency of the matter.

The opinion shall be delivered by the majority laid down in Article 148(2) of the Treaty. The votes of the representatives of the Member States within the committee shall be weighted in the manner set out in that Article. The chairman shall not vote.

The Commission shall adopt measures which shall apply immediately. However, if these measures are not in accordance with the opinion of the committee, they shall be communicated by the Commission to the Council forthwith. In that event:

The Commission shall defer application of the measures which it has decided for a period to be laid down in each act adopted by the Council, but which may in no case exceed three months from the date of communication.

The Council, acting by a qualified majority, may take a different decision within the time limit referred to in the previous paragraph.

FINAL PROVISIONS

Article 32

1. Member States shall bring into force the laws, regulations and administrative provisions necessary to comply with this Directive at the latest at the end of a period of three years from the adoption of the Directive.

   When Member States adopt these measures, they shall contain a reference to this Directive or be accompanied by such reference on the occasion of their official publication. The methods of making such reference shall be laid down by the Member States.

2. Member States shall ensure that processing already underway on the date the national provisions adopted pursuant to this Directive enter into force, is brought into conformity with these provisions within 3 years of this date.

   By way of derogation from the preceding subparagraph, Member States may provide that the processing of data already held in manual filing systems on the date of entry into force of the national provisions adopted in implementation of this Directive shall be brought into conformity with Articles 6,7 and 8 within 12 years of the date on which this Directive is adopted. Member States shall, however, grant the data subject the right to obtain, at his request and in particular at the time of exercising his right of access, the rectification, erasure or blocking of data which are incomplete, inaccurate or stored in a way incompatible with the legitimate purposes pursued by the controller.

3. By way of derogation from paragraph 2, Member States may provide, subject to suitable safeguards, that data kept for the sole purpose of historical research are not brought into conformity with Articles 6, 7 and 8 of this Directive.

4. Member States shall communicate to the Commission the provisions of national law which they adopt in the field covered by this Directive.

Article 33

The Commission shall report to the Council and the European Parliament at regular intervals, starting not later than three years after the date referred to in Article 32(1), on the implementation of this Directive, attaching to its report, if necessary, suitable proposals for amendments. The report shall be made public.

The Commission shall examine, in particular, the application of this Directive to the data processing of sound and image data relating to natural persons and shall submit any appropriate proposals which prove to be necessary, taking account of developments in information technology and in the light of the state of progress in the information society.

Article 34

This Directive is addressed to the Member States
Done at Brussels,

For the European Parliament	For the Council
The President	The President

Working Document: Preliminary views on the use of contractual provisions in the context of transfers of personal data to third countries

Adopted by the Working Party on 22 April 1998
The use of contractual provisions in the context of transfers of personal data to third countries

1. Introduction

In the discussion document adopted by the Working Party on 26 June 1997 entitled 'First Orientations on Transfers of Personal Data to Third Countries— Possible Ways Forward in Assessing Adequacy,' the Working Party promised to examine in its future work the circumstances in which ad hoc contractual solutions may be an appropriate means of securing protection for individuals when personal data are transferred to a third country where the level of protection is not generally adequate. This document is intended to provide a basis for such an examination.

The data protection directive (95/46/EC) establishes the principle in Article 25(1) that transfers of personal data to third countries should only take place where the third country in question ensures an adequate level of protection. Article 26(1) sets out certain exemptions to that rule. These exemptions are not examined in this paper. The purpose of this paper is to examine the additional possibility for exemption from the 'adequate protection' principle of Article 25 set out in Article 26(2). This provision allows a Member State to authorize a transfer or set of transfers to a 'non-adequate' third country 'where the controller adduces adequate safeguards with respect to the protection of the privacy and fundamental rights and freedoms of individuals and as regards the exercise of the corresponding rights'. The provision goes on to specify that 'such safeguards may in particular result from contractual clauses'. Article 26(4) also gives a power to the Commission, acting in accordance with the procedure laid down in Article 31, to decide that certain standard contractual clauses offer the sufficient guarantees envisaged in Article 26(2).

The idea of using contracts as a means of regulating international transfers of personal data was not of course invented by the directive. As long ago as 1992 the Council of Europe, the International Chamber of Commerce and the European Commission were jointly responsible for a study on the issue. More recently an increasing number of experts and commentators, perhaps noticing the explicit reference in the directive, have made comments on the use of contracts in studies and articles. Contracts have also continued to be used in the 'real world,' as a means of dealing with data protection problems arising from the export of personal data from certain EU Member States. They have been widely used in France since the late 1980s. In Germany the recent example of the 'Bahncard' case involving Citibank received a considerable amount of publicity.

2. The Use of Contracts as a Basis for Intra-Community Flows of Data

Before examining the requirements of contractual provisions in the context of data flows to third countries, it is important to clarify the difference between the third country situation and that pertaining within the Community. In this latter case, the contract is the mechanism used to define and regulate the split of data protection responsibilities when more than one entity is involved in the data processing in question. Under the directive one entity, the 'data controller,' must take the principal responsibility for complying with the substantive data protection principles. The second entity, the 'processor,' is responsible only for data security. An entity is deemed to be a controller if it has the decision-making power over the purposes and means of the data processing, whereas the processor is simply the body that physically provides the data processing service. The relationship between the two is regulated by Article 17(3) of the directive, which stipulates that:

the carrying out of processing by way of a processor must be governed by a contract or legal act binding the processor to the controller and stipulating in particular that:

*the processor shall act only on instructions from the controller

*the obligations set out in Paragraph 1 (the substantive provisions regarding data security), as defined by the law of the Member State in which the processor is established, shall also be incumbent on the processor.

This elaborates on the general principle established under Article 16 that any person acting under the authority of the controller, including the processor himself, must not process personal data except on instructions from the controller (unless required to do so by law).

Where personal data are transferred to third countries it will also normally be the case that more than one party will be involved. Here the relationship in question is between the entity transferring the data (the 'transferer') and the entity receiving the data in the third country (the 'recipient'). In this context one purpose of the contract should still be that of determining how the responsibility for data protection compliance is split between the two parties. However, the contract must do much more than this: it must provide additional safeguards for the data subject made necessary by the fact that the recipient in the third country is not subject to an enforceable set of data protection rules providing an adequate level of protection.

3. The Objective of a Contractual Solution

In the context of third country transfers, therefore, the contract is a means by which adequate safeguards can be provided by the data controller when transferring data outside of the Community (and thus outside of the protection provided by the directive, and indeed by the general framework of Community law) to a third country where the general level of protection is not adequate. For a contractual provision to fulfil this function, it must satisfactorily compensate for the absence of a general level of adequate protection, by including the essential elements of protection which are missing in any given particular situation.

4. The Specific Requirements of a Contractual Solution

The starting point for assessing the meaning of 'adequate safeguards,' as used in Article 26(2), is the notion of 'adequate protection' already developed at some length in the "First Orientations . . . " discussion document.

This document sets out an approach consisting of a series of basic data protection principles together with the three further requirements: that there be a good level of compliance with these principles in practice, that support and help be available to individual data subjects in the exercise of their rights, and that an appropriate means of redress be available to the injured party when the principles are not complied with.

The Substantive Data Protection Rules

The first requirement of the contractual solution is, therefore, that it must result in an obligation on the parties to the transfer to ensure that the full set of basic data protection principles set out in the "First Orientations" paper apply to the processing of the data transferred to the third country. These basic principles are:

1. the purpose limitation principle—data should be processed for a specific purpose and subsequently used or further communicated only insofar as this is not incompatible with the purpose of the transfer. The only exemptions to this rule would be those necessary in a democratic society on one of the grounds listed in Article 13 of the directive (e.g. national security, the investigation of criminal offences).

2. the data quality and proportionality principle—data should be accurate and, where necessary, kept up to date. The data should be adequate, relevant and not excessive in relation to the purposes for which they are transferred or further processed.

3. the transparency principle—individuals should be provided with information as to the purpose of the processing and the identity of the data controller in the third country, and other information insofar as this is necessary to ensure fairness. The only exemptions permitted should be in line with the Articles 13 of the directive, or Article 11(2) which allows organisations who have not collected data directly from the data subject to be exempted from the requirement to provide information if to do so would be impossible or involve a disproportionate effort

4. the security principle—technical and organisational security measures should be taken by the data controller that are appropriate to the risks presented by the processing. Any person acting under the authority of the data controller, including a processor, must not process data except on instructions from the controller.

5. the rights of access, rectification and opposition—the data subject should have a right to obtain a copy of all data relating to him/her that are processed, and a right to rectification of those data where they are shown to be inaccurate. In certain situations he/she should also be able to object to the processing of the data relating to him/her. The only exemptions to these rights should be in line with Article 13 of the directive.

6. restrictions on onward transfers to non-parties to the contract—further transfers of the personal data from the recipient to another third party should not be permitted, unless a means is found of contractually binding the third party in question providing the same data protection guarantees to the data subjects.

Furthermore in some situations additional principles must be applied:

1. sensitive data—where 'sensitive' categories of data are involved (those listed in article 8), additional safeguards should be in place, such as a requirement that the data subject gives his/her explicit consent for the processing.

2. direct marketing—where data are transferred for the purposes of direct marketing, the data subject should be able to 'opt-out' from having his/her data used for such purposes at any stage.

3. automated individual decision—where the purpose of the transfer is the taking of an automated decision in the sense of Article 15 of the directive, the individual should have the right to know the logic involved in this decision, and other measures should be taken to safeguard the individual's legitimate interest.

The contract should set out the detailed way in which the recipient of the data transfer should apply these principles (i.e. purposes should be specified, data categories, time limits for retention, security measures, etc.). In other situations, for example where protection in a third country is provided by a general data protection law similar to the directive, other mechanisms which clarify the way data protection rules apply in practice (codes of conduct, notification, the advisory function of the supervisory authority) are likely to be in place. In a contractual situation this is not so. Detail is therefore imperative where the transfer is based on a contract.

Rendering the Substantive Rules Effective

The "First Orientations . . ." document sets out three criteria by which the effectiveness of a data protection system should be judged. These criteria are the ability of the system to:

1. deliver a good level of compliance with the rules. (No system can guarantee 100% compliance, but some are better than others). A good system is generally characterised by a high degree of awareness among data controllers of their obligations, and among data subjects of their rights and the means of exercising them. The existence of effective and dissuasive sanctions is important in ensuring respect for rules, as of course are systems of direct verification by authorities, auditors, or independent data protection officials.

2. provide support and help to individual data subjects in the exercise of their rights. The individual must be able to enforce his/her rights rapidly and effectively, and without prohibitive cost. To do so there needs to be some sort of structure or mechanism allowing independent investigation of complaints.

3. provide appropriate redress to the injured party where rules are not complied with. This is a key element. It must involve a system which provides impartial judgements and which allows compensation to be paid and sanctions imposed where appropriate.

The same criteria must apply in judging the effectiveness of a contractual solution. Clearly this is a major though not impossible challenge. It is a question of finding means which can make up for the absence of oversight and enforcement mechanisms, and which can offer help, support and ultimately redress to a data subject who may not be a party to the contract.

Each of these questions must be examined in detail. For ease of analysis, they are taken in reverse order.

Providing Redress to a Data Subject

Providing a legal remedy to a data subject, (i.e. a right to have a complaint adjudicated by an independent arbiter and to receive compensation where appropriate), by way of a contract between the 'transferer' of the data and the 'recipient' is not a simple question. Much will depend on the nature of the contract law chosen as the national law applicable to the contract. It is expected that the applicable law will generally be that of the Member State in which the transferring party is established. The contract law of some Member States permits the creation of third party rights, whereas in other Member States this is not possible.

As a general rule, however, the more the recipient is limited in terms of his freedom to choose the purposes, means and conditions under which he processes the transferred data, the greater will be the legal security for the data subject. Bearing in mind that we are dealing with cases of inadequate general protection, the preferred solution would be for the contract to set down the way the recipient is to apply the basic data protection principles in such detail that, in effect, the recipient of the transfer has no autonomous decision-making power in respect of the transferred data, or the way in which they are subsequently processed. The recipient is bound to act solely under the instructions of the transferer, and while the data may have been physically transferred outside of the EU, decision-making control over the data remains with the entity who made the transfer based in the Community. The transferer thus remains the data controller, while the recipient is simply a sub-contracted processor. In these circumstances, because control over the data is exercised by an entity established in an EU Member State, the law of the Member State in question will continue to apply to the processing carried out in the third country, and furthermore the data controller will continue to be liable under that Member State law for any damage caused as a result of an unlawful processing operation.

This type of arrangement is not dissimilar to that set out in the "Inter-territorial Agreement" which resolved the Citibank 'Bahncard' case mentioned earlier. Here the contractual agreement set out in detail the data processing arrangements, particularly those relating to data security, and excluded all other uses of data by the recipient of the transfer. It applied German law to data processing carried out in the third country and thus guaranteed a legal remedy to data subjects.

There will of course be cases where this kind of solution cannot be used. The recipient of the transfer may not be simply providing a data processing service to the EU-based controller. Indeed the recipient may, for example, have rented or bought the data to use them for his own benefit and for his own purposes. In these circumstances the recipient will need a certain freedom to process the data as he wishes, thus in effect becoming a 'controller' of the data in his own right.

In this kind of case it is not possible to rely on the continued automatic applicability of a Member State law and the continued liability for damages of the transferer of the data. Other more complex mechanisms need to be devised to provide the data subject with an appropriate legal remedy. As mentioned above, some legal systems allow third parties to claim rights under a contract, and this could be used to create data subject rights under an open, published contract between transferer and recipient. The position of the data subject would be further strengthened if, as part of the contract, the parties committed themselves to some sort of binding arbitration in the event of a data subject challenging their compliance. Some sectoral self-regulatory codes include such arbitration mechanisms, and the use of contracts in combination with such codes could be usefully envisaged.

Another possibility is that the transferer, perhaps at the moment of obtaining the data initially from the data subject, enters into a separate contractual agreement with the data subject stipulating that he (the transferer) will remain liable for any damage or distress caused by the failure of the recipient of a data transfer to comply with the agreed set of basic data protection principles. In this way the data subject is granted a means of redress against the transferer for the misdemeanors of the recipient. It would be up to the transferer to then recover any damages he was forced to pay out to the data subject, by taking action for breach of contract against the recipient.

Such an elaborate three-way solution is perhaps more feasible than it might appear. The contract with the data subject could become part of the standard terms and conditions under which a bank or a travel agency, for example, provide services to their customers. It has the advantage of transparency: the data subject is made fully aware of the rights that he has.

Finally, as an alternative to a contract with the data subject, it could also be envisaged that a Member State lay down in law a continuing liability for data controllers transferring data outside of the Community for damages incurred as a result of the actions of the recipient of the transfer.

Providing Support and Help to Data Subjects

One of the main difficulties facing data subjects whose data are transferred to a foreign jurisdiction is the problem of being unable to discover the root cause of the particular problem they are experiencing, and therefore being unable to judge whether data protection rules have been properly followed or whether there are grounds for a legal challenge. This is why an adequate level of protection requires the existence of some sort of institutional mechanism allowing for independent investigation of complaints.

The monitoring and investigative function of a Member State supervisory authority is limited to data processing carried out on the territory of the Member State. Where data are transferred to another Member State, a system of mutual assistance between supervisory authorities will ensure that any complaint from a data subject in the first Member State will be properly investigated. Where the transfer is to a third country, there will in most cases be no such guarantee. The question, therefore, is what kind of compensatory mechanisms can be envisaged in the context of a data transfer based on a contract.

One possibility would be simply to require a contractual term which grants the supervisory authority of the Member State in which transferer of the data is established a right to inspect the processing carried out by the processor in the third country. This inspection could, in practice, be carried out by an agent (for example a specialist firm of auditors) nominated by the supervisory authority, if this was felt to be appropriate. A difficulty with this approach, however, is that the supervisory authority is not generally a party to the contract, and thus in some jurisdictions may have no means of invoking it to gain access. Another possibility could be a legal undertaking provided by the recipient in the third country directly to the EU Member State supervisory authority involved, in which the recipient of the data agrees to allow access by the supervisory authority or a nominated agent in the event that non-compliance with data protection principles is suspected. This undertaking could also require that the parties to the data transfer inform the supervisory authority of any complaint that they receive from a data subject. Under such an arrangement the existence of such an undertaking would be a condition to be fulfilled before the transfer of data could be permitted to take place.

Whatever the solution chosen there remain significant doubts as to whether it is proper, practical, or indeed feasible from a resource point of view, for a supervisory authority of an EU Member State to take responsibility for investigation and inspection of data processing taking place in a third country.

Delivering a Good Level of Compliance

Even in the absence of a particular complaint or difficulty faced by a data subject, there is a need for confidence that the parties to the contract are actually complying with its terms. The problem with the contractual solution is the difficulty in establishing sanctions for non-compliance which are sufficiently meaningful to have the dissuasive effect needed to provide this confidence. Even in cases where effective control over the data continues to be exercised from within the Community, the recipient of the transfer may not be subject to any direct penalty if he were to process data in breach of the contract. Instead the liability would rest with the Community-based transferer of the data, who would then need to recover any losses in a separate legal action against the recipient. Such indirect liability may not be sufficient to encourage the recipient to comply with every detail of the contract.

This being the case it is probable that in most situations a contractual solution will need to be complemented by at least the possibility of some form of external verification of the recipient's processing activities, such as an audit carried out by a standards body, or specialist auditing firm.

5. The Problem of Overriding Law

A specific difficulty with the contractual approach is the possibility that the general law of the third country may include requirements for the recipient of a data transfer, in certain circumstances, to disclose personal data to the state (the police, the courts or the tax authorities, for example), and that such legal requirements might take precedence over any contract to which the processor was subject. For processors within the Community this possibility is evoked in Article 16 of the directive which requires processors to process data only on instructions from the controller unless required to do so by law. However, under the directive any such disclosures (which are by their nature for purposes incompatible with those for which the data were collected) must be limited to those necessary in democratic societies for one of the 'ordre public' reasons set out in Article 13(1) of the directive. Article 6 of the Amsterdam Treaty also guarantees respect for the fundamental rights set out in the European Convention for the Protection of Human Rights and Fundamental Freedoms. In third countries similar limitations on the ability of the state to require the provision of personal data from companies and other organisations operational on their territory may not always be in place.

There is no easy way to overcome this difficulty. It is a point that simply demonstrates the limitations of the contractual approach. In some cases a contract is too frail an instrument to offer adequate data protection safeguards, and transfers to certain countries should not be authorised.

6. Practical Considerations for the Use of Contracts

The preceding analysis has demonstrated that there is a need for any contractual solution to be detailed and properly adapted to the data transfer in question. This need for detail as regards the precise purposes and conditions under which the transferred data are to be processed does not rule out the possibility of developing a standard contract format, but it will require each contract based on this format to be completed in a way which matches the particular circumstances of the case.

The analysis has also indicated that there are particular practical difficulties in investigating non-compliance with a contract where the processing takes place outside of the EU and where no form of supervisory body is provided for by the third country in question. Taken together, these two considerations mean that there will be some situations in which a contractual solution may be an appropriate solution, and others where it may be impossible for a contract to guarantee the necessary 'adequate safeguards'.

The need for detailed adaptation of a contract to the particularities of the transfer in question implies that a contract is particularly suited to situations where data transfers are similar and repetitive in nature. The difficulties regarding supervision mean that a contractual solution may be most effective where the parties to the contract are large operators already subject to public scrutiny and regulation. Large international networks, such as those used for credit card transactions and airline reservations, demonstrate both of these characteristics and thus are situations in which contracts may be most useful. In these circumstances, they could even be supplemented by multi-lateral conventions creating better legal security.

Equally where the parties to the transfer are affiliates or part of the same company group, the ability to investigate non-compliance with the contract is likely to be greatly re-inforced, given the strong nature of the ties between the recipient in the third country and the Community-based entity. Intra-company transfers are therefore another area where there is a clear potential for effective contractual solutions to be developed.

Main Conclusions and Recommendations

Contracts are used within the Community as a means of specifying the split of responsibility for data protection compliance between the data controller and a sub-contracted processor. When a contract is used in relation to data flows to third countries it must do much more: it must provide additional safeguards for the data subject made necessary by the fact that the recipient in the third country is not subject to an enforceable set of data protection rules providing an adequate level of protection.

The basis for assessing the adequacy of the safeguards delivered by a contractual solution is the same as the basis for assessing the general level of adequacy in a third country. A contractual solution must encompass all the basic data protection principles and provide means by which the principles can be enforced.

The contract should set out in detail the purposes, means and conditions under which the transferred data are to be processed, and the way in which the basic data protection principles are to be implemented. Greater legal security is provided by contracts which limit the ability of the recipient of the data to process the data autonomously on his own behalf. The contract should therefore be used, to the extent possible, as a means by which the entity transferring the data retains decision-making control over the processing carried out in the third country.

Where the recipient has some autonomy regarding the processing of the transferred data, the situation is not straightforward, and a single contract between the parties to the transfer may not always be a sufficient basis for the exercise of rights by individual data subjects. A mechanism may be needed through which the transferring party in the Community remains liable for any damage that may result from the processing carried out in the third country.

Onward transfers to bodies or organisations not bound by the contract should be specifically excluded by the contract, unless it is possible to bind such third parties contractually to respect the same data protection principles.

Confidence that data protection principles are respected after data are transferred would be boosted if data protection compliance by the recipient of the transfer were subject to external verification by, for example, a specialist auditing firm or standards/certification body.

In the event of a problem experienced by a data subject, resulting perhaps from a breach of the data protection provisions guaranteed in the contract, there is a general problem of ensuring that a data subject complaint is properly investigated. EU Member State supervisory authorities will have practical difficulties in carrying out such an investigation.

Contractual solutions are probably best suited to large international networks (credit cards, airline reservations) characterised by large quantities of repetitive data transfers of a similar nature, and by a relatively small number of large operators in industries already subject to significant public scrutiny and regulation. Intra-company data transfers between different branches of the same company group is another area in which there is considerable potential for the use of contracts.

Countries where the powers of state authorities to access information go beyond those permitted by internationally accepted standards of human rights protection will not be safe destinations for transfers based on contractual clauses.

Index

ABOUT THE AUTHOR

Curtis D. Frye is Principal of Technology & Society, LLC, an electronic commerce and policy analysis firm in Portland, Oregon. Earlier, he was an analyst with The MITRE Corporation and Director of Sales and Marketing for Digital Gateway Systems. A specialist in the interaction of advanced communications technologies and society, particularly the Internet and the communities that have formed around it, Mr. Frye is also a successful writer, with several books, online courses, articles, and numerous book reviews on his personal bibliography.